A SCANDALOUS HISTORY
OF THE ROMAN EMPERORS

A SCANDALOUS HISTORY
OF THE ROMAN EMPERORS

Anthony Blond

Robinson
LONDON

To Mary Hesketh & to Georgia de Chamberet

Constable & Robinson Ltd
3 The Lanchesters
162 Fulham Palace Road
London W6 9ER

First published in the UK by Quartet Books Limited 1994

This edition published by Robinson,
an imprint of Constable & Robinson Ltd 2000

A copy of the British Library Cataloguing in
Publication data is available from the British Library.

ISBN 1-84119-173-6

Printed and bound in the EU

❖ CONTENTS ❖

Contents

✦ ACKNOWLEDGMENTS ✦

To my wife, Laura, for her chapter on Roman food, to Auberon Waugh, editor of *The Literary Review,* who let me write notices of these Emperors' biographies, and to James Fergusson, who suggested they be written up into a book; to Lord Bridges, who introduced me to the British School in Rome and to the kindness and hospitality of the Director and the Deputy Director of that admirable institution; also to the archive department of the British Film Institute.

❖ BIBLIOGRAPHY ❖

There isn't one. Publications are acknowledged in the text. I have used the Ancient Roman historians and am indebted to Penguin, not only for the relevant Penguin Classics but also for *Who's Who in the Ancient World* by Betty Radice, which Anthony Blond published in hardback in 1971. The glossaries in the historical novels of Colleen McCullough, *The First Man in Rome,* etc. (Century), are superb works of clarity and scholarship. *Rome in Africa* by Susan Raven, now in its third edition with Routledge, has become a classic, and the Falco novels of Lindsey Davis (Century) are a delightful way of slipping painlessly into the mores of Ancient Rome.

✦ APOLOGY ✦

There is nothing original in this book. Even my view that the Emperor Caligula was not mad, just very bad and very dangerous to know, is allowed by his latest biographer.

The unexpected behaviour of the famous and infamous in Ancient Rome, which I may have pointed up in these pages, came from mostly standard sources; what I hope has been fresh is the approach. Cicero revealed himself as a Rachmanlike slum landlord in a letter to his friend Atticus. The loan of money at 48 per cent by Brutus, 'the noblest Roman of them all', is a matter of Senatorial record. Julius Caesar's disdainful preoccupation with his despatch box at the Games was witnessed by thousands and recorded by a few. The picture of his great-nephew, Augustus, friendless and bored in his old age, watching small boys playing dice in his little house on the Palatine Hill, hoping his wife has found him a virgin for the afternoon, is my emphasis but not my invention; indeed Ancient Rome was so literate, so lively and so malicious that the amateur historian has no need to invent anything, unlike, say, the mediaevalist. (My favourite anecdote has a very modern ring. One of Nero's aunts was very mean. She let it be known that she did not 'appreciate' – as New Yorkers say – one young man around town saying she sold old shoes. He sent back a message. 'Tell her I didn't say she sold them; I said she *bought* them!')

Tiberius, Augustus' stepson and son-in-law, was the next Emperor and essentially the most scrupulous and conscientious of the bunch, and the misanthropy which soured him only came from his bitterness at being forced (by Augustus) to abandon the only human being he loved – his wife. (Augustus, by the way, was certainly not poisoned by his wife, Livia, as seen on television. They had lived together for forty years and did not particularly like each other, but she had no reason to murder him, like two other Empresses, the succession of her son, Tiberius, being secure.)

Hating Rome, and indeed all mankind, Tiberius took his revenge by bequeathing as Emperor the 'serpent' (his word) Caligula, his great-nephew, who, inevitably assassinated, was succeeded, illegally, by his uncle Claudius, not the dithering benevolent figure of recent impersonations but the most cunning and ruthless of the Julio-Claudian clan. Poisoned by a dish of his favourite mushrooms, and finished off by his doctor, Claudius was succeeded by his seventeen-year-old nephew, a golden boy who did not breathe freely until he had murdered his mother.

(An explanation for their appalling conduct must be that these characters, with the exception of the first two, Caesar and Augustus, who had loving parents, endured such traumatic childhoods as would make a social worker of today vow to get them off any charge.)

The first five years of Nero's fourteen-year reign were notably benign, guided by Seneca, hero of Classics masters down the ages, whose enforcement of his usury provoked the bloody rebellion of Boadicea, Queen of the Iceni and Commander-in-Chief of the English, who appealed to the Emperor Nero. (This lady was coeval with St Paul, so, with Seneca as link, they would all have known about each other.) Nero, historically unpopular for trying to eliminate an unappealing sect of Jews, not yet known as Christians, was the most charming of these Emperors, the most visionary and the only aesthete. He was of course cruel – Romans were – but this twentieth century, with Auschwitz as its visiting card, has no right to point a finger at the first. Nero tried to abolish the Games, and his proposal that he stop a war by appearing before the army of the enemy and bursting into tears should be an idea considered for contemporary heads of state by the United Nations.

Finally a word about the essays, which are intended to set the background against which the leading characters perform. I have included – perhaps a piece of self-indulgence – one on Rome and her Jews, relatively more numerous than they are today but ignored by Ancient Roman historians and not much dealt with by the moderns. Further I have not really well understood the religions of the Romans but I sense that neither did they. I see I have omitted the *haruspices,* the practice of divining the correct course of actions by examining the entrails of an animal. I remember the Roman general thus warned against his proposed attack ignoring the advice and winning. I believe the only 'ism' Romans believed in was that of *pragma.*

To our eyes now, Ancient Rome does not appear so ancient or so far away. It was nearer in spirit to turn-of-the-century Manhattan – with its polyglottery, very rich and very poor – and in its power-broking and denunciations, to contemporary Washington, capital of the present number-one world power.

This book is the personal view of an amateur and will therefore contain inaccuracies, for which I apologize. I have snuffled round Roman vestiges in England, France, Italy and Israel (once with the late General Yadin). I published a book on Aphrodisias but I have not yet been there, or seen much of Rome in North Africa, though reading Susan Raven is a fine substitute for a visit. Patrolling the perimeter of the Circus Maximus in Rome, I noticed one side was dug into the rock of the Aventine Hill and I fancied I heard the echo of the din made by the very early morning crowd claiming their free seats for the chariot races which so annoyed Caligula, trying to sleep in his palace on the top of the Palatine Hill opposite.

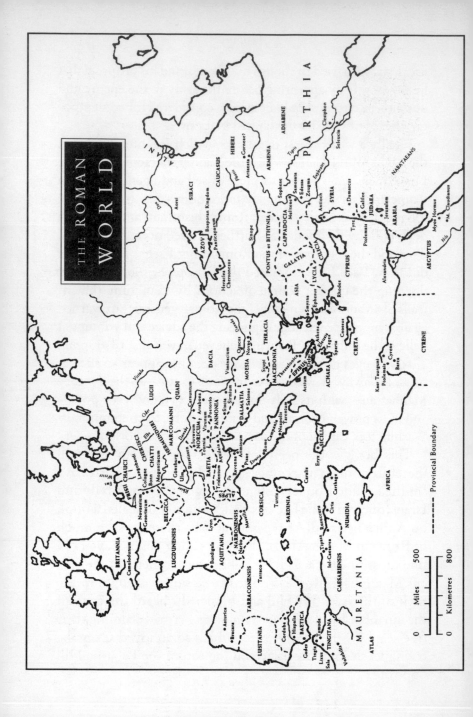

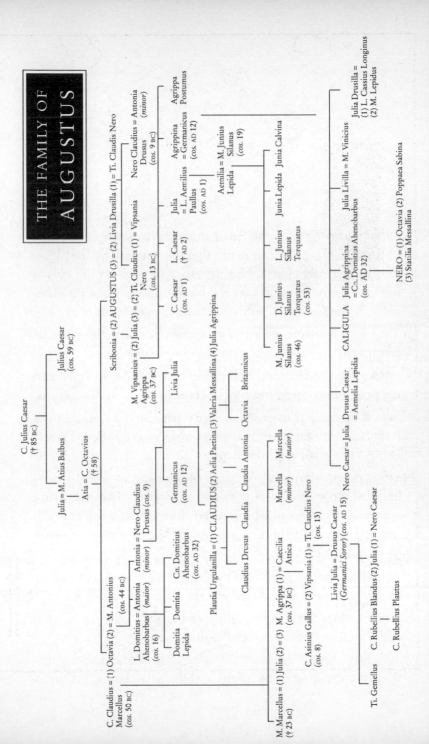

THE FAMILY OF AUGUSTUS

✦ GLOSSARY ✦

AEDILE magistrate in charge of the infrastructure of the city of Rome. Originally four in number (two elected by the plebs, two by the patricians). Not an essential step on the *cursus honorum* – the political career – but because of their involvement in the Games, a way of getting into the public eye.

AFRICA to Romans only the countries bordering the Mediterranean.

AGER PUBLICUS the land belonging to the state, in Italy and the provinces, leased out by the censors or given to veterans.

ALLIES OF ROME title given to a city friendly to Rome in the Italian peninsula; nations further afield were called 'Friend and Ally of the People of Rome'.

AMPHORA the standard container of the ancient world, a two-handled jar with a narrow neck for storing or transporting anything which could be poured, like grain, wine and oil; holding an average of nine gallons in Greece and six to seven pints in Rome.

AQUILIFER the top soldier in the legion who carried the silver eagle and was expected to die rather than surrender it.

ASIA western Turkey, including the islands of Lesbos, etc., and the cities of Smyrna and Ephesus.

ASSEMBLY there were three: 1) the Centuriate, ancient un-wieldy, consisting of the plebs and the patricians together in their classes. Elected consuls, *praetors* and *censors* and passed laws. 2) The Assembly of the People, arranged in the thirty-five tribes of Rome, summoned by a consul or praetor. Elected the *quaestors*, the *curule aediles* and the tribunes of the soldiers, with the patricians. Passed laws and had trials. 3) The Plebeian Assembly, no patricians, passed laws and conducted trials. In all Assemblies the block vote was operated.

AUCTORITAS authority plus prestige, credibility and influence.

AUGURS elected priests to the official College of, to check out whether a proposed undertaking – anything from a war to a marriage – had the approval of the gods.

BARBARIAN any non-Roman, originally any non-Greek.

CAMPUS MARTIUS military training ground outside the city walls to the north-west, with space for horticulture, depots for wild animals, temples and mausoleums.

CENSOR this office was the zenith of a respected political career, to which only a consular (q.v.) could be elected, for five years. The two censors controlled the membership of the Senate, the equestrian order, and awarded state contracts, apart, of course, from coping with the

CENSUS which was the roll call of every male Roman citizen, with his tribe and status, brought up to date every five years.

CISALPINE GAUL Gaul from this, the southern, Roman, point of view. Conquered by an Ahenobarbus ancestor of Nero, securing for Rome the territory from north-west Italy to the Pyrenees.

CITIZEN a Roman citizen could not be flogged or punished without a trial and had the right of appeal *(vide* St Paul). He could be conscripted at seventeen and was entitled to the corn dole.

CITRUS WOOD no longer extant and not to do with lemon trees

but cut from the roots of the cedars of Lebanon; the most coveted and valuable wood for cabinet makers in the ancient world. Table tops were mounted on ivory legs; Seneca had a lot of them.

CLASSES there were five official classes in Rome, according to economic status; the 'head count' did not have any, therefore no vote.

CLIENTELA every grand Roman patron was attended in the morning by a group of hangers-on or dependents, 'clients', who were treated by him with consideration or hauteur according to his mood or nature, but the relationship was important to both parties, crucial between former master and freedman.

CONSCRIPT FATHERS senators enjoyed this designation because it reminded them of their antiquity.

CONSUL the top job in Rome under the Republic, with limitless power, and an office to which Emperors were frequently elected. Strictly speaking a Roman could not be elected consul before the age of forty-two. Two were elected annually and their names, with the abbreviation 'cos', were used to date events.

CONSULAR (noun) a former consul who would be used to govern provinces, become censor, etc.

CUNNUS root of the English word 'cunt' and the French 'con'.

CURSUS HONORUM the four steps of a political career – senator, quaestor, praetor, consul.

CURIA place where the Senate met, in our period not fixed.

CURULE CHAIR a grand stool made of ivory, sometimes inlaid with gold, for the use of magistrates and above, with curved legs in the shape of an X.

DELATOR a citizen who denounced another, usually one of

substance, to ingratiate himself with the powers that be and get a rake-off *(vide* MAIESTAS).

DEMAGOGUE rude word from the right for a politician of radical views who often hired thugs *(vide* Clodius and Milo).

DENARIUS the origin of our penny (1d), a silver coin the size of a dime.

DIGNITAS crucial to a Roman of any standing, his reputation, his worth, his everything. It was for the sake of his *dignitas* that Caesar crossed the Rubicon.

ERGASTULA barracks where slaves in chain-gangs working *latifundia* (landed estates) were locked up at night.

ETRUSCANS were an older race than the Romans, who took over many of their beliefs. They lived in that swathe of Italy on the west, between the rivers Arno and Tiber. Maecenas was an Etruscan prince.

FASCES outward and visible sign of authority in Rome, these bunches of birch rods were borne before a magistrate by lictors, whose number indicated the level of his power, from two for an *aedile* to twenty-four for a dictator. Outside the *pomerium* (boundary) of Rome an axe was included in the bundle, meaning the official could execute as well as scourge . . .

FORUM any open-air space where people congregated, also a market place.

FREEDMAN a slave who had been given, or had purchased, his freedom, but see 'CLIENTELA'.

FREE MAN a man born free anywhere in the world.

GENS (noun, fem.) clan in Rome – e.g., Julia, Claudia (this book is about the Julio-Claudian clan), Livia, Cornelia, etc.

GLADIATOR a professional performer with the sword, who

fought before an audience, not intentionally to the death, several times a year.

GOVERNOR used loosely in this and other books on Roman history to mean consul, *praetor* or other official who ruled a province in the name of the Senate or Emperor for a year or more.

GREECE was never even a geographical expression in Roman times, being depopulated and politically *déclassé*. (The Athenian Empire only lasted for thirty years.) Roman Emperors patronized, in every sense, the Greeks.

IMPERATOR originally the commander of a Roman army, then a great general hailed for his victory by his army, then a title used only by Emperors.

IMPERIUM area of power and degree of authority, vested in an individual and renewed annually.

INSULA apartment building in Rome, where most people lived, separated from the next *insula* by a street or alley. A rich family might have the whole of a ground floor of a five-storey building, the street-facing spaces being let as shops and the higher, the cheaper, the more dangerous and the most insanitary floors being subcontracted to a slum landlord.

KNIGHTS substantial Roman citizens, members of the equestrian order, who became in our period the businessmen of Rome – as opposed to the patrician senators who were not supposed to be 'in trade'. In the early days of the Republic the knights had to supply and maintain a horse as part of a unit of cavalry for the city's defence, but it became an indicator of status – 400,000 *sesterces* a year – and political entitlement.

LEGATES the Roman army did not categorize ranks into as many grades as ours (from lieutenant to field-marshal); legates were senior officers at the level of senator, reporting to the general and senior to military tribunes.

LEGION the essential Roman army unit, akin in *esprit de corps,* tradition and reputation to our regiments but fixed at around 6,000 men made up of ten cohorts of six centuries each. They were variously rowdy, riotous, rapist, indisciplined or balanced and trustworthy, depending. A legion was a complete unit, like a modern division with its own artillery, auxiliaries and cavalry.

LEX (noun, fem.), e.g., Lex Pompeia, called after the consul Pompey Strabo, passed by the Plebeian Assembly, which enfranchised communities in Cisalpine Gaul. Laws were inscribed in bronze or stone and stored in the temple of Saturn.

LICTORS the beadles, beefeaters, escorts of Roman magistrates who carried the *fasces* (q.v.). They had to be citizens but were not well paid and relied on tips.

MAGISTRATES general term for the elected officers of the Senate and People of Rome (SPQR – *Senatus Populusque Romanus* – still engraved on the manholes).

MAIESTAS treason (cf. *lèse-majesté),* a dangerous and much abused law by Tiberius through to Nero in our period.

MANUMISSION the act of freeing a slave. Theoretically the freedman became a Roman citizen but was usually too poor to vote as he was placed in one of the unenfranchised classes.

MENTULA correct Latin for male organ *(vide* PENIS).

NOBLEMAN as distinct from PATRICIAN (q.v.). A consul and his descendants became noblemen and this was a way of diluting the exclusivity of the old aristocracy, *vide* the English custom of converting politicians into peers of the realm.

PATERFAMILIAS head of the family, who in early Rome could execute his daughter if he smelt wine on her breath and sell his son into slavery. Augustus, when pushed, availed himself of these ancient, terrible rights.

PATRICIANS the early Roman aristocracy which adhered to its

prestige and privileges for hundreds of years, producing consuls, *praetors*, senators, generals and governors, whoever was in power. As in eighteenth-century England, when there were only 150 members of the House of Lords, they were all related and alone could hold certain priesthoods; however, throughout our period their power is fading in the face of the 'new men' and the imperial freedman.

PENIS (vulgar) name for the male organ *(vide* MENTULA).

PLEBS nothing derogatory about being plebeian, embraced every citizen who was not patrician.

POMERIUM the religious boundary enclosing the city of Rome within which no one could be buried.

PONTIFEX MAXIMUS head priest of the state religion; not a full-time job, but brought with it a grace and favour house with the Vestal Virgins.

PRAETOR second highest job in the state, eight of them in our period, often provincial governors.

PROLETARII the lowest, classes, also the 'head count'.

PUBLICANI 'publicans' of the New Testament, tax farmers under the republic. The system generated abuse and was cleaned up by the Emperors.

PUBLIC HORSE in Rome (as in the Middle Ages) a horse cost as much as a Bentley; 1,800 were supplied by the state to the most important knights, becoming a mark of distinction for a family, which handed them down through the generations.

QUAESTOR the first step on the *cursus honorum,* a tax official who was elected for a year and had to be thirty, like a senator. There were sixteen of them and they served in the treasury in Rome or were seconded to the provinces.

QUIRITES a civilian as opposed to a soldier (cf. Julius Caesar's opening remark to his disaffected veterans).

ROSTRA prows of ships used for ramming but became our 'rostrum' because the prows of the defeated fleet of the Volsci were stuck on to the speakers' platform in the Forum.

SENATE senior advisory and occasionally legislative and debating chamber in Rome, whose numbers wobbled up and down from 100 in the days of the kings to 300 in the Republic (when they were appointed by the Censors) to 600 under the Empire at the discretion of the Emperor. Senators had to be rich and were mainly landowners, often with estates all over the Empire. They were often usurers and Brutus, 'the noblest Roman of them all', once took advantage of a thinly attended session to put through a guaranteed loan to some Cretans at 48 per cent interest for himself. The Senate controlled the treasury, foreign affairs, declarations of war and could dominate in an emergency, even against an Emperor, e.g., in outlawing Nero. Unlike its imitators in other countries, the Senate did not have its own building but could be convened in different places, like a privy council.

SESTERCES abbreviated as HS, the commonest Roman currency, worth a quarter of a *denarius*.

SUBURA the slummiest section of Rome, where nevertheless Caesar had his family *domus;* polyglot, including Jews and the first synagogue.

TALENT about twenty-five kilos of metal not necessarily gold or silver.

TOGA impressive but awkward garment worn by Roman citizens on formal occasions; like a large bath-sheet and held by the left hand. Colleen McCullough, now a scholarly writer of historical novels, has proved that a Roman so attired could not have worn underpants as he would have found it impossible to pee. Togas only came in one size, were always made of light wool but were decorated variously for Emperors, triumphant generals, magistrates, priests and for those in mourning – black.

TRIBE thirty-five in number of which sixteen were ancient, patrician *gentes.*

TRIBUNE an official. The term was used of military officers, magistrates, senior civil servants at the treasury, elected representatives of the plebs with powers of veto. Tribunicial *potestas* voted to Emperors gave them overriding powers.

TRIUMPH voted by the Senate to a successful general; occasions when the city of Rome went *en fête*, wallowed in self-glorification, food, drink, loot and the blood of their enemies. Often the preliminary to a *coup d'état;* Augustus restricted Triumphs and Nero, fatally, perverted them.

TUNIC standard top for a Roman male, distinguished by stripes of colour according to rank. The *tunica modesta* was used to burn the Christians for Nero's garden parties.

VESTAL VIRGINS six girls of gentle birth chosen as children of seven or eight to be brought up in chastity and serve the goddess Vesta for thirty years. Their persons were sacrosanct and any lapse on their part was punished by being buried alive.

VILLA a large country house, originally at the centre of an estate but in our period built in agreeable spots, like Antium, for pleasure and holidays by the sea. They were always grand.

ROMAN SOCIETY

✢ SEX ✢

The omnipotent *paterfamilias,* enforcing chastity on his sons with the threat of death if they did not obey; the formidably pure matron, like the mother of the Gracchi; the censorious Cato the Elder, who held that a husband had the right to kill a man found in his wife's bed; all were part of Roman legend at the beginning of our age, the time of Augustus, but their image had faded.

The DIY element in Roman justice had been replaced by the courts. The *matrona* Lucretia might blush in the presence of Brutus on being quoted an epigram of Martial, but she had her own copy in the bedroom, and Cato was said to go to the theatre – smutty music-hall – only so that he could be seen to leave it.

The sexual temper of the age was randy, permissive and tolerant of fairly bad behaviour, but not vicious or orgiastic. The sources for this opinion – the poets Horace, Virgil and Ovid, the writers Martial, Petronius and Juvenal, the historians Tacitus, Suetonius and Dio and, somewhat surprisingly, Cicero, from his lawyer's addresses and his letters – used by modern scholars, with your author limping behind, describe every variety of sexual activity, but contain no reference to group sex – *partouses.*

The interested modern eroticist might also be puzzled by Roman indifference to female breasts – boys', yes – lesbians and masturbation. There is no Latin word for dildo and the constantly self-replenishing pool of slaves in Rome – willing or unwilling, it did not matter – surely made masturbation unnecessary.

In Rome, attitudes and even laws obtained which inhibited sexual excess, but pederasty, prostitution, pimping and pornography were never criminal. Wife-beating is not recorded and rape was more talked about and threatened than prosecuted in either sense.

The free-born Roman constructed for himself a sexual personality, a macho image, derived from the God Priapus,* who was depicted displaying his organ – his weapon – massive, ensconced in huge balls, as boldly as Jupiter his thunderbolts. Priapus was a potent, talking phallus, celebrated by the poets, who stood in his garden, a potter's field, threatening expected intruders with his sickle in one hand and – more often employed – his powerful penis in the other. He raped women in the normal way and boys through the arsehole but men were subjected to *irrumatio*.

Another work** I have consulted lists 800 Latin words for sexual organs and other orifices and vessels, and the use to which they could be put – for there was no activity unknown to, or beyond, the Roman appetite, except perhaps 'rimming'. Rimming (the theme of a privately circulated

---

* This chapter depends greatly on *The Garden of Priapus* (OUP, 1983) by Amy Richlin, an avowed feminist and the Professor of Classics and Women's Studies at the University of South California. She writes, however, with charm and translates (as well as James Michie, whom I have also used) the works of Horace and Martial. Her book is inflammatory and should be kept in a cool, dry place, out of reach of children.

** *The Latin Sexual Vocabulary* by J.N. Adams, Johns Hopkins University Press, 1982.

poem by the late W.H. Auden), for which, again, I cannot find a Latin word, is seriously indelicate. I cannot repeat the advice of Dr Johnson, in the same quandary, to a young lady, to 'ask your mother', because mother would not know. An open-minded (I nearly said open-mouthed) homosexual who knows Japan, might. In defence of this proclivity one can only say – as the Roman playwright Terence, not Horace, remarked – *'Homo sum; humani nil a me alienum puto'* ('I am a man so consider nothing human foreign to me').

Mr Adams states there is no English equivalent to the Latin transitive verb *irrumare*. It means to fuck someone in the mouth, quite different from fellating them or sucking their cock or clitoris. Penis, by the way, was a four-letter word for the Romans (avoided, for instance, by Cicero), *mentula* being the acceptable form. *Irrumatio* was the ultimate humiliation a Roman could inflict on another and to be accused of taking pleasure in being so performed upon was the worst insult available to Roman writers. It was one used by the Emperor Augustus in his famous obscene epigram directed at Antony. The first and last lines of Catullus' defence on his erotic poetry are thoroughly priapic, viz., *'Pedicabo ego vos et irrumabo'* ('I will bugger you and fuck your mouths').

Women were not threatened or abused in this way. Towards women the Roman was loving, tender, generous, persuasive, jealous and possessive but rarely gallant and never chivalrous. The knighty Christian concept of chivalry would have baffled the Romans (*vide* Julius Caesar's treatment of the glamorous Gaul Vercingetorix). Their ideal woman had 'skin as white as wax, sparkling eyes, sweet breath, lustrous dark or auburn hair' (never yellow or red), 'a scented sensuous lissome body and a shaved clitoris, glowing like a pearl'. (To be the ultimate ideal, she should be sixteen.) All these attributes are culled from Roman poets. She should also be buxom, in the old English sense of being obliging both round the house and in bed, and sober (Roman gels only drank water), not extravagant or too made-up, with a graceful carriage and able to dance – but not too well.

The Romans had always been, unlike contemporary sophisticated peoples like the Jews, monogamous. However, divorce was easy and the attendant litigation over marriage settlements, dowries, inheritance and custody kept the lawyers rich, happy and popular. The Roman chose his bride for her looks, her consanguinity (she was often a cousin) or her political connections – or for a combination of all three. Marriages therefore, especially in politically dominant and Imperial families, were arranged. Nevertheless, or perhaps because of this, they were often happy and endured, but not so often discussed as those which were not, and did not.

The Romans loved gossip. How they would have enjoyed the telephone! Cicero, so different from the ponderous and indignant orator presented by generations of Latin masters, was fascinated by the affairs of his sons' ex-mistresses. When a Roman marriage 'broke up', they used the expression, as we do, in a passive sense, as if a bad-tempered wind had picked up the marriage vessel and smashed it to the ground. The former partners might behave in a 'civilized' way towards each other. The poetess Lucretia, prized by Professor Richlin, remarks that her marriage lasted fifteen years and that she was still remarkably fond of her husband. How like an Upper-East-Side New Yorker!

The husband was not expected to be faithful and there is no reference in Roman literature to 'cheating on the wife' nor to the 'scarlet woman' stealing his affections. In a city packed with prostitutes – and a bored married woman could register as one with the city *aediles* – there was no need for such carryings-on. Upon marriage a Roman was expected to put aside his boy and his *concubinus* but, if he could afford it, it would be normal for him to employ a – traditionally, pretty – cup-bearer. Wives' comments on this tradition are not recorded.

Horace advises a young unmarried man, with a bob or two, to seek relief with a prostitute and not with a girl of the same class, in order to avoid affronting the *matronae*. ('Do you need a gold cup for your thirst?') He describes the fate of those, forced through lack of means to pursue 'free' sex, who are caught in adultery by the master returning unexpectedly to his country house. 'One throws himself headlong from the roof . . . another is beaten with whips to the point of death . . . another gives money for his bodily safety.' Not for him, says Horace smugly, the fear of 'while I'm fucking, the door being broken in, the dog barking and having to beat a retreat barefoot, in an unbuttoned shirt'. It has been said of Horace, as of Virgil, that he could not have been in such danger, his inclinations lying elsewhere. (The curious and successful defence by a man found in a married woman's bedroom – that he was looking for a slave boy with whom he was in love – is part of Roman history.)

The Romans were not infernal sex machines geared to gratifying lust. They did not treat, like upper-class Victorian and Edwardian English gentlemen, the lower class as their brothel. The six plays of Terence, who died in 159 BC, have been performed for 2,000 years, and still are by the boys, and I suppose now girls, of Westminster School. They are peopled by courtesans, their pimps, eunuchs and maids – Ethiopians being favourite for their fine bones – by the young gentlemen of Athens, loaded with debt and love for a 'music-girl', their cheeky servants, ancestors of Figaro, and by grumpy papas, whose bark was always worse than their bite, turning up in the last act to sort things out. Music was the least of the girls' accomplishments. They were quite young, the idyllic age of sixteen, and their young men were expected to pay for their lessons. The plays of Terence are frothy but full of affection – of brothers and friends for each other, of fathers for their sons, of servants for their masters (and for servants, read slaves) and of a well-born young man for a lowly music-girl, the sort which ends in marriage. That the Romans could delight in the mores of Terence shows surely that they would not have approved the cynicism of *Les Liaisons Dangereuses* or the ethic of the blockbuster sex novel, put together off Madison Avenue and powered by the Harold Robbins' formula of money/power/sex/violence/money/power . . . From this the Romans would have detached sex, for though 'private', i.e., sexual, life was very much not a man's own affair, but was used by anyone who dug up the details for use in character assassination in a trial,* in graffiti, lampoons, letters to friends or loud remarks at a party, public knowledge of it never destroyed (or made) a career.

Exposure of a Roman's deviant sexual behaviour did not reflect on his ability to govern nor did it automatically terminate a political career, as has occurred to British politicians caught kerb-crawling, spanking rent-boys or visiting the basement-flat property of a Chancellor of the Exchequer, controlled by a lady flagellant . . . Indeed Julius Caesar, who was known as a young man to have been the toy-boy of an Oriental prince and later to have become a promiscuous

* Of Cicero's attack on Verres, the corrupt governor of Sicily, Professor Richlin has this to say: '. . . a peculiar recurring accusation was that he was involved in homosexual debauchery . . . The Verrine accusations have the morbid appeal of all narratives of atrocity and resemble sadistic pornography . . .' – so much for a favourite classical text.

'bald-pated adulterer', sung about by his soldiers, went on to be deified. Antony, exhibited as a boy for sale in a woman's toga, the garb of a prostitute, became a triumvir and would have been, had he not lost the Battle of Actium with Cleopatra, the ruler of the world.

For a Roman to be a known homosexual did not affect his social or political progress provided he was circumspect, did not let his desires appear obsessive, did not behave outrageously in public – did not, in other words, 'frighten the horses'. Though the ancient Greek patented *meeden agan* – nothing to excess – they were notorious for ignoring that precept. Diogenes masturbated in public. Phryne, the most powerful courtesan in Athens, accused of orgying at the sacred mysteries of Eleusis, was stripped naked before the Athenian Assembly with the words, 'You who believe that the good are beautiful must believe that the beautiful are good!' She got off. Alcibiades, the Athenians' star, died under a shower of their arrows. They were bored by his umpteenth betrayal. Excess was in fact the characteristic of the Athenian Empire, which lasted only thirty years; moderation that of the Roman, which lasted for centuries.

Further, a Roman homosexual should not pursue his ultimate sexual goal – anal penetration – with a free-born boy, lest it affect his character. The passive role, reinforcing through economic domination the dread and contempt in which it was held, was reserved for slaves. Inevitably the relations between a Roman and his freedmen were made awkward, if they had served him in this way in their past.

Most Romans with leisure and money were bisexual. Of our five Emperors only Claudius was certainly not. Such indifference was unusual. A later Emperor, the goody-goody Marcus Aurelius, was considered unreal for not responding to a compliment on the beauty of his male slaves.

More love poetry was written to and about boys than women or girls. (There is none between male lovers.) Virgil, 'the supreme poet of the Empire and the Roman people', told in his most passionate and lyrical lines, in the second *Eclogue,* the sad tale of Corydon and his love for Alexis, a slave boy, designed for buggery as a Porsche is for speed – and costing as much. Virgil, so rumour had it, was a homosexual but again this did not diminish his prestige among contemporaries nor the admiration of his Emperor, Augustus.

The charm of boys as they advanced towards puberty and on to manhood was vigorously celebrated and enjoyed. Unlike today, when enthusiasts have to check them out dangerously and often illegally, they were freely on view in the baths of Rome. Men's eyes would fall easily on a 'cute pair of balls'. The appearance of a spectacularly well-hung young man or *a fortiori* a boy – the beau ideal – would be greeted with applause. Dragging back could be expensive and there are sad little poems about an erection collapsing when a Roman reflected on the cost of further pursuit. Boys were – and were expected to be – petulant, demanding, indifferent and faithless. Serving at table they should play the Ganymede; epicene, tender and flirtatious, but later that night the Priapus, 'stuffing the master's dinner further down his backside'.*

---

* This quotation is from Juvenal but it must have been common practice, for Seneca, when writing about slaves from the Stoic point of view, has the following: 'Another, who serves the wine, must dress like a woman and wrestle with his advancing years: he cannot get away from his boyhood, but is dragged back to it; and though he has already acquired a soldier's figure, he is kept beardless by having his hair smoothed away or plucked out by the roots, and he must remain awake throughout the night, dividing his time between his master's drunkenness and his lust – in the bedchamber he must be a man, at the feast a boy'.

Romans did not allow themselves the gooiness of homosexual sentiment. They did not romance about the Theban 'army of lovers'. They were practical in this matter as in every other. Boys were lovely but tricky and finally disposable and replaceable like the succession of poodle puppies required by the lady in Aldous Huxley's novel *Point Counter Point*. We do not know the extent of loving between men in Rome but we can guess, suspect or (why not) hope. The Dictator Sulla had a satisfactory affair with an actor, synonymous with male prostitute, throughout his explosive career. We can be sure that love between men was thought to be a preference, never a perversion.

In Praise of Older Women would not have sold in Ancient Rome. A nasty niche is reserved in the Roman Chamber of Sexual Horrors for the voracious older woman, rich enough to buy men or employ eunuchs, pathics or slaves to satisfy her 'itching, desiccated cunt'. (That word by the way has a respectable Latin root.) Women were more generally feared than idolized. Juvenal's description in his sixth *Satire,* the most vitriolic piece of misogyny in the ancient – or, one would have thought, any other – world on the behaviour of a Roman wife, is designed to discourage matrimony. If a man wants a chaste wife, says Juvenal, he must be mad, for a woman will try to run his money, friends and slaves, will try to gossip with important men, will, if literary, act superior, will take, as lovers, actors, musicians, even eunuchs and pretend to be jealous to conceal her own adultery. If upper-class, she will refuse to have children, and if rich, will wear too much make-up. (Fards, then as now, cost a fortune.) Juvenal does comment that good women are boring.

No Roman wife behaved as badly as Messalina. She consumed lovers recklessly but also had an appetite for anonymous sex, posing as a prostitute in a brothel. When her husband, the Emperor Claudius, was snoring safely in his bed, she sneaked out into the streets wearing the red or yellow wig of a slave and accompanied only by her maid. (A *nostalgie de la boue* was frequently indulged in by high and mighty Romans, to the dismay of their security men.) She would stand naked in the doorway of a room in the brothel, her nipples titivated with gold paint, welcoming all until the early hours, when she would creak back to the palace, grimy with lust and dirt. Though spectacularly wicked she was also stupid, and caught in an inept plot against the Emperor, having gone through a form of marriage with her lover, she was finally put down.

Of course, most Roman wives did not have a slave flogged to give them an appetite while they were being dressed for dinner (or while choosing material for a new set of curtains), nor did every well-heeled husband abuse his slave boys, and the prurience of the satirists describing this behaviour surely contains a sliver of disapproval. The ancient world might have considered some twentieth-century activities, like the purveying of 'snuff movies', inhuman, though Romans took an unashamed and guiltless pleasure in the display of cruelty, perhaps not understanding how much of their pleasure was sexual.

❧ SLAVERY ❧

Slavery is as old as mankind, indeed an early sign of human organization. The absence of slavery in the modern First World is a recent phenomenon. Declared illegal by an English judge in the seventeenth century, abolished in the United States and Russia in the nineteenth, slavery flourished a hundred years ago in parts of Latin America, notably Brazil (*The Masters and the Slaves* by Gilberto Freyre, published by Knopf in 1956, is one the most remarkable books on any subject).

Slavery still exists in Arabia, where auctions have been recorded recently, and, by extension, in Eaton Square, London SW1, where indentured Filipino girls are found sobbing in the streets, complaining about their attempted rape by the sons of their employers.

We react to revelations of slavery or of quasi-slavery – child labour in the Far East, for example – with horror, but this reaction is only as old as the existence of the motor car, say a hundred years. For the Romans in our period, from the birth of Julius Caesar to the death of Nero, the last of his clan (37BC–AD 68), slavery was a mostly unquestioned part of life. The behaviour of human beings towards each other, however inhumane, always has its *justificatif*. Geneticists from California were invited to Germany by the Nazis to justify the concentration camps. The institution of slavery had the most respectable apologists: Aristotle approved, subject to 'no outrage, no familiarity', limitations which were spectacularly ignored. Euripides, the great humanitarian, 'could not conceive of its abolition', a view shared by the Hellenist Jewish philosopher Philo. The Stoics considered slavery to be an external accident about which nothing could be done. Hannah Arendt, the existentialist political theorist, explains in *The Human Condition:* 'The institution of slavery in antiquity . . . was not a device for cheap labour, nor an instrument of exploitation for profit, but rather an attempt to exclude labour from the conditions of a man's life.'

Put the other way, the ancient world considered some tasks, essential to life, so disagreeable that they could and should not be performed by proper human beings, so slaves were invoked to perform them. Therefore slaves cannot be considered as completely human. They were 'tame animals', interested only, said Euripides, in filling their stomachs. Under Roman law, because slaves do not naturally tell the truth, their evidence in court was only allowed if obtained under torture. When a slave was freed he rejoined his 'nature' – i.e., was transmuted from a *res* to a *persona.*

Seneca – playwright, philosopher, tutor to Nero – was alone in disapproving of slavery and of the bloodletting of the Games, but then he was a very rare and a very rich man. Seneca's contemporary in Rome, St Paul, with whom fifth-century Christians invented a correspondence, said easily: 'We are all slaves before God.' It was not until the reign of Trajan, nearly fifty years later, that the institution was thought to be 'unnatural', and not until the Emperors Antoninus Pius and Claudius Aurelius that a slave could complain of ill-treatment and that the power of life and death was removed from the masters.

A Roman of senatorial rank could be a soldier, an administrator or an advocate (unpaid) but never a business-
man in a regular way, though speculation was, strangely,
considered OK. The poorer Roman citizen, the plebeian,
who had only his vote to sell, would never sell his labour.
So all the *work*, physical and mental, was performed by
slaves. They were doctors, secretaries, book-keepers, major-
domos. Both sides used slaves as soldiers in the Civil Wars,
Emperor Augustus as Imperial Guardsmen. Gladiators and
actors almost had to be slaves, which explains the downfall
of the Emperors Caligula and Nero, whose performance in
these roles, though they delighted the plebs, engendered
the fatal distaste of the Roman upper classes. The first was
murdered by young nobs and the second outlawed by senatorial decree.

A man born into this world was weaned, coddled, taught,
fed, entertained and indeed often loved by a variety of slaves
from the cradle to the grave. Long-serving slaves were
manumitted on his deathbed – Seneca's was the classical
example – and the rest were left as part of his estate. Slaves in
Rome were completely inside society and indeed often, if a
play on words is permissible, inside their owners. By the
end of our period few families in Rome were not laced with
slave blood, which may have diminished Roman *severitas*
but also made Romans more tolerant. Rich people bought
handsome slaves of all sexes for pleasure and display just as
randy duchesses in the eighteenth century relished a
well-turned calf in a footman or a groom both for public
contemplation and for private enjoyment. Marcus Aurelius,
listing the austere attitudes of indifference to sensual pleas-
ures of his adoptive father, Antoninus Pius – a remarkable
pair of pure Emperors – adds that he did not notice 'the
beauty of his slaves'.

The field slave or mining slave did not fare so well; one Roman matron, a big landowner, the Mrs Helmsley of her day, maintained it was cheaper to work her slaves to death and replace them than to feed them properly. If slaves wrote love poems they have not come down to us. There are moments in Latin literature describing the love and affection of masters for their slaves of which Virgil's second *Eclogue* is the most famous. The desperate love of Corydon for Alexis is told at length and heart-wringingly. Alas the pampered slave boy belongs to another. Such a beauty in the open market would have cost 24,000 *denarii* – the cost of a Porsche today. A run-of-the-mill slave at this time, at the beginning of our millennium, cost only 500 *denarii* and his day's labour half a *denarius*, but the poets were not interested in such fellows. The size of the Empire and the extent and variety of its conquests meant that slaves, shuffled anonymously in the markets, could have come from anywhere and be anybody. Virgil's contemporary, Horace, writes to a friend:

> Dear Phocoan Xanthias, don't feel ashamed
> Her family's undoubtedly royal; perhaps
> She's mourning some palace's cruel collapse.

> (Horace, *Odes*, Book 11, iv, tr. James Michie,
> Penguin)

The reason for the *Lex Aelia Sentia,* which prohibited the manumission of slaves under thirty by masters under twenty, can be imagined. A slave in Rome had many routes to the 'status' of freedom, which gave him liberty but not citizenship. Then he could wear the conical little hat of liberty, revived in the French Revolution. He might purchase his manumission from his master with his *peculium* (literally 'private property', usually an accumulation of tips). He might earn his freedom through public service in the fire brigade or as a street cleaner. But the most common way of manumission was from the affection or deathbed gesture of the master. Cicero, whose manumitted slave Tiro edited his letters, claimed that it should only take six years for a slave to become a freedman and then, if he were shrewd and industrious, he could become a millionaire like Trimalchio – the exuberant party-giver satirized by Petronius and filmed by Fellini. Pliny records one freedman who became rich enough to leave 4,116 slaves in his will.

Members of the Roman intelligentsia were often descended from slaves. The father of Horace was a freedman who became a tax-collector or possibly an auctioneer's assistant but in a substantial enough way to leave him the competence of a gentleman. Epictetus, the stoic philosopher, was slave as a boy to Epaphroditus, one of Nero's courtiers.

Of course, the life of slaves, even in Rome, could be heavy with humiliation and cruelty. Ovid writes of porters being chained in Rome. Vedius Pollio, a Roman aristocrat, fed his slaves to his lampreys for 'trivial offences'. The 400 slaves (a large enough number to have included *silentarii* – slaves employed to keep the others quiet) of the household of the Prefect Pedanius Secundus were led off to execution by soldiers, through a sullen crowd, after one of them had murdered him.

In the early days, the concept of slavery – of one man helping another till the soil – could be described by the historian Mommsen as 'innocent'. But as the numbers of slaves increased so did the Romans' fear of them. Laws relating to slavery under Nero, for instance, were both repressive, through fear, and humane, through a sense of justice. The law under which the 400 slaves of Pedanius Secundus were executed in AD 61 had been initiated by Augustus but the classical schoolmaster's favourite, Seneca, so famous for his clemency, did not even attend the agonizing debate in the Senate deciding that the law be enforced in this case (Professor Michael Grant suggests that the slave who murdered his master may have been in love with him!). The Senate's decision was truly Roman: the law was cruel but clear, it had to be implemented.

The supply of slaves came mainly through conquest. Men, women and children from defeated Italian towns were the earliest source. Then Rome was flooded by the entire population of Sardinia and the phrase 'cheap as a Sardinian' became current. As the Empire expanded, slaves were shipped in from all over the world and the flow only stopped, as Gibbon pointed out, with the completion of the Roman system of conquest. The international big business of slavery was centred on the little Cycladic island of Delos, where the turnover of 10,000 slaves a day was recorded in the time of Augustus. Before they were suppressed, kidnappers and pirates dumped slaves anonymously on to Delos. Julius Caesar was himself kidnapped and held to ransom, as a young man. As a general in Gaul he records selling (the sale of slaves was the general's perk) 53,000 Aduatuci (defeated Gallic tribesmen) in one day. Perhaps he needed the money to repay Crassus . . .

There was no uniform for slaves in case they should realize how many they were. The system was based on force and was occasionally broken by greater force. Sicily was the first scene of effective slave revolts. In that unblessed island, chain-gangs of slaves, mainly Greeks, were used by bulk farmers to run the grain business, which supplied more than half the Roman market. In 104 BC, under the consulship of Marius, the mad young son of a Roman knight, one Titus, armed 500 slaves with weapons being auctioned off by a gladiatorial school and in no time had an army 4,000 strong. This revolt was put down and all participants executed. The second Sicilian revolt lasted longer. Two slave kings emerged – one called Salvius, an Italian freedman and snake charmer, the other a Greek called Athenio – and raised an army of 60,000 well-armed slaves and 5,000 cavalry, but enthusiasm and indignation cannot glue armies together for ever. It was not until the revolt of Spartacus in 73 BC that the Romans were seriously threatened by 'their enormous slave population', which outnumbered them three to one.

Spartacus and his ultimate destroyer, Crassus, were the stuff movies are made of: one noble, forgiving, heroic, the other greedy, cruel and charmless, the unacceptable face of Roman capitalism. Crassus, a slave trainer and dealer on an enormous scale, bought houses when they were on fire at a cut-down price – otherwise he refused to put them out. He financed Caesar and was the third man in the triumvirate with Caesar and Pompey. After four years Crassus defeated Spartacus and lined the Appian Way with the crucified bodies of rebellious slaves.

Spartacus passed into Roman folklore as a bogeyman, like Napoleon, and was used to frighten the children. Voltaire described his struggle as 'possibly the only just war in history'. But history belongs to the conquerors. Roman history was played against a backdrop – painted bloody and brooding, occasionally lit by charm and consideration – of innumerable slaves. They were essential to the life of their masters and their lives were not always a living death. They were also essential to the economy of the Empire and without them the roads, bridges, ports, aqueducts, amphitheatres (though some were built by soldiers), triumphal arches, markets and public baths could not have been built or maintained. Maintenance is the essence of civilization and without slavery Rome could not have been civilized.

✦ THE ROMANS ✦
AND THEIR JEWS

The Romans may not have liked their Jews but they never attacked them with that committed hatred characteristic of Christian (and other) rulers in Europe from the Middle Ages to the first half of the twentieth century. Judaism, one of many cults around for Romans looking for fresh religious experience, was respected; Jews were not.

The religion was puzzling and unintelligible, the habits of its practitioners distasteful and inconvenient. 'They worship nothing but the clouds and the sky . . . they despise Roman laws . . . they have this man Moses . . . they smell of candles and tunny fish tails . . . they practise circumcision . . .' (wrongly supposed to increase sexual potency), complained Juvenal. And on the seventh day, the Sabbath, they absolutely refused to budge, rendering them unsuitable for military service. 'No Jew on the Sabbath,' wrote Augustus to Tiberius (getting it wrong), 'fasted as seriously as I did . . .'

Throughout our period, from Julius Caesar to the Emperor Nero (both venerated by the Jews), their privileges and exemptions were confirmed and honoured throughout the Empire, and, when challenged by officials or rival subjects, were usually upheld. The annual levy of a drachma, paid by Jewry in the Diaspora to the temple in Jerusalem, was transmitted intact, even during a hard currency crisis in Rome. A centurion who raised his skirt and farted, to show his contempt, in the Temple precinct was reduced to the ranks. Roman standards bearing eagles, or bulls, had to be covered when paraded through Jerusalem.

Recent excavations in Aphrodisias,* near Smyrna in Turkey, have revealed an inscription in the stalls of the amphitheatre which reads, 'reserved for His Imperial Majesty's loyal Jewish subjects'. Aphrodisias, a city as large as Pompeii, was destroyed by earthquakes in the seventh century and vanished from history. Like every other town in the Empire, Aphrodisias had its quota (though there were no restrictions as that word implies) of Jews, and an inscription in creamy white marble, for which the place was famous, lists seventy, mostly with non-Jewish-sounding names, which suggests proselytes – on whom, again, there was no restriction.

Of the 4 million Jews in the Roman world (more, relatively, than in ours), half had emigrated, mostly voluntarily and happily, from Judaea. One explanation for their numbers may be that unlike many peoples in the ancient world they did not practise infanticide. They spoke the language of the country where they had settled – often Greek, though they were not Hellenized. They could read, but not necessarily understand – never a rabbinical requirement – the law and their prayers in Hebrew. Like overseas Chinese in Europe today, but emphatically not in the takeaway context, they were everywhere.

Marseilles, a Greek colony, had thousands of Jews centuries before Christ. Jews may have been in England with the Phoenicians, exploiting the mines of Cornwall. They deferred to no central religious authority (unlike the equally ubiquitous

---

* *Aprodisias, City of Venus Aphrodite* by Professor Kenan Erim, Muller, Blond & White, 1986.

Roman Catholics of our day) and their only common link was a sentiment for Jerusalem, realized in the obligatory temple tax of one drachma* a year. Jews were particularly strong in Alexandria, feuding with the Greeks and interrupting the Games. They were also prominent in Antioch, Cappadocia, Pontus, Phrygia and Pamphylia – everywhere in fact visited by Paul on his journeys. When he arrived, under praetorian escort, in Rome in AD 62, he would have found 40,000 Jews and fourteen synagogues. The first swathe of Jews, thousands of them, had arrived as prisoners-of-war in Pompey's triumphal procession 100 years before in 61 BC, and were sold into slavery as part of the successful general's perks. But as we have seen (*vide* chapter on slaves), with a bit of *nous* and application a slave in Roman times could be manumitted, and once they were free they had settled down on the wrong side of the Tiber – in what is now Trastevere – as butchers, bakers, candlestick-makers, in any kind of métier except that of moneylending, which was enjoined upon them by the Christians in a later era. Some gained unpopularity (and were occasionally banned) as fortune-tellers. A Jewish actor (as we have already seen, a questionable profession) who welcomed

* Historians have an awkward task calculating the contemporary equivalent of such sums, especially because of the rate of inflation over the last fifty years and the different values of a pre-industrial society. Clothes, for instance, were vastly more expensive. People were murdered for a cloak. In one of his letters Paul asks for the return of one he left behind. A poor country like Sri Lanka is a present indicator of the levels of the ancient world. There labourers are paid by the day the equivalent of a dollar, which is enough for a family to survive on. The drachma, always used by Josephus and the same as the silver Roman *denarius* (the origin of the 'd' which stood for our former penny) was also a day's wage. A talent was worth 60,000 drachmas, so when Herod in his bankrupt (and charming) early days offered 300 talents to ransom his brother Phasael he would have had to find 1.5 million sterling in today's money.

Josephus to Rome had insinuated himself into Poppaea's circle, probably as master of (a certain kind of) 'ceremonies' at the palace.

Paul rented a flat near the praetorian barracks, and lived there for two years, at his own expense, practising without let or hindrance the gospel of Our Lord Jesus Christ – to paraphrase the last two verses of the Acts. He would have been the only Jew on the block. One wonders what happened then. Legends abound. Paul might have died before the fire of Rome in AD 64, but it is unlikely that he could have survived Nero's persecution of the Christians – as they were not yet called – because although they did not, of course, start the fire (nor did Nero) it suited the Emperor to pretend that they had. Poppaea, the Emperor's mistress and eventual wife, was not a Jewish proselyte but favoured Jews and protected them against the accusation of arson which fell so savagely on the Christians, a sect indistinguishable, to the Romans, from the Jews.

Few Romans could, or would, have said 'some of my best friends are Jews'. The Emperor Gaius could have and should have because Herod Agrippa *was* his only friend, but being Caligula he didn't and indeed planned a grotesque insult, which nearly broke Agrippa's heart (*vide* chapter on Caligula). Jews in the Roman Empire, however successful, rarely assimilated with the powers-that-were, unlike the Jews of South Africa or at the court of Edward VII during the British Empire.

Only one Jew, a nephew of Philo the philosopher and historian from Alexandria, abandoned his religion and became Prefect of Egypt, as well as Prefect of Police and Corn and of the Praetorian Guard, one of the top jobs in the Empire. Josephus, of whom much more anon, having changed sides in the Jewish War, boasted of his Roman acquaintance; but the family which fraternized consistently with the Julio-Flavian dynasty was that of Herod the Great, who weren't really Jews at all.*

Herod came from Idumaea, the biblical Edom, the bottom left-hand corner of what is now Israel, inland of the Gaza Strip. The Herod of the New Testament, he who massacred the Innocents, gross, cruel and stinking, like Henry VIII at the end of *his* life but with four more wives, has left an impression of horror difficult to dent. Immobilized by advanced arterio-sclerosis, paranoiac and communicating with his family, it would seem, only through torture and assassination, it is amazing that he survived so long, but as a young man this handsome, athletic and kind Arab – not many princes in his day bothered to ransom their younger brothers – managed to convince the Romans *and* the Jews he was the only figure in the landscape they could trust. He was trusted by and loyal to Antony and then, in spite of being penniless, was believed by the new conqueror, Octavian (Augustus), who added to his dominions and trusted him as completely. By the age of thirty-six, through charm, daring and political genius – much of which consisted in out-bribing the bribers – he became the King of Judaea, 'the friend of Caesar, the most distinguished non-Roman in the Roman world, known throughout

* Herod visited Rome three times in his life and was always welcomed and honoured at court. His sister Salome had an affair with the Arab regent Syllaeus and in her wish to marry him was backed by her friend, the Empress Livia. Berenice was a friend of the Empress Antonia, Caligula's grandmother, with whom Herod Agrippa stayed in Rome. She also paid his debts when he went to see Caligula on Capri with the Emperor Tiberius. According to Gibbon, his sister Berenice (famous, like the Duchess of Windsor, for her jewels) was loved by Vespasian Titus and, aged fifty, had to be prised from the arms of his younger brother Domitian.

the Empire for his wealth, his splendour and his magnificence'.*

His money came not from taxation and, though he was the biggest spender in the ancient world, and second to the Emperor Hadrian the biggest builder, he was never in debt. Through his mother, whose father was a merchant in Petra – not then a picturesque spot with rose-red walls, but the most profitable trading-post in the world – he controlled the traffic from the East to the Mediterranean, owned the palm and balsam groves round Jericho, ran on Augustus' behalf the copper mines in Cyprus and split the profits with him, and lent money to other local kings.

Though not a Jew, he professed and marketed Judaism (although the spiritual element eluded him) with as much zeal and on a greater scale than any Jewish king since Solomon. (The institution of monarchy, 'fashionable in modern times', as Gibbon sourly remarks, was a Jewish invention.) He rebuilt the Temple in Jerusalem within an enclosure covering thirty-five acres, greater than the area of the Acropolis, and filled it with colossal buildings. The Temple was begun in 19 BC and not completed till AD 64. The little Old City of today's Jerusalem, cosy if tortured, encircled by Saladin's intact wall, is a fraction of the size of Herod's and is without an edifice of any remark. Herod's city was staggering. Here is Sir Charles Wilson, quoted by Stewart Perowne, on the Royal Portico, which he investigated 100 years ago: 'It is almost impossible to realize the effect which would be produced by a building longer and higher than York Cathedral, standing on a solid mass of masonry almost equal in height to the tallest of our church spires: and to this we must add the whiteness of stone fresh from the mason's hands.'

---

* Quoted from *The Life and Times of Herod the Great* by Stewart Perowne, Hodder & Stoughton, 1986 – a wonderful book.

Within his kingdom, Herod created 'western' cities like Caesarea, and the fortress Masada, where he planned to retreat in case of heavy trouble from his own subjects. Synonymous with munificence internationally, like a Carnegie, a Rockefeller or a Rothschild, Herod spread his *euergetai* – good works – throughout the Empire, repaving Antioch with marble, presiding at great expense over the Olympic Games and constantly giving hand-outs to good and bad causes.

One of his subjects, born just before his death, must have been awed by Herod's development of Jerusalem. The young Galilean from Nazareth – not a highly rated place in his day – may have contemplated its gardens and palaces with resentment, for he was not invited in. Jesus' only rich friend was Lazarus, in nearby Bethania (Bethany), whose hospitality he was able to repay with the ultimate gift – life. His overturning of the money-changers' tables outside the Temple would have been regarded by the fat cats of Jerusalem as a Republican Senator would consider a raid on the souvenir shop at Fort Knox today.

The special relationship between Rome and Jerusalem, the Imperial family and Herod, could not survive his death and in AD 6, Judaea was annexed as a province and subsumed by Syria. Through the reigns of Tiberius, Caligula, Claudius and Nero, Herod the Great's dominions were chopped about and administered by governors or procurators of no particular account, certain of whom are known to us for their appearance in the New Testament. Pontius Pilate was corrupt, bad-tempered and tactless; Felix, who imprisoned Paul and whom he disdained to bribe, was bent; Festus, who wanted to acquit Paul, was straight; the worst was Cestius Gallus, the legate of Syria whose behaviour at Passover in Jerusalem in AD 66 provoked the Jewish War.

The Jewish War, which lasted six years – a long time if the relative strength of the parties is considered, especially since the Jews spent much of their energy fighting each other – was painful and exasperating for the Romans and catastrophic for the Jews. If Josephus is to be believed,* and there is no one else to turn to since the usual sources – Tacitus, Suetonius, Dio Cassius – are either brief, silent, contemptuous or not extant, the Jews brought their final solution on themselves.

Josephus worked on his *History of the Jewish War against the Romans* from the comfort of a large house in Rome, a large income and the friendship of the Emperors Vespasian and his son Titus. His objectivity was therefore dimmed by his circumstances, but the history is exciting and readable and has been a steady seller for nearly 2,000 years. It was especially popular in Victorian households.

Aged nineteen, son of a middle-class Jewish family with property in Jerusalem, Josephus, having studied both the Sadducees and the Essenes, became a Pharisee. In the war he was appointed commander in Galilee, one of the six regions into which the country had been divided, but at the Siege of Jotapata, which he was defending, he changed sides – like John Churchill, first Duke of Marlborough, on the eve of the Battle of Sidgwick, but after more thought and with more copious explanation. Josephus maintains in his history that the Romans held him in such esteem that they thought the war would be virtually over when they secured his person. He surrendered to 'an old friend', the tribune Nicanor, having addressed his comrades-in-arms as follows: 'Why, my friends, are we so anxious to commit suicide? Why should

---

* As E. Mary Smallwood, editor of Josephus' *History of the Jewish War,* truly a Penguin Classic, observes, 'In the absence of external controls we must perforce accept Josephus' word, however uneasily.'

we make those best of friends, body and soul, part company?' So Josephus opted out of a provincial war into Roman history. On meeting Vespasian, he prophesied for him the imperial purple and, if he is to be believed, became one of Vespasian's 'kitchen cabinet', steering him in the 'year of the four Emperors' towards his destiny.

Meanwhile the war, even after Josephus' defection to the Romans, continued. The war had begun well enough for the Jews, who had taken advantage of the disarray and rebelliousness in the provinces, caused by Nero's rackety behaviour towards the end of his reign, to attack the occupying power. (When concentrating, Nero had been capable of quite effective foreign policy.) One Sabbath day in September AD 67 the legate Cestius, a greedy bloodthirsty brute, was booted out of Jerusalem, losing in the process 5,300 infantry and 480 cavalry. Among the dead was the commander of the 6th Legion. Jewish losses were negligible. Romans would not have been astonished by the success of the Israeli army though they would have been surprised by its discipline and its unity with the state, for though the Jews of their day fought with daring and often fanatical courage, they were dangerously disorganized. After the Roman débâcle 'many prominent Jews fled from the city, like swimmers from a sinking ship' (Josephus), and here we must distinguish the factions, who hated each other as much as they hated the Romans.

The Sadducees were the hereditary high priests, no more religious than the *noblesse* of the *ancien régime* who monopolized the plump offices of the Church in France. They were property-owners who employed hard men to collect their rents. From their palaces on Mount Zion,*

---

* '. . . beautiful for situation, the joy of the whole earth . . .' from Psalm XLVIII, traditionally sung on Mondays.

special only because it was the highest point in the city and attracted the first rain, they could walk along a covered way to the Temple. The Sadducees, perhaps because they could not credit that it could be an improvement on the one they enjoyed, did not believe in the afterlife and being anxious at all costs to preserve their earthly position co-operated (like Vichy) with the occupying power. They thought they were there for ever, but as Abram Levy, Haham of the Sephardic congregation in London, asked: 'Where are the Sadducees now?'

Needless to say, the Sadducees were often at odds – politically, socially and economically – with the Pharisees, who were priestly, scholarly, intellectual, bourgeois, believers in the letter and spirit of the Law. Their attention to hygiene, for instance, amounted to the obsessive. Saul, who was a prize Pharisee before he became Paul, joked that the Pharisees would have washed the moon had they been able to. The self-appointed monitors of society, they interpreted, practised and guarded the Law, notably from the often unintentional insults of the occupying power, and were not always so narrow in this role as they are cast in the Gospels. Professor Hyam Maccoby, the most tolerant and readable of modern Jewish scholars, maintains that the Pharisees and the Sanhedrin were not continuously hostile to Jesus, nor to his followers after his death, indeed that occasionally friendly references to both peep through, uncensored, in the Gospels. Professor Maccoby claims that Jesus *was* a Pharisee. (Alas for the Jews, he is their most famous man.)

Nothing Jesus is reported to have said conflicted with the Jewish law he had come 'to fulfil and not to destroy'. The same Dr Abram Levy told me the only doctrinal difference between Jesus and Judaism is the Christian emphasis on forgiveness. Jews are not obliged to be so agreeable, being a people known, as Disraeli put it, 'never to forgive an injury, nor forget a benefit', but equally they do believe that the Sabbath is made for man and not man for the Sabbath, which means that considerations of serious illness or danger take precedence.

None of the above, of course, would have been of any interest to the Romans, in whose literature the only reference to Jesus is in Josephus, and that a forgery. Awareness of followers of the cult of Jesus – the term 'Christian' was not current till long after his death – being separate from other Jews, cannot be detected till the fire of Rome and they were not systematically persecuted till the end of the century. Anatole France has a story which may well describe the effect of the new religion on the Roman mind at the time of Nero. Anxious to know more about the background of the followers of Jesus, the Foreign Office (as it were) sent a young man to question Pontius Pilate, the governor who had him crucified, now in retirement in Baiae (Naples). Pilate is delighted at the opportunity to talk shop and evades the matter in hand with a series of reminiscences in the vein of I-wonder-what-happened-to-him? Finally, exasperated, the young diplomat asks Pilate directly to tell him about Jesus of Nazareth, founder of this new subversive cult which is giving trouble to the authorities. Pilate looks puzzled.

'– whom you had crucified,' repeats the young man, 'thirty years ago.'

'Rappelle pas,' says Pontius Pilate.

The followers of Jesus, the disciples of his brother James, the 'Jerusalem Christians', as historians called them later, may have fought the Romans in the Jewish War, but they are – tactfully, perhaps – nowhere mentioned.

Another sect with whom early Christians have been (mistakenly) compared were the Essenes. Though there is no monastic arm in Judaism, monasticism and monkish habits, coming from the ashrams in India around 1,500 BC, were adopted by colonies of Jews and of these, since the discovery in 1947 of scrolls around the north-west corner of the Dead Sea, the colony in the caves at Qumran is the most famous. We know now that the Essene community there was destroyed by Vespasian after his capture of Jericho in AD 68. Josephus describes them thus:

> The Essenes profess a severe discipline ... They eschew pleasure-seeking as a vice and regard temperance and mastery of the passions as a virtue. Scorning wedlock, they select other men's children and fashion them after their own pattern ... contemptuous of wealth, they are communists to perfection ... each man's possessions go into the pool ... Men to supervise the community's affairs are elected by a show of hands, chosen for their tasks by universal suffrage.

Apart from their misogyny, Josephus could be describing Chassids in North London or the Bronx, and apart from their silence and severe piety, an early Kibbutz in Israel. Certainly, like latter-day *kibbutzniks*, the Essenes were famous for their fighting capacity, their only personal possession being a knife.

In the Jewish War the Romans also came up against the Zealots and the Sicarii, so-called from the daggers hidden on their persons. During the Siege of Jerusalem, Titus found three factions fighting each other and occasionally successfully combining against him. As Josephus explains, 'Men highly organized and trained to fight according to the book and in obedience to orders are more quickly demoralized by unorthodox and enterprising tactics.'

Finally, after hundreds of thousands of Jews had died through slaughter or starvation in every corner of the once wealthy kingdom of Herod, and after the capture of his fortress Masada, where the Romans found corn, wine, oil, pulses and dates, in a perfect state, hidden by Herod 100 years before, resistance by Jews expired. It had been an unequal fight. As Josephus had warned his compatriots, the Romans were destined to rule the world. 'What corner of the earth escaped the Romans, unless heat or cold made it of no value to them?' God was on the Roman side.

Titus, son of Vespasian, fulfilled the prophecy of Jesus (recorded after the event), that not one stone in Jerusalem should remain on top of another, by levelling Herod's city. Only the tower Herod built for Mariamne I, the wife he loved and murdered by mistake, was left standing. Perhaps Titus wanted to leave a souvenir, perhaps he liked it. It is still there.

Vespasian and Titus, like all successful Roman generals, were reasonable towards the reasonable. We have seen how they treated Josephus. Unnecessary trouble should be avoided. Romans would always deal. When Rabbi ben Zakkai had himself smuggled out of besieged Jerusalem in a coffin and explained to Vespasian that he had not planned on a martyr's death, he was allowed to start a theological college in Sfad. Titus, returning to Jerusalem, was, according to Josephus, appalled at the destruction he had ordered but reflected that the Jews had only themselves to blame. Those in the Diaspora were made to pay for the folly of the homeland by having their annual levy to the Temple in Jerusalem diverted to a temple dedicated to Jupiter in Rome, but in no other way.

When the not-so-good citizens of Antioch besought Titus to revoke the privileges of Antioch's Jewish community, the second richest in the Empire next to that of Alexandria, Titus refused. Robin Lane-Fox, in *Pagans and Christians* (Penguin, 1988), points out that for centuries of the common era the synagogue in a Roman city remained a more substantial and prominent building than the Christian 'house church'. But the destruction of the Temple in Jerusalem was a trauma from which the Jews have never recovered. It has never been rebuilt; the sacrifices detailed at length in the current Jewish Book of Common Prayer have never been performed; the Sanhedrin has never sat.*

This chapter began with the observation that the Roman world was not averse to new religious experience. Judaism had now been tainted by its connection with an unpleasant little war; an alternative was waiting in the wings.

The whole of Rome turned out for the Triumphs of Vespasian and Titus. (The Senate had voted them one each but they decided to combine.) The Roman Triumph was a triumph of organization and glory. Every stop was pulled out. By AD 71, the end of our period, the choreography, as it were, was fine-tuned. The Triumph was an amalgam of display, religiosity, terror, feasting and debauch. Only the Romans could have invented it. It was also a superb instrument of foreign policy, demonstrating to client kings, allies and potential enemies the power and the generosity of Rome – and the cruelty, for the Triumph ended with the execution of the principal enemies, who had formed part of the procession.

Mark, the youngest of the Gospel writers, is said to have witnessed the Triumph for the Jewish War. If he did he would have seen the treasures of the Temple, the richest in the world, paraded through the streets of Rome: the golden vessels and the golden trumpets, the altar of solid gold, the five scrolls of the Pentateuch, the *menorah* in solid gold with its seven branches – the latter two the most holy objects in Israel: Also in the procession was Simon the Zealot, the invincible hero of the Siege of Jerusalem, in chains, walking to his execution. Mark must have decided that a new religion could not succeed if it offended Rome.

* In 1808, Napoleon convened a Sanhedrin to dignify Jews with proper names but they suspected it was just a tax ploy.

✦ ROMAN LAW ✦

Roman Law bound Rome like Roman cement. Its genius was its complexity and its fairness, which gained it acceptance for thirteen centuries by millions of people. It lasted from Romulus in 753 BC to Justinian in AD 535, when 3 million judgements were finally consolidated into sixteen volumes by sixteen commissioners. In the realm of jurisprudence, Roman Law is rivalled only by the English and the First World still responds to one or other of these systems.

The power of Rome grew through conquest, followed by treaties, and a process by which local gods and local laws were subsumed by Rome. The British, when collecting their Empire through annexation and the spoils of war, were not so respectful of 'native' rights; for instance, after a career such as his in Africa, Cecil Rhodes would have been prosecuted for extortion* had he been a Roman. Indeed it was with this

---

* Extortion *(repetundae)* was big business, both ways, with the Romans, and it became recognized in a law of 122 BC, the Lex Acilia, passed by a friend of the reformer Gaius Gracchus, that provincials had to be effectively protected against the unreasonable depredations of their Roman governors. A permanent court was set up, organized by the knights *(equites)*, who drew on a pool of their order for juries. Judaea was a hot but profitable seat, because of the wealth of Jerusalem, for Roman officials, and Pontius Pilate, who we now know to have been a prefect, not just a procurator, was constantly being complained about. Philo quotes

charge that Cicero, champion of the Republic in its dying days, leapt into Roman history to prosecute Verres, a governor of Sicily.

Cicero, darling of Classics masters, is most eloquent in his analysis of Roman Law – whose twelve tables schoolchildren had to learn by heart – and in the preaching and practice of the Republican virtues of dignity, probity, industry, virtue, respect (for authority) and prudence, which are all Latin words and Roman concepts. He could also be a thumping bore and wrote the worst hexameter extant:

O fortunatam, natam me consule Romam

which has been neatly translated as, 'How fortunate of Rome to date/her birthday from my consulate', and his penchant for self-congratulation and his long letters of advice must have contributed to his being purged, after the *coup* which brought Octavian (later Augustus), Antony and Lepidus into power as dictators.

The establishment of that triumvirate was, in typical Roman fashion, enacted by the Senate with 400 centurions and soldiers hovering around to help them make up their minds; for the seizure of power in Rome was always cloaked with legality, and the Senate, which finally disposed of Nero, remained an institution respected by tyrants, until the arrival of the 'African' Emperor Severus.

Roman Law, in the beginning, was based on the authority of the *paterfamilias*, the head of the family, who had the right, until the end of the Empire, to sell his children. It was he who insisted on *boni mores* – dutiful service, chastity and

---

Agrippa as calling him 'inflexible, heartless and obstinate'. Pilate was never prosecuted but was recalled in AD 36 for what really amounted to lack of tact on a monstrous scale.

respect for superiors. He could and did punish adultery in his children with death. The Romans were always monogamous, though later divorce was easy. Strangely, there is no trace of primogeniture, although a Roman must ensure his posterity, otherwise enjoy no happiness in the grave. Hence the frequency of adoption, because the upper classes were far from philoprogenitive – which led Augustus, as part of his campaign to restore 'old-fashioned values', to give tax concessions to citizens who produced three or more children, rather like the almost free rail travel and state benefits for large families in present-day France.

The original Roman *paterfamilias* was the incarnation of the law. There was one law for the patricians and none for anybody else. Between these patricians – who belonged to a *gens* (like the *gens Julia* of our first five Emperors), of which there were 300, which was in turn one of the thirty *curiae* making up the three tribes of Ancient Rome – there was at first no need for complicated laws of contact, because a Roman's word – to another Roman – was his bond.

Each was a legal personality with a lot of land in the centre of Rome – his *heredium* – to which the family clung throughout the generations; and as they grew with Rome, so they attracted a *clientela,* a group of dependents – poorer citizens and freedmen – whom they protected in return for votes or willingness to participate in a claque in court.

Freedmen and 'foreigners', which were soon the majority in Rome, could only sue in the courts via a Roman *paterfamilias,* so it was essential to belong to a *clientela* right up until Caracalla – he of the Baths – enfranchised all free men in the Empire. Roman lawmakers moved in great strides to deal with the problems, and the benefits, of increasing population and prosperity. At first one of the magistrates, called a *praetor,* interpreted the tables of the law in Rome; after the conquest of Sicily there were four, with Spain six; Sulla the Dictator made eight and Caesar, sixteen; they began to create case law with their decisions, which were posted on a white board *(album)* displayed in the Forum.

More through the influence of Seneca than of Christianity, Roman Law softened with time, until even slaves gained certain rights. A creditor could no longer seize the son of a debtor and put him in irons. Debt, and the means of its recovery, often by a patrician from a small farmer, had been the cause of the greatest riots in early Rome. At that time it was not only legal, but a religious duty to revenge murder of a kinsman with another death. This law is now only observed by the Mafia. However, a citizen could still kill a thief if he came by night or, in the daylight, carried arms.

Laws like this, which came from the original twelve tables, could be chanted by schoolboys, but later legislation regulating, say, repossession of mortgaged property or restitution for damage done by a slave to another citizen's mule or alienation by a trustee of a minor's fortune had to be studied, together with the art of rhetoric, in law schools throughout the Roman world. Cicero studied under Scaevola, who was an *augur* (one of twelve interpreters of Roman religion) and was, more to the point, *the* expert on Civil Law. He went on to take instruction under Philo the Academician, then attended the lectures on rhetoric of Apollonius Molon in Rhodes, and finally he toured Greece, improving his lung power. His subsequent successes in political trials gave him (a *novus homo,* without family connections) enough support among the electorate – the knights, the country grandees, the smart young men about town – to become a consul. So success at the bar, like success on a military campaign, was the first step in the *cursus honorum,* which led to the top of the Roman state.

Our five Emperors all, in their fashion, respected the laws of Rome. Augustus, who had, as Octavian, proscribed 2,000 knights and 300 senators in 43 BC, became the benign father of the state, whose mission it was to restore the institutions of the Republic, so battered by the civil wars in which he was the only winner. He followed the forms of the Republic and in being elected consul thirteen times demonstrated that his authority came from the Senate and People of Rome.

The Roman term *imperator* was given to a general by the acclaim of his troops, whereas the superior king figures of modern history derive their status from the Judaeo-Christian ritual of being anointed with oil by a priest, in early days under instruction from the Almighty. Emperors in Rome never claimed divine right and had to wait for death to be deified. They believed in *vox populi – vox dei*, that the voice of the people expresses the will of God (and not, as revolutionaries would have it, the other way round); they insisted that the people, that is to say the legislators, had to approve their most outrageous actions.

This explains the amount of time the successors of Augustus spent terrorizing the Senate. Nero, having failed to arrange a fatal accident for her, had his mother killed but legalized matricide by inventing a conspiracy which she was supposed to have mistress-minded. As we shall see, he even managed to convert the event into a Triumph. And consider Caligula, always billed as the monster of the classical world; feckless, whimsical and cruel, he would have approved the dictum of his latest (American) biographer, that while power corrupts, absolute power is more exciting. In fact, making his horse into a consul never happened, and was his joke anyway. His thirty-nine named victims were carefully chosen and were fewer than those of the Emperor Claudius (who couldn't be kept out of the courtroom).

Caligula despised the Roman people which is why he was wished on them by his predecessor, Tiberius, equally contemptuous, but less amusing and amused; but he respected their laws. By modern standards – Hitler executed 10,000 Germans after the July plot – Roman Emperors were restrained in their treatment of conspirators, having no secret police and only rarely holding trials in camera. In fact, Caligula practised 'open government', in that when reintroducing the *Lex Maiestatis* (discouraging *lèse-majesté* – offences against his sacrosanct person) he had the terms set out on a bronze tablet. He published his accounts, lifted censorship and even published the names of the clients at his brothel on the Palatine. (Another of his terrible practical jokes.)

The Roman Empire could not have lasted so long had its subjects not believed in the efficacy and eventual justice of Roman Law. One of its most famous citizens, Saul of Tarsus, knew exactly what he was doing when he appealed unto Caesar.

❧ THE ROMAN ARMY ❧

Colonel de Gaulle, in his revealing book – like Hitler and Franco* he stuck to his principles – *Le Fil de l'épée (The Way of the Sword)*, published in 1932, praises the army as the embodiment of a nation's will. He wrote. 'France was created by the sword. Our fathers entered history via the sword of Brennus [he of the Brenner Pass, *ed.*]. Roman armies brought them civilization. The fleur-de-lys, symbol of the nation's unity, is but a javelin framed by lances.' De Gaulle and his admirer (but not his friend) Churchill were the last statesmen to believe in blood. Both had experienced the First World War at its most disagreeable, Churchill with his battalion – he had asked for a brigade – and de Gaulle who had been present at Verdun where the mutiny had been put down by another future head of state, Pétain; but if the experience had dismayed them it had not discouraged them. The Roman Army – and still less the Japanese – would not have tolerated trench warfare. The Roman soldier respected his life and would not have obeyed a commander who did not share that view. Both would have regarded the grumpy deference of the British tommy and the sentimental sacrifice of the French *poilu* – in their hundreds of thousands – as unprofessional.

In equating a nation with its army, de Gaulle is thinking like a Roman; indeed to contemporaries the Roman army

---

* Who both showed their hands early on in book form.

was the religion of Rome, and Rome the religion of the army. With good reason, since the vulnerable city of Rome had achieved hegemony in Italy through force of arms (and some cunning) wielded by its volunteer citizen foot soldiers assisted by knights, riding, without stirrups, small horses paid for out of the public purse. The Republic conquered most of the world with a professional army essentially of heavy infantrymen, and the Empire maintained, consolidated, monitored and only slightly aggrandized those possessions which stretched from Mauretania (Morocco) to Armenia, and Thebes in Lower Egypt to Luguvallium (Carlisle). The addition of Britain by the Emperor Claudius was expensive and would not have been approved by Augustus. In his day the Roman world contained a population of about 45 million controlled by an army totalling, with auxiliaries, 400,000 men, who (with weapons less sophisticated than the 500,000 Americans recently in the Gulf) kept the world at peace. When the Roman soldier was not fighting – most of the time – he was building. Nowhere is this military activity of peaceful construction better illustrated than in North Africa where Legio III Augusta (originally 100 men) was stationed for more than a century, and where, as Sir Mortimer Wheeler once observed, the remarkable thing was that nothing remarkable happened.

When de Gaulle wrote of the civilizing mission of the Roman army in France he cannot have meant its original and at times genocidal subjugation of Gaul under the command of Julius Caesar, who gained a lot of his money and much of his reputation (*pace* his unchivalrous treatment of the brilliant young Vercingetorix) there. De Gaulle must have been thinking of the Roman roads, the aqueducts (like the Pont du Gard), the temples (like the Maison Carrée in Nîmes, perhaps the most perfect building in the Western world,

erected at the beginning of the millennium in honour of
Augustus' two young grandchildren and heirs) and the
almost intact amphitheatre in the same city, where I saw
the Davis Cup in 1991. All these were constructed by engineers, architects and surveyors attached to the Roman army,
using Roman cement and blocks of building stone cut and
joined by Roman soldiers. De Gaulle was thinking too of
that system of law and order, inspired by and imposed on
their world by the Romans, so fair that it justified, in the
fullest sense, their regime, whose rarely invoked sanction
was the Roman army. For though the Empire was gained
by force, consensus secured it. In our period – from the
accession to power of Octavian to the death of Nero – and
so on for centuries, the Roman army never had to face an
equal enemy.

'*Delenda est Carthago*', 'Carthage has to be destroyed',
grim old Cato had declared, and it was. Then followed the
three civil wars when Roman soldiers fought each other.
Caesar and his son-in-law Pompey joined battle and hostilities culminated in the victory of Octavian, Caesar's
great-nephew, at the naval battle of Actium against Antony
and Cleopatra. With Octavian's change of name to Augustus,
the Pax Romana, secured by the Roman soldier who swore
an oath to him as 'Imperator' (Commander-in-Chief) on
joining up and renewed his oath annually on New Year's
Day, had begun. From this moment on, none but the Emperor
could be called Imperator and none but the Emperor could
be voted Triumphs. Before, popular generals were hailed
Imperator and could be voted Triumphs by the Senate.
Augustus made sure that no bold general could ever again
cross the Rubicon and threaten Rome. The Roman army
became an army of defence, regionally based and too static
to form the basis of a military *coup*.

This potential role passed to the Praetorian Guard in Rome, created by Augustus to protect the *princeps,* but increasingly, if not 'Emperor-makers', a force whose approval (usually simply secured by 'donatives') was a *sine qua non* of accession, legal or slightly dodgy, by successive and successful candidates for the principate (each of whom upped the ante). The Praetorian Guard, stationed at the centre of power like the Brigade of Guards in London, was not supposed to wear uniform off-duty and unlike – but who knows? – the Brigade, constituted the dirty-tricks department of the Empire. Nero, when other tricks failed, used one of its number to despatch his mama. Equally he himself was killed by a centurion from the Praetorian Guard and the two tribunes, Chaeraea and Sabinus, who struck the first and second blows slaying his predecessor Caligula had also been from the Praetorian Guard. Finally, of course, the Praetorian Guard, in a scene beloved of Hollywood, auctioned off the Empire. Oddly it didn't go for very much – sold to Didius Julianus for 6,250 *denarii,* about five years' full pay, the rate for the job of Emperor paid a century-and-a-half before to Claudius. The Praetorians probably never got their money, for the excellent Severus, one of the best later Emperors, marched on Rome and remodelled the Guard.

The Praetorian Guard was the first of the tripartite Roman military system, which included the fleets of *Milsenum* and Ravenna and the volunteer fire-brigade – the *vigiles* – serving in which was a six-year route to citizenship. The Romans were not very keen on boats, which were unsophisticated compared to their curtained, marbled, centrally heated houses. Their sea, the Mediterranean, was thick with pirates until cleaned up by Pompey, and command of ships was vested in the senior army officer on board, leading to the unthinkable situation (to the British mind) when St Paul in his action-packed (and free) sea voyage could and did take over. Rome produced no Nelson.

The second part of the Roman military system consisted of the legions, each 5,500 men strong, which varied only between twenty-five and thirty in number for 300 years. The Order of Battle given by Tacitus for the year AD 23 looked like this: Rhineland 8; Spain 3; Africa 2 (including the Legio III Augusta); Egypt 2 (one of which, the XXII Deiotariana, was chewed up by the Jewish guerrillas under Simon Bar-Kochba in AD 132 which provoked Hadrian, then obsessed with promoting his drowned lover Antinous as a god, to settle the problem of the Jews, who had their own particularly jealous and exclusive God, once and for all); Syria 4; Pannonia 2 (inferior and superior, a large area south of the Danube and north of Dalmatia); Moesia 2 (Bulgaria and the eastern part of what was Yugoslavia); Dalmatia 2. Missing from this list are legions XVII, XVIII and XIX lost by Varus in AD 9 in the forests of Germany. The numbers were never used again. To the total must be added three or sometimes four legions needed to keep Britain quiet, since that island, together with Germany, Parthia and Judaea (rewritten by Hadrian as Palestina), was a trouble-spot for the Romans.

In a sense the Roman army was only defeated by its own success, for the Pax Romana lasted so long and engendered such prosperity that a military career ceased to be attractive, and when the sturdy volunteer infantrymen were replaced by listless conscripts, it was overwhelmed by hordes of barbarian horsemen. (Given a choice men have always preferred to spend their lives as tinkers, tailors, rich men, even poor men and beggarmen – the role of most Jews in the Empire – than as soldiers or sailors.)

In the early days of Rome the soldier was a young man between eighteen and twenty, over five foot, five inches in height, neither a slave nor an ex-slave, with no criminal record, who signed on for twenty-five years' service, whereafter he could expect to retire with a wife, farm and Roman citizenship. From the moment he took his *viaticum,* equivalent of the Queen's shilling but worth much more, and swore the oath, the army because his life. Unless he was pretty dim and not armed with a letter of introduction, or never bothered to ingratiate himself with his centurion (to this day Greeks bring their officers apples), he would be allowed off stone-cutting fatigue and encouraged to practise what in my time in the British army was called a 'trade' or, if he were able to manage the three 'r's, to go into the 'office' and become a *librarius* or clerk. In the Roman army a trade could be that of ditcher, farrier, glassfitter, limeburner, woodcutter or plumber, and a clerk might be responsible for soldiers' money left on deposit (in AD 89 in Mainz, this mounted up to a point where a legion nearly financed its own rebellion) or work in the surveyors' or architects' departments. Here is a letter from one Julius Apollinaris, writing in his native Greek (Latin was the official language of the army) to his father from Egypt in AD 107:

> I'm getting on all right. Thanks to Sarapis I got here safely and so far haven't been caught by any fatigues like cutting building stones. In fact, I went up to Claudius Severus, the governor, and asked him to make me a *librarius* on his own staff. He said, 'There's no vacancy at present, but I'll make you a *librarius legionis* for the time being, with hopes of promotion.' So I went straight from the general to the *cornicularius.**

---

* Senior NCO under a centurion, in charge of clerical duties.

Not all recruits to the Roman army had such a cushy time as this artful Greek dodger. Basic training was deliberately arduous, featuring twenty-mile route marches with a heavy pack, PT with long and high jump, weapon training with dummy wooden shields and staves twice the service weight (with gladiators as instructors) and wooden-horse vaulting, eventually in full armour. The Roman soldier carried an awful lot of kit, including, to quote Josephus: '. . . a lance, a round shield, as well as a saw and a basket, an axe together with a leather strap, a sickle and a chain and rations for three days'.

His enemies – the Celts, the Germans, the Parthians – exhibited more dash in battle, and none more spectacular than Boudicca (Boadicea), outraged daughter of the King of the Iceni (Suffolk), in her amazing chariot, but 'for steady onward pressure and determined stands his training had made the Roman soldier usually invincible'. He was famous for his obedience and stamina but he also had a mind of his own and would not perform unless he could respect his general; witness the consistent success of Julius Caesar, even when outnumbered, and the catastrophe of the elderly banker Crassus. Julius Caesar wooed, cajoled, bullied and bribed his soldiers and in return they responded to his magic by following him wherever he led them, for it was never boring and often profitable. They sang rude songs about him and if they resented his punishments they never mutinied. Crassus was more than just a very rich man – how else could he have become a triumvir with Caesar and Pompey? He had suppressed the rebellion of the romantic Spartacus, when all around were losing their nerve; he had made a fortune out of dealing in slaves; and the means whereby he acquired real estate – buying up the estates of those proscribed by Sulla, and waiting for property to catch on fire – have not endeared him to history. His plan to conquer Parthia was a classic in doomed unmilitary behaviour. He was too old, Parthia was too far away, he was impatient and resorted to the press-gang for troops. He set sail in the stormy season from Brindisi, losing ships and men in the crossing. Finally he ignored public opinion (in the ranks of his dispirited army) and quarrelled publicly with his commanders. This tragic expedition ended in farce when in a mock triumph the victorious Seleucids paraded some pornography found in the luggage of one of Crassus' officers. His own head was delivered to the Parthian king Orodes when he was in the middle of a play.

The episode points up the Roman passion for the pursuit of glory through arms – as if Charles Clore, dissatisfied with his millions, had decided to mount an expedition against Ho Chi Minh. But Crassus with all his money and power could not have raised the wind for such an outing if the will and the discipline of the Roman army had not been there to harness. The will was part of the Roman belief that the world was theirs to conquer and that other nations, even the Greeks, were inferior. The discipline was the work of the centurions. Military tribunes, often young men taking the compulsory first step in a political career, and generals, appointed by the Senate for a term and for a specific task, might, as they were designed to, come and go, but the centurion was the hard, permanent core of the Roman army.

Reorganized by Marius, the man from the sticks, the Republic's most successful and popular general, the army turned the citizen into a volunteer, professional soldier, more literate and numerate than any before or since. Marius invented the cohort of 600 men, which, times ten, constituted a legion. He organized a system of pay and allowances which became standard throughout the Empire and endured for centuries. He gave the legions their eagles, gave the soldiers their laundry allowance and burial funds with something over for the regimental dinner.

He also weighed them down with equipment so that they were known as 'Marius' mules'. The 'whole armour of God', to use the expression used by St Paul, consisted, apart from 'the belt of truth, the breastplate of righteousness, the shield of faith, the helmet of salvation and the sword of the spirit', of a pike and a dagger which together with the rest of his kit weighed about forty-five pounds, today's standard baggage-allowance for air travel. The Roman soldier 'messed' in groups of six or ten (the sources differ) and lived on wheat (which was turned into porridge or bread), salt and some not very nice wine. He might add some vegetables but rarely meat, except for the occasional bacon. The original of St George, it will be remembered, was a wholesale pork butcher in Cappadocia, whose Christianity was irrelevant until he was lynched by the Roman soldiers for supplying rotten meat. 'The profession was mean,' says Gibbon in one of his best footnotes, 'he rendered it infamous.' A soldier's first step on the ladder of promotion would be to become the head man of his mess, or an orderly; then he would become the centurion's second-in-command, then a centurion. His only route to officer status was to move up the centuriate to the first cohort. Then he would be made a knight and would retire, as it were, with directorships. Centurions literally directed the traffic of the Empire; an indication of the busyness of Antinous' home town Bithynion (now Boli in north-west Turkey and buried under the main road to Ankara) was that it needed two centurions to control the traffic. Retired centurions were in demand for decorative positions (today members of the Royal Corps of Commissionaires tend to be retired company sergeant-majors) or to be in charge of security in a large household. The Roman army trained some soldiers as *questionarii* – torturers – someone had to do it.

A centurion in full rig, with a crest on his helmet, greaves on his shins, his scale armour clanking with medallions from campaigns all over the known world, and carrying in his right hand the vine rod of authority with a nasty little switch at the end, was, for most people, the visible symbol of Roman power and, as we know from the New Testament, the nearest to them. An officer and gentleman would never pass through the rank of centurion, and indeed the distinction between him and the other ranks has been emulated in all modern armies except the Israeli, which functions more like that of one of the early states of Greece. Under the Republic, twenty-four young men were elected annually by the *Comitia* (the Assembly of the Plebs) to serve in the legions of the consuls, also elected, so the link between the army and politics was strong. Too strong thought Augustus, so he added to each legion 120 horses for the young gentlemen to ride – not very effectively because they had no saddles or stirrups – and allocated six tribunes to each legion to serve as aides-de-camp rather than as commanders. A well-connected young officer – and only exceptional men like Marius got anywhere if they were not – would be taken up by the general, perhaps an old boyfriend of his aunt, and mess with him and then be appointed colonel of a regiment of auxiliaries. These were the third prong in the Roman military system – the Praetorian Guard and the legions being the first two – and were equal in number, but not prestige, to the legions.

Auxiliaries were what we might call 'colonial' troops, recruited in the provinces, sent elsewhere, less well paid, longer serving, but ending up with citizenship and a vote for themselves and their family, a more generous dispensation than that afforded to, say, the Gurkhas, who fought for the British in two world wars. (In 1991 when so many English and Scottish regiments were reduced or abolished it was suggested that the Foreign Office compensate these fierce little fellows, who had had to be restrained from presenting their British commanding officers with the genitalia of their enemies in the trenches of the Somme.) As we know, the Roman soldier was essentially a heavy infantryman and the functions of cavalrymen, archers and slingers were often performed by auxiliaries. It was all part of the 'artful system' of the 'artful founder', phrases used by Gibbon three times in describing the remodelling of the army by Augustus. He realized that local affiliations could be dangerous, so Gauls served in Spain and Macedonia and Spaniards served in Britain and Judaea. So Romanized was Gaul that no legions were needed there.

Mobility within the Empire was one of its greatest achievements. The Roman roads were so good that Harold was able to march (down Ermine Street) from Yorkshire to Hastings in three days. British roads, on the other hand, were so bad that George III, having once been overturned, never in his long reign ventured further north than York.

Long distances therefore were no bother to the Roman army, so cohorts – they were never called legions – of auxiliaries, often using their own tribal weapons and sometimes with special skills, like the slingers from the Balearics, the horsemen from Numidia (Algeria) and the archers from Crete, could be moved readily around the Roman world. They were always commanded by Roman tribunes or prefects, were supposed to understand orders in Latin and could eventually benefit from the perks of the Roman legionary. The eighteenth- and nineteenth-century Englishmen, steeped at Eton and Winchester in Roman history – did not one cable the Foreign Office from India, *peccavi* ('I have Sind')?

– copied the 'artful' system of Augustus. William Pitt, in inventing the Highland regiments, was following a Roman precedent.

The discipline of the Roman army was legendary, retailed with relish and approval by nineteenth-century historians echoing their Roman predecessors Livy and Polybius. Most famous, or infamous, was the punishment of decimation, whereby one in every ten soldiers in an offending cohort was chosen by lot to be clubbed or stoned to death by soldiers from another cohort. In fact it didn't happen very often and hardly at all in the Empire, though Octavian had employed it in the Dalmatian War of 34 BC. (He was not, as we shall see, a very nice man.) Caligula, of course, tried to inflict decimation but his orders were ignored. Flogging was a more usual punishment and, for larger bodies of men, the substitution of barley for wheat in the diet; this latter, with a reduction of share of booty, was the favoured punishment of Julius Caesar. A modern German historian propounds the view 'that mutiny and insubordination were surprisingly prevalent in the Roman army . . . that the Roman legionary arrogated to himself an independence of thought and action which was far beyond that with which the Roman soldier is generally credited'.*

Here is an account** of a mutiny worth retailing. The Emperor Claudius, who was not stupid as Gibbon would have us believe, nor amiable as portrayed by Charles Laughton, had decided to invade Britain. Julius Caesar had pointed the way in 55 and 54 BC, but he had not known about the lead mines which, together with wheat and slaves, could

---

* *The Roman Soldier* by G.R. Watson, Thames and Hudson, 1969.
** *Roman Britain* by R.G. Collingwood and J.N.L. Myres, OUP, 1937.

make the operation 'wipe its face', as they say in the City. Besides, his predecessor, Caligula, made a fool of himself by pretending to invade the island – the fleet never sailed – and to restore imperial pride, teach the barbarians a lesson, employ some under-extended legions and get himself a Triumph, Claudius assembled a force of 40,000 men consisting of the legions from the Rhine and one from Pannonia (roughly where Austria is now). But as the historian Dio recounts, the army flatly refused to face an ocean voyage 'outside the world'. When he heard of the mutiny, Claudius sent his top freedman, Narcissus, who was in charge of the new secretariat he had instituted (a sort of Army Council), to sort it out. The soldiers were not impressed. They were used to a pep talk from their *imperator* at the outset of a campaign; to be addressed by an ex-slave, one can hear the centurions grumbling, was too much – or too little. They shouted him down with the sort of jeering reserved for the Saturnalia, when slaves dressed up as masters and vice versa, like the Roman soldiers at the Antonia in Jerusalem, crowning Jesus King of the Jews with twigs from kindling. Nevertheless, Narcissus must have turned them round because the mutiny evaporated and the legions went on board.

The crucial battle was a two-day affair, unusual in ancient warfare, at the Medway (whose existence the Roman General did not expect), and the first day went badly for him. But the second went well, especially when the Emperor turned up with a contingent of his Praetorian Guard and a detachment of elephants. The inscription cut on the triumphal arch celebrating his victory states Claudius suffered no losses; at Colchester eleven kings had submitted to him. Not finding any existing town grand enough to constitute the capital of this new and peaceful province, the Emperor founded Verulamium (St Albans). After three weeks, having left complicated instructions for the administration of Britain, he returned to Rome, where he added to his names that of 'Britannicus'. He also had his Triumph.

A Roman Triumph was a terrible thing. It was the ultimate beano for the legionaries, who paraded through the city with sticks instead of swords and gorged themselves afterwards on oysters from Baiae (Naples), freshwater eels, capons, ducks, piglets and kids and had their fill too of gilded prostitutes. They also received a *donativum*, a present of money. The procession followed a prescribed route: assembling in the west of the city on the Campus Martius (cf. Champ de Mars in Paris), it went through a special gate called the Porta Triumphalis, through the Circus Maximus, where it was cheered by a crowd of 150,000 people and ended at the temple of Jupiter Optimus, which the triumphant *imperator* entered to offer the god the laurels of victory.

Floats were drawn through the streets depicting highlights from the campaign and the vanquished were paraded in their finery and with their captured treasures displayed. Jugurtha, King of Numidia, cut a splendid figure at the Triumph of Marius, in his purple robes, his golden jewelled necklaces and bracelets flashing in the sun, his head encircled with a white diadem. He was led in his chains to the Tullianum, Rome's only execution cell, divested of all his finery (which was handed piece by piece to a clerk of the treasury) and, clad only in a loincloth, jumped into the pit beneath. Rather than face such a humiliating end, the defeated Mithridates, hero of Mozart's first opera, had himself killed.

There is a legend that Mark, the youngest of the Gospel writers, witnessed Titus' Triumph to celebrate the capture of Jerusalem and was so affected by the sight of the high priest in chains on a Roman cart, surrounded by the treasures of the Temple, that he resolved never to incur the wrath of Rome. The triumphant generals laid trophies taken from the enemy in temples, where Roman soldiers could honour them, in ceremonies of which the regimental services, victory parades and state – or as they used to say 'public' funerals of great warriors like Wellington and Churchill, which take place at St Pauls in the City of London, are reminiscent. In Rome the temple of Jupiter was not far from the temple of Juno Moneta, where the mint was housed. It is interesting that while poets lie with kings in the Royal Peculiar of Westminster Abbey, the monuments to the victories which made the British Empire are in the church built in the City of London, where the money is, to celebrate England's status as a great power.

Rome peaked at a Triumph. While voices were raised, occasionally, at the excesses of the Games or the institution of slavery, no one criticized the expense, the grandeur, the arrogance, the triumphalism of a Triumph, not even Cicero. Rome, which kept a copy, on a bronze tablet, of each individual soldier's record of service, never forgot that Triumphs were achieved on his back. Nero forgot and it cost him his life.

❧ THE BLOODY GAMES ❧

The Roman Games descended from the Greek, whose inspiration had been religious, international and pacific. They had begun at Olympia in 776 BC and lasted unchanged for 1,000 years until banned by the spoilsport Christian Emperor Theodosius. The winning athletes won only token awards but, sneered Cicero, were more celebrated in Greece than were victorious generals. Roman Games, though attended by a whiff of religion and originally featuring athletic events like the foot-race, javelin throwing and the pentathlon, developed along quite different lines, becoming bloody, political and expensive. In our period, they included fights to the death between every kind of wild beast, between men (criminals and, later, Christians) and beasts, and, of course, between men and men – gladiators, professional killers.

The passionate entertainment of Romans was the chariot race where, although accidents did occasionally happen – to a too-successful jockey just before a big race – death had no part. The chariot race was essentially Roman. Romulus and Co. raped the Sabine women in a hippodrome at races in honour of an ancient rural deity, Consus, and throughout the history of the Roman Empire there were annual games called the Consualia. In the end there were at least fifty circuses in the Empire and they are still being unearthed. The largest was the Circus Maximus, where the Great Fire started, in a boutique, in AD 64; it was rebuilt by the Emperors Domitian and Trajan to seat 150,000 spectators, becoming the model (with dimensions of 640 by 190 metres) for circuses throughout Europe. They can be seen, or bits of them, at Arles, Vienne, Trier, Antioch (which held 80,000 and where the film *Ben Hur* was shot) and Carthage. Private circuses were built by the rich, like nine-hole golf courses, for their friends. The younger Pliny had one on his Tuscany estate.

The centre of the Circus Maximus was used for the exhibition of trophies and prisoners-of-war, works of art and spectacular loot, like artefacts from Karnak (cf. Cleopatra's Needle in London or the lions in the Piazza di San Marco in Venice). Nothing was too grand for the greatest display of power, speed and danger in Rome, relished and anticipated with excitement by all ranks – slaves, freedmen, citizens, knights, senators and the Emperor and his friends. Everyone could sit and free seats were allocated for the poor. Caligula complained about being kept awake by the noise of the common people claiming their places in the middle of the night before the Games next morning – so much more fun than Wimbledon.

The charioteers were beloved and imitated. Children played with chariot toys, like they play with the models of cars sold all over the world today. Later they rode in carts drawn by sheep or donkeys, pretending to be charioteers, like Caligula and Nero, a contemporary of the dreaded Boadicea, 'married' one at a famous orgy. They were of modest origin, sometimes slaves, but were admired like Nigel Mansell and Sir Lester Piggott rolled into one, and they made, relatively, much more money (tax free). One called Diolus, with 1,462 wins, made 36 million *sesterces*, say £15m in today's money; another, Scorpus, subject of an epigram by

Martial,* was given fifteen sacks of gold in an hour. The chariots were divided into teams, White and Red, then subdivided into Green and Blue. Romans and their Emperors were intensely partisan for their favourite teams: Caligula lunched with the Greens, Caracalla had the jockey of a rival team murdered.

The horses – two, rarely three and, in a *quadriga* like the bronze on top of the arch by Apsley House on Hyde Park Corner, four – bred, and trained until they were five years old, in studs in Cappadocia, Sicily, Spain and North Africa, were also famous, and the judgement of the animal on the inside left of a *quadriga* was crucial when it came to cutting corners. There was no time for pit stops, so slaves threw buckets of cold water on the overheated axles of the chariots when they turned. By the time of Caligula, when spectators could watch and bet on twenty-four heats in a day, the four chariots circulated fourteen times, covering about five miles, so the axles must have got quite hot.

No statistic could be produced to show the number of Spaniards who go home after a bullfight and do not beat up their wives, but we do not have to be psychologists to understand the catharsis, the soothing of the savage breast, induced after hours of witnessing the bloody deaths of animals or human beings, *a fortiori* the crueller, the more protracted, the more ritualized. Julius Caesar invented the bullfight as another course in the sadistic banquet of the Roman Games. Oddly, he exhibited indifference, at the height of his power, when he attended the Games, publicly looking through his papers instead of down at the gore below, attracting the kind of comment which a prime minister might if he were to be

---

* In one race he made more money 'pulling' his horses than if he had won.

seen glued to his despatch box at a Cup Final at Wembley. However he did understand, as a young man on the political make, the brownie points to be scored by paying for gladiators. As an aedile, the first office on the political ladder, he showed off (borrowing the money from Crassus) by fielding 300 pairs. Gladiators also doubled as bodyguards and were used by Caesar's buddy and fixer, Clodius, for the political and gang warfare which marked the last years of the Republic and made Romans more easily accept the discipline imposed by Augustus.

Gladiators, who had performed originally as part of a funeral offering from a pious son in memory of his parent, had become so significant that there was even a profession, *auctoreamentus gladiatorium,* and the trainer, the *lanista,* of gladiators (a synonym in Etruscan for butcher or executioner) could become rich and powerful, though never socially acceptable; for though Romans, 'from first to last spectators, and not, like the Greeks at their best, actors', hugely enjoyed the combat, they were not proud of their gladiators. None, for instance, ever figured on a coin. They were, however, admired, and lovesick tributes have been found on the walls of Pompeii. Occasionally, like the pugs in eighteenth-century England, they survived, and have been caricatured limping through the salons of older and voracious Roman ladies, with their rheumy eyes, scarred bodies and missing ears, objects of contempt, not compassion.

Pliny was bored by the Games; Cicero was in favour, with reservations; Claudius, a gibbering, snivelling weakling, but, as we shall see, immensely cunning, adored them as much as the most voyeuristic of his subjects; Caligula was obsessed by gladiators and once fought an opponent armed with a wooden sword, only to despatch him in due course with a real one. Only Seneca protested.

Here is a well-known extract from one of his letters:

I've happened to drop in upon the midday entertainment of the arena in hope of some milder diversions, a spice of comedy, a touch of the relief in which men's eyes may find rest after a glut of human blood. No, no, far from it. All the previous fighting was mere softness of heart. Away with such bagatelles: now for butchery pure and simple! The combatants have nothing to protect them: their bodies are utterly open to every blow, never a thrust but finds its mark. Most people prefer this kind of thing to all other matches, whether part of the programme or by special request. Naturally so. The sword is not checked by helmet or shield. What good is armour? What good is swordsmanship? All these things only put off death a little. In the morning men are matched with lions and bears, at noon with their spectators. These pit butcher actual against butcher prospectively and reserve the winner for another bloody bout, death is the fighters' only exit. 'But this, that, or the other fellow has committed highway robbery!' Well? 'And murder!' As a murderer, then he deserved what he's getting: what's your crime, unlucky creature, that you should watch it? 'Kill! Flog! Burn! Why does he jib at cold steel? Why boggle at killing? Why die so squeamishly?' The lash forces them on to the sword. 'Let them have at each other in the nude – get in at the bare chest!' There's an interval in the display. 'Cut a few throats meanwhile to keep things going!' Come now, can't you people see even this much – that bad examples recoil on those who set them?

The joy in cruelty, the cruel joy wafting up from this hostile telling of the Romans at play, shows that the crowd was sadistic, like many crowds, though that concept, with its sexual undertones and subsequent possible feelings of guilt, would have been, like masochism, unknown. The Roman lust for blood was equally uncomplicated and prodigious. Tigers and lions were first introduced to the arena in 184 BC and were an instant hit. Cicero wrote that the 'wild beasts were magnificent', though he noticed the crowd felt sympathy towards the elephant. Respect for wild animals is a very modern phenomenon and the Romans felt none. There were, after all, in the Empire, plenty more lions, tigers, bears, ostriches, and even crocodiles, where they came from. They cost a lot to assemble and were only offered at *munera* – the extravagant shows mounted by grandees like Pompey and Agrippa and, of course, the Emperors – as opposed to the *ludi,* attended daily by Caligula,* where deaths were only human. (These, especially the sea battles, when thousands fought to the end on artificial water, could mount up and yield a satisfying glut of blood.)

The Roman Games, beginning as pious memorials, ended in an impious killing, when a (subsequent) Christian martyr, a monk called Telemachus, endeavoured to interpose himself between two gladiators in the year AD 402. The presiding *praetor*, who had probably paid for the event, had him instantly despatched, but when the current Emperor, Honorius, heard of this unhappy interruption, as it might have been represented, he banned the Games and they were never revived.

The elected officials – the *aediles*, *quaestors* and *praetors* who ran Rome and the Empire – were obliged to pay for the Games and were voted money by the treasury, but if they did not double it they could be accused of embezzlement – a

---

* The morning of his assassination, he opened the Games by sacrificing a flamingo, whose blood sullied his toga.

very Roman arrangement. The Games were as significant a feature of Roman life for high and low as the baths, the aqueduct (which the poor would illegally tap into) and the dole. Citizens used the occasions to voice with impunity their grievances to officials and to the Emperor. Everyone knew how much they cost and who had paid what. The public of the Games was the public of the electors, and friends of a young *aedile* on the first rung of the political ladder would stump up so that their chum could put on a good show.

Finally; many Roman citizens had no regular employment and spent their day gossiping, cadging, watching trials and so on – all, unless they were rich, outside and not in the dirty, smelly tenements where they slept. Since holidays increased from two months at the beginning of the Empire to three under Tiberius, four in the second century and six in the late Empire, there could have been no better way of passing the time than attending the Games.

JULIUS CAESAR AND THE JULIO-CLAUDIAN EMPERORS

✦ JULIUS CAESAR ✦

Julius Caesar grew up when the Senate and People of Rome constituted the most powerful state on earth, when the over-crowded capital could barely contain the millions of inhabitants of whom only a quarter were citizens entitled to the corn dole, when the ancient Roman virtues of modesty and probity were being smothered by the fruits of conquest, where the checks and balances in government created over 400 years were strained by civil war, the prescriptions and proscriptions of dictators, the demands of victorious generals and their land-hungry veterans.

Cicero believed a consensus of high-minded citizens (senators), with the plebs kept in their place, electing even higher-minded officials (consuls like himself), could still govern Rome and its provinces. Julius Caesar was one of those high-spirited Romans who believed only in themselves, in their sole capacity to restore law and order.

In modern terms, Cicero was on the right, *optimate,* and Caesar on the left, *popularis.* In their opposing views they represent the conflicts of the later Republic, which was finally finished off when Caesar's great-nephew Octavian became the Emperor Augustus. However, even he believed in the Republic; and the slogan of all who led an army to march on Rome was, 'The Republic is in danger. Follow me, I can save it.'

Marius, the country squire with no Greek, the populist general who remodelled the army; Sulla, his impoverished aristocratic protégé, once down to one slave, who turned on his patron and became dictator; Pompey the Great; Mark Antony the triumvir; Julius Caesar and Octavian: all professed belief in republican principles as they murdered them and each other. Sulla hounded Marius to death; Caesar fell out with his fellow triumvir Pompey and caused his death; Brutus, Caesar's friend and former companion at arms, 'the noblest Roman of them all', with Cassius, another friend, assassinated Caesar; Octavian, in revenge, killed them both, provoked Antony's suicide and left Cleopatra to kill herself. Only Sulla retired to die in his bed, and Augustus lived long enough for his crimes to be forgotten and for him to become, on the instant of his death, a god. Sulla, coming from nowhere, was the most successful, Augustus was the most effective, but Julius Caesar was the most famous.

Gaius, his first name *(praenomen)*, Julius, his clan *(gens)*, Caesar, his nickname *(cognomen)*, was the boldest man in history. 'Caesar' simply meant head of hair, ironic because both he and his great-nephew suffered from baldness – Caesar treasuring the right to wear a laurel wreath on his and Augustus wearing a sombrero-like straw hat to conceal his. Caesar was a bald dandy, Augustus wore homespun from the looms of his household women.

Julius Caesar was blessed with a patrician mother, Aurelia, who had enough money to set him up on the *cursus honorum* – a political career – and lived long enough, till seventy, to see her boy conquer Gaul. It is unlikely that he was delivered by a 'Caesarean' because although that operation sometimes saved the child, the mother rarely survived. Caesar was a graceful, courteous young man with strong but delicate features and the eyes of an eagle. His grandfather, also Gaius

Julius Caesar, had married his granddaughter Julia to the country squire Marius, who had jumped from his provincial background to a governorship in northern Spain. There he acquired mines and was therefore rich but not well enough connected to make consular rank. In exchange for her hand, Marius paid for her brother's first step on the political ladder as *aedile* (town councillor) and dowered her – a standard Roman arrangement. It worked. Marius grew in political credibility and honoured his understanding with his in-laws, making Julius Caesar a priest of the cult Jupiter,* at the age of nineteen.

In the same year he married a daughter of Cinna, another strong man in Rome – not a tactful move because Cinna's star was fading and his enemy, the implacable and victorious Sulla, demanded he divorce. Caesar refused and was only saved by his mama, who lobbied the influential Vestal Virgins. Caesar never obeyed any other man and this early gesture was typical. When a successful general he continued to take risks, appearing like an OAS parachutist behind enemy lines without an escort, climbing aboard an enemy ship by himself, threatening alone an entire nest of pirates with crucifixion, armed only with audacity, with boldness as his only friend.

---

* The cults of Rome are confusing but Jupiter was the top god. The finale of a Triumph took place at his temple at the end of the Via Sacra. Each cult celebrated its own festival and since the Romans were fond of spectacles and ceremonies and in the absence of tabloids and TV this was the only way a politician could get his face known to the electorate. Later, through bribery, using money borrowed from Crassus, Caesar had himself elected *pontifex maximus* (latin for Pope) and this office, coupled with his dramatic life and death, inspired miracle plays about him in the Middle Ages. With this job went a nice town house next to the Vestal Virgins, more agreeable than the old family *domus* of the *gens Julia* in Subura, now a slum.

Dodging Sulla's long arm he joined the army and won a medal for saving another soldier's life at the siege of Mytilene, then he went to Bithynia to serve under – malicious tongues said literally – the client King Nicomedes. A whiff of homosexuality lingered around Caesar throughout his life, refuted by his most doting biographer, John Buchan; but how about this, rather sweet, vignette from Suetonius:

> While *praetor* in Africa he protected a nobleman's son named Masintha ... with such devotion that he caught Juba (the king's son) by the beard. Masintha was arrested but Caesar rescued him ... and harboured him in his own quarters for a long while. At the close of this *praetorship* Caesar sailed for Spain, taking Masintha with him. The *lictors* ... and the crowds ... acted as a screen and nobody realized that Masintha was hidden in Caesar's litter.

(Whatever became of Masintha?)

Caesar had begun his political career, traditionally, as a prosecutor in the law courts, but was unremarkable, so decided to go to Rhodes to study oratory under Cicero's tutor Apollonius Molon. On the way he was captured by pirates, who plagued the Mediterranean – the Romans were never too good at sea – until destroyed by Pompey. Then followed the incident related above with Caesar insisting on upping the ransom from twenty to fifty talents, displaying (typically) his insolence, dependence on others for money, his resolution and his triumph – for he did indeed return to crucify his captors, having first considerately had their throats cut.

He returned to Rome in a fast ship, dreaming of power and nearly thirty years of age. He became *aedile*, attacked the establishment in the form of Pompey and Crassus, bom-

barded the plebs with money and became *quaestor* and super-
intendent of the Appian Way, offices which allowed him to
show off with silver cages the wild beasts at the circuses.
Cicero spotted the 'deep and dangerous designs under the
smiles of his benignity' (Plutarch). 'I perceive an inclination
for tyranny in all his projects, but on the other hand when I
see him adjusting his hair with so much exactness and scratch-
ing his head with one finger I can hardly think that such a
man can conceive so vast and fatal design as the destruction
of the Roman Commonwealth.' (Nicely observed!)

At thirty-four he was given a command in Spain but until
the campaigns in Gaul he was better known in Rome as a
demagogue than as a soldier. In the last years of the Republic
a man who aimed for the top of the greasy pole of politics
needed an army to hoist him there and keep him there. For
an army he needed a command and a campaign. The Roman
army nearly always won. The failure of Crassus in Parthia,*
graveyard of greater military reputations, was exceptional.
A general with legions in a provincial command which could
always be extended had more power, for a longer term, than
a consul who stayed in Rome. He could make or break kings
and chieftains, conclude treaties, determine frontiers, raise
and pocket taxes, extort protection money (a favourite of
the Duke of Marlborough) and make a fortune from the sale
into slavery of prisoners-of-war – his personal perquisite.
Roman generals frequently exceeded their brief, though communications between them and the Senate were quite as efficient as those between Chatham and his generals, or Pitt the
Younger and his admirals in the eighteenth century. Once *en*

* Parthian shot: a horseman in real or pretended flight turns round in
the saddle and launches a shot. One such did for poor, or rather rich, old
Crassus.

poste, a Roman general might decide it was in the best interests of the Senate and People of Rome to turn on tribes hitherto recognized as 'Friends and Allies' – an official designation – and to cross frontiers in pursuit of more territory and loot; for if the Romans believed that as the only civilized power they had the right to conquer, their more basic motives were immediate treasure and continued tribute. A successful campaign would be sanctified by the erection of a temple in the Campus Martius containing the trophies (body armour) of the defeated enemy, and the general's ego satisfied by his being acclaimed *imperator* by his troops and by his Triumph, in whose associated fun (and games) the plebs would also share.

Caesar spent a sixth of his life – nine years – in Gaul. The fighting was sporadic, often savage and intense, occasionally tedious as in the siege of Alesia, now Alise Ste Reine in Burgundy. Caesar won because his legions were professional and the forces of the Gallic tribes – gigantic, brave and bloodthirsty men – were easily demoralized; greedy, factious and encumbered by their women and children. Though Gaul was nearer to Italy than Spain only Cisalpine Gaul – roughly the plain of Lombardy and 'the Province' (roughly Provence) – were Romanized. The Gauls were temperamentally the opposite of the Romans, being impatient, volatile, gallant and credulous. When introduced to wine by the Romans, they became so enthusiastic that they would exchange a slave for an *amphora.*

In the Vatican Museum is a larger-than-life statue of a captured Gallic chieftain. He is bearded, with heavy moustaches, clad in baggy breeches and leggings, a cloak over his shoulders secured by a giant silver clasp on his left breast; his head is lowered and he has an expression of bafflement and great sadness on his face – not surprising since his hands, held in front of him, are bound at the wrists. (Such was the affectation of the *nouveaux riches* in Rome that this ruined prince might have ended up as a cook.) In the past Gauls had mounted their own expeditions, sacking Rome in 390 BC. The Belgae had invaded and settled south-east England three centuries later. The exploits and characteristics of these barbarians were recorded by historians and would have been known to Caesar.

'Gaul,' as every young Latin scholar knows, 'is divided into three parts . . .' This sentence begins Julius Caesar's account of his conquest in *De Bello Gallico* and often concludes the knowledge many people have of the ancient world, but the quotation is worth continuing because it is an excellent précis of the geography and demography of the country he had decided to subdue, and an example of the general's clear, clipped style. (One can see that he was not cut out to be a lawyer.)

> . . . three parts, inhabited respectively by the Belgae, the Aquitani and a people who call themselves Celts, though we call them Gauls. All of these have separate languages, customs and laws. The Celts are separated from the Aquitani by the river Garonne, from the Belgae by the Marne and the Seine. The Belgae are the bravest of the three peoples, being farthest removed from the highly developed civilization of the Roman Province, least often visited by merchants with enervating luxuries for sale, and nearest to the Germans across the Rhine, with whom they are continually at war. For the same reason the Helvetii are braver than the rest of the Celts; they are in almost daily conflict with the Germans, either trying to keep them out of Switzerland or themselves invading Germany.

(Caesar, *The Conquest of Gaul*, Penguin, p. 28)

Gaul, like much of northern Europe in 58 BC, was a forest (Latin: *foris est* – is outside) so until the Romans built roads, troop movements, without maps or compasses, were tricky, especially at night, one of Caesar's favourite resources. Further, communications between armies depended on one swift horseman, who might, as we shall see, not always get through. Then, too, nature had not been tamed – consider the modern motorway, impervious to natural hazards save earthquakes, floods and hurricanes – and soldiers were often as fearful of the landscape as the enemy.

The outcome of a battle depended both on the discipline and determination of the men and the skill of the commander. Crucial in the Roman army was the centurion. A good old pro – and there were few instances of bad centurions – could dispose personally of twenty barbarians and, by his example, change the course of battle, so it did not signify if the Romans were outnumbered on the field as they usually were. When a young military tribune was killed, from a family known to Caesar (which was why he was there), he was sad, but when a centurion fell, Caesar wept. Often in his account he refers to them by name (they only ever had two) and gives them loving, long citations, observing how much better they fought when he was watching them, though he was often in the thick of the battle himself and once ordered his horses away so that he could retreat. As the historian of his own actions, he was fair and uncompetitive, not skating over his mistakes, acknowledging the skill and even the eloquence of his enemies, though of course *De Bello Gallico* was designed as party political propaganda – the party being himself.

His first campaign was against the Helvetii, which entire people was on the march, quitting the Swiss fastnesses for 'the good land and high standard of life of the Rhone valley'. Outnumbered two to one, he forced them to give battle near the site of Autun, a city later founded by his great-nephew Augustus, where there are still Roman remains. (It was here that he dismissed the horses.) He routed the Helvetii and was particularly proud of the victory because one of their tribes, the Tigurini, had fifty years before killed a Roman general, Lucius Piso, who had been the grandfather of his father-in-law, another Lucius Piso; so 'Caesar was able to avenge a private injury as well as that done to his country.'

He then moved in 55 BC to the Rhine to crush two German tribes whose chiefs had come to confer with him in his camp. He treacherously locked them up and massacred their leaderless armies, justifying this action, which was deplored in the Senate by Cato and co., by saying that the Germans were such a serious threat to Gaul and the safety of Rome itself that normal behaviour did not apply. The principle of 'divide and rule' was more of a political idea than a reality, for the Romans, unlike the British in India, had to work hard to sustain their hegemony, which depended on a system of alliances and client kings. They were obliged, therefore, to protect their allies. The Sugambri, in the north-east, had been harassing the Ubii, allies of Rome who lived a little further up the Rhine – which Caesar called 'the limit of Roman sovereignty' but which he had to cross in order to teach them a lesson. 'A crossing by means of boats was both too risky and beneath the dignity of a Roman Commander,' he wrote – a very Caesarean sentiment and turn of phrase – so he built a bridge just outside modern Coblenz.

A model of this bridge, constructed by the Italian School of Military Engineers, is on display in the Museum of Roman Civilization in Eur, a bleak high-tech town without pedestrians, outside Rome. Caesar was proud of his bridge which he describes in such detail that it was easy for the descendants of his engineers to reproduce it. ('. . . the whole structure was so rigid that, in accordance with the laws of physics, the greater the force of the current the more tightly were the piles held in position.') He crossed the bridge, built in ten days, burned the villages, farms and crops of the offending Sugambri, recrossed the bridge, destroying it behind him, and considered, having spent a total of eighteen days behind the Rhine, 'that he had done all that honour or interest required'. When one reflects on the palaver about crossing the Rhine in the Second World War this is quite a classy comment.

The Roman soldier was trained to be flexible; he was first a navvy, breaking stones and building roads being the principal occupation of the ordinary recruit, but he might specialize in operating engines of war, like the battering ram, whose business end was indeed a mass of iron in the shape of a ram's head, or the gigantic catapult, which Caesar designed himself, or the portable siege tower, or the harpoon which he used in a sea battle against the Veneti, a tribe on the Atlantic coast of Brittany who had dared to kill his ambassadors. Their tall ships with sails and rigging out-manoeuvred the Romans in their oar-powered flat-bottomed boats but in the middle of the battle the wind dropped – Caesar's luck – and as Caesar commented 'after that it was a soldiers' battle' which the Romans won. The punishment he meted out was severe; their leaders were executed and the entire population sold into slavery.

Caesar used the same ships to invade Britain in 55 BC. The Brits heard him coming and offered hostages, usually a ploy to gain time. He sent Commius, whom he had made King of the Atrebates, and who, like the Belgae, occupied territory on both sides of the channel (the 'ocean' as the Romans called it), roughly Normandy, and Wilts and Berks, to announce his imminence. He landed at Dover. Caesar wrote in *De Bello*

Gallico: 'The natives sent in their cavalry and chariots, which frightened the Romans who were quite unaccustomed to this kind of fighting.' (How odd to hear Caesar crying 'foul'.) But the Romans' oar-powered boats, which *they* had not seen, frightened the Britons even more. Then Commius returned with a message that the opposition to Caesar's disembarkation had all been a terrible mistake, the fault of the common people, who had now all been sent home to tend to their fields. Peace was proposed and hostages offered. Like Genghis Khan, Caesar often conquered through his advancing reputation, so much more economic than troops. Caesar returned to Gaul having experienced difficulties with the unfamiliar high tides, so different from the Mediterranean, dealt with the Morini (Pas-de-Calais), who had thought to profit from his reported problems, and sent a suitable despatch to the Senate, who decreed a holiday of twenty days. In fact the expedition had been a failure; only two of the tribes ever sent hostages.

Next year's invasion was better arranged. In 54 BC, with five legions and 2,000 cavalry, he landed at Deal and found a worthy opponent in Cassivellaunus (Cadwallader?), King of Herts, Essex and Middlesex, who had been elected to command – the British were then democratically organized. Again Caesar complains that the British deployed their chariots in an 'unfamiliar, daring and unnerving' manner. In retaliation the Roman soldiers plodded on, burning the countryside, while their leader concluded deals with the odd dissident chieftain, until both sides had had enough. Cassivellaunus promised hostages and tribute and Caesar withdrew.

Why had he gone there in the first place?

His army had been large enough to conquer a country a fifth the size of Gaul, but again he had retreated. Perhaps he had been put off by the woad, the curious marital habits and the appalling Druidic customs – including human sacrifice – of the native Britons, apart from being unnerved by their chari-oteers. The conquest of Britain was abandoned for a century.

Besides, Caesar had to hurry back to deal with Ambiorix, chief of 'an obscure and insignificant' tribe in Picardy, but acknowledged by Caesar to be an eloquent and ingenious fellow. His general Sabinus, his tribunes and first-grade centurions had agreed to a parley outside their camp, a fool-ish move one might have thought, in retrospect, when they were overwhelmed and massacred. The standard-bearer threw his eagle over the ramparts and fought to the death, survivors crept back into the camp and committed suicide. It was the worst defeat in Gaul. Caesar had not been there. Worse followed. Encouraged by this unexpected success against the invincible Romans, Ambiorix raised the flag for a general revolt and besieged the winter camp of Cicero. Still Caesar was not there. Messengers sent to him were captured and tortured in front of the besieged Roman soldiers. Finally a Gaul who had deserted to Cicero persuaded his slave, 'by the promise of freedom and a large reward', to carry a despatch to Caesar, on receipt of which Caesar told his *quaestor* Crassus to march through the night to relieve Cicero, sending him a message (in Greek) via a javelin which stuck unnoticed in the ramparts for two days.

The Gauls were 60,000 strong, the Romans 7,000. Through feints Caesar manoeuvred the enemy into a disadvantageous position on the wrong side of a valley, then he struck. The Gauls panicked and fled, throwing away their arms. At the post mortem Caesar blamed Sabinus but praised Cicero – though one can sense him saying something sharp under his breath; one must remember that the Gallic campaign, though long and arduous, was part of his design to gather enough political clout (and money) to bid for supreme power in

Rome, and he would have avoided in his despatch any offense to another politician, the other Cicero. The Gallic tribes were so restless that Caesar decided he could not risk spending the winter, as was his habit, in northern Italy, attending to the assizes and less solemn pursuits.

De Bello Gallico is a sparse narrative written with 'a sharp pen in sharp ink' and does not of course refer to its author's extra-marital and extramural activities, which we know to have been intense from Suetonius' list of his mistresses, which, in the fashion of the times, included the wives and daughters of his friends. An attractive man of power, lecherous and susceptible, he must have found ample distraction when not actually on the war-path, as the bawdy ballad sung by his soldiers at his Triumph – 'lock up your daughters, Romans, our bald-pated chief is on his way' – suggests.

In 53 BC Caesar had dealt with the Treveri (around Trier), but in 52 BC Vercingetorix, destined to become Caesar's most glamorous and formidable opponent in Gaul, decided to strike back. He had heard that Caesar was in trouble in Rome. Publius Clodius Pulcher was a bad lad from a grand family (his sister Clodia, mistress of the poet Catullus, was also a bad girl). He was Caesar's trusty in the business of political gang warfare, in opposition to Pompey's man, T. Annius Milo (hostilities had intensified after the break-up between the two leaders in 54 BC). Both specialized, in Tammany Hall fashion, in delivering the vote. (Clodius was feminine enough in looks to disguise himself as a woman and penetrate a party given by the Vestal Virgins. Caesar's wife had been involved and in the resulting scandal he divorced her, as she was not 'above suspicion'.) Clodius had been murdered by Milo's gang. Caesar was therefore fighting on two fronts, the political in Rome and the military in Gaul. For the moment, the latter became his priority.

Vercingetorix came from Arvernia (the Auvergne) and his father was only prevented from being elected king of the Gallic tribes by assassination. Energetic, eloquent and ruthless, he had been chosen commander-in-chief of eight tribes and gave Caesar a lot of trouble with his scorched-earth policy, realizing, after three defeats, that he could not expect to beat the Roman army in the field. The Roman soldier was not a gourmet but he had to have his porridge, and if the grain had been burned . . .?

Caesar describes the forces and the campaign of Vercingetorix as carefully as his own – one is reminded of the German General Staffs research into the character of the American commander General Patton, in the Second World War – and mentions without remark or bitterness that he 'turned round' his friend Commius, whom he had made a king, but who arrived at the siege of Alesia with a quarter of a million men and cavalry three miles long. In the battle – which was, like Waterloo, 'a dam' close-run thing' – Caesar, wearing his scarlet cloak, saved the day with a cavalry charge. Vercingetorix's speech to the Gallic Assembly on the following day indicates the extent of the victory. 'I did not undertake the war for private ends, but in the cause of national liberty, and since I must now accept my fate I place myself at your disposal. Make amends to the Romans by killing me or surrender me alive as you think best.'

Of course Caesar wanted this glittering young man alive and well for his Triumph, and indeed kept Vercingetorix in cold storage for six years against this event; when the time came he may or may not have tried to prevent his execution, for, as even Buchan admits, Romans were not strong on gallantry or compassion. From this battle every soldier earned one prisoner-of-war, which he could sell as a slave.

There were few survivors of the Eburones' rebellion, which Caesar was determined should be the last in Gaul for some time. It was. Roman legions and auxiliaries cut a swathe of terror from Bordeaux to Provence, from Switzerland to Belgium, destroying every building, killing every cow belonging to rebellious tribes. In this campaign he was helped by 'young' Brutus and Mark Antony so the policy of inflicting Pax Romana on the Gauls was not just Caesar's idea. The terror worked. The tribe who started this final rebellion delivered their leader to Caesar, who, 'normally averse to harsh punishment', had him flogged to death, the punishment reserved for a rebellious *subject* as opposed to an enemy.

Though in Rome one of the *'populares'*, Caesar approved the excuse of the apologetic and finally submissive tribes, that their rebellion had been due to the influence of demagogues from the proletariat. Whatever their politics at home, Romans always supported the establishment abroad, granting citizenship only to the rich – as to the father of Paul of Tarsus in Cilicia, who had the wool monopoly. When he judged Gaul truly conquered, Caesar distributed presents to loyal collaborators and encouraged the conquered in the pursuit of the Roman way of life. This worked, for within three generations the bearded and belligerent Asterix became the urbane, clean-shaven Q. Tullius Crassus, as it were, giving dinner parties for the local garrison officers in his newly built villa, complete with mosaics, murals, central heating and curtains, such as are currently being excavated on an island in a graceful curve of the Vienne, in Limoges, just half an hour up the road from where I am writing. Indeed Gaul quickly grew to be the Romans' favourite province. The Emperor Claudius was born in Lugdunum (Lyons), Hadrian was acclaimed Emperor in Lutetia, the capital of the Parisii, and the rue St Jacques, Paris's exit to the south, which leads, like all roads, to Rome, is a Roman road. It was from Rome that France learned the art of making vintage wine, an art rediscovered in the eighteenth century by a Dutchman, who worked out that sulphur had to be added to grape juice to kill the spoiling bacteria. The Romans cleansed their wine barrels with fire and were able to seal promising wine in *amphorae* for twenty years. Ausonius, Professor of Rhetoric in Bordeaux, had a boyfriend who went 'walkabout' – as Australians say of Aborigines who go absent without leave – and being a man of influence asked Rome to find him. Discovered in a bar in Barcelona, the boyfriend refused to return but sent a message to Ausonius saying, 'Cultivate your vineyard.' (Hence Chateau Ausone.*)

The Gallic Wars over, Caesar's enemies in Rome, notably the consul Metellus, tried to relieve him of his legions. While campaigning, the Triumvirate, of which he was a third, had not worn well. Pompey's affection had gone with the death of his wife Julia, whom he had really liked, and he declined another alliance with Caesar's family. (Marriages at this level in politics were purely political.) Crassus, the elderly backer, had creaked off to Parthia (Rome's *bête noire*), where he had been defeated and decapitated; his head, delivered to Athens, had been kicked around on a stage. (In better times Pompey had repaid Caesar's IOUs to Crassus with a special tax on Asia.) Without an army (as Caesar observed later, surveying the Roman dead after the battle of Pharsalus, where he defeated Pompey), a general was no better than a felon. ('*Hoc voluerunt*,' he also said – 'It was their idea.') The Senate voted Pompey sole consul and at the trial of Milo, his man, for the

---

* I am indebted to the late Israel (Lord) Sieff for this anecdote, which I'm sure is true.

murder of Clodius, Caesar's man, he menaced the court with soldiers. (There was no police force in Republican Rome.) Milo had hired Cicero to defend him but it was the great advocate's only failure and when he sent his client the speech he had been unable to deliver, Milo replied from exile in Marseilles that he was glad, because otherwise he would not be enjoying the local mullet.

The Civil War was not so much the result of the rivalry between Caesar and Pompey but that of the Optimates and the Populares. The Senate had voted, 370 to 22, on a proposal from Caesar's new spokesman, an impoverished patrician called Curio, that both Pompey and Caesar relinquish their commands. Pompey dithered, then, prompted by Metellus, agreed to take command of all land-forces in Italy. Caesar was menaced. He had to act. He left Ravenna and seized a little town called Ariminum (Rimini); there he slipped out of a dinner party with a few friends in the middle of the night and crossed a little stream, whose whereabouts is now unknown, but which history records was the Rubicon, muttering, it is said, 'The die is cast' – for he had crossed the Italian border. His first action was to 'liberate' some horses in a meadow on the other side. The Civil War had begun.

Caesar had a winning reputation and though he started with one legion and no money, troops were drawn to him like iron filings to a magnet. He took his fill of money from the treasury in the Forum and sent friendly messages to Pompey. He met Cicero, the intellectual doyen of the Optimates, and let him join, in perfect safety, his rival. The war spread to Africa and Spain, then to Greece, Egypt and Asia (western Turkey), but Caesar prevailed. Unlike previous dictators, to which special office he was elected in 46 BC, he behaved with courtesy and clemency to his defeated fellow Romans. At home he used his exceptional powers to relieve debtors and recall exiles. When Pompey fled to Egypt, after losing the final battle in Thessaly, and was murdered by the advisers of the ten-year-old king, Caesar mourned him with the rest of the Roman world.

The boy king had a sister, a Macedonian like all the Ptolemies, at eighteen more witty than pretty, but full of charm, dash, ambition and courage. Enter Cleopatra. She had been seen off by her brother's faction but when she heard that the new conqueror had arrived in Alexandria she contrived to have herself smuggled into the palace and presented to Caesar. So began the world-famous affair. But they did not, as legend has it, spend the next two months cruising down the Nile, for though Caesar was enchanted by the beguiling princess, he had other, less agreeable, things to do. The son of Mithridates had invaded the Roman province of Cappadocia and Caesar defeated him in a lightning campaign summed up in a scrap of graffiti on a cartwheel subsequently displayed in Rome (where he was badly needed): *Veni, vidi, vici.* Caesar's *mots* were always pithy, never endearing.

The dreaded Milo, gang-leader of the Optimates, had returned to Rome and his debt laws were being sabotaged. His own veterans were so grumpy that they had marched on the capital demanding their demob pay and Caesar returned just in time to halt them with a speech beginning, '*Quirites*' – citizens – meaning that he could no longer think of them as his soldiers. He saw Cicero, dismounted and walked with him for 'several furlongs'. He had to cross to Africa to squash Pompey's father-in-law, then to Spain to deal with Pompey's sons. The Senate voted him his fifth consulate and at each victory, more honours, more Triumphs, more titles, including 'Liberator' and finally, in February 44 BC, that of 'Dictator Perpetuus'. (Unlike Augustus he declined none of them.) The month Quintilius was renamed, after him, July. For some

Romans all this was too much. In February the Ides of March were not far off.

Caesar enjoyed power and its trappings. He would have liked to run the Republic for ever and said that Sulla was an idiot to have resigned his dictatorship. More than the *auctoritas* and *potestas* of his position he revelled in his *dignitas* – the esteem of his peers – and it had been to preserve this that he had crossed the Rubicon. He did not want to be King or Emperor in Rome, nor had he wanted to start a dynasty. Indeed he made it an offence for anyone to hail him as King, rejecting a royal wreath when it was offered to him saying, *'non Rex sed Caesar sum'* ('I'm not Mr King I'm Mr Caesar'). Octavian, his adopted son and great-nephew, was his testamentary, not his political heir, and it was not Caesar's intention that he should parley himself into becoming the Emperor Augustus.

Caesar was not, like his predecessors (Marius and Sulla) or his successors (Octavian, Tiberius, Caligula, Claudius and Nero), dictators before him, and Emperors after him, in a dynasty he unknowingly founded, ever cruel, vindictive or greedy. No proscriptions followed his victories over other Romans, no son was deprived of his patrimony, no husband was contemptuously cuckolded – and most of those who struck the twenty-seven blows which killed him on 15 March 44 BC were his friends. Caesar was a radical but not a dreamer. His measures were practical, like the reform of the calendar which still endures, the autonomy for the municipalities, the rationalization of the corn dole (similar to the thinking behind the proposal to abolish the child allowance for the better off in Britain today), the codification of Roman Law, a new harbour at Ostia, draining marshes, founding twenty new towns, changing the oligarchic city state of Rome into a serious and efficient capital – first of Rome then of the

Roman world – and so on and so forth. When he was killed he was planning to extend the Roman world and particularly wanted to subdue Parthia and avenge his friend Crassus. He had maddened the Optimates by increasing the number of officials – the *aediles* from four to six, *quaestors* from forty to sixty – and bumping up the Senate to 900, to include businessmen, loyal Gauls and even centurions, thus broadening the powerbase and diminishing the perquisites and profits of the aristocracy. It was for these measures, coupled with increasing arrogance and irritability in the last months of his life, that he was killed.

Caesar might have disdained a crown but his manner was often regal and his flip *hauteur* was wounding. The Games bored him – but did he have to be seen in his box reading his papers? A group of senators with a swathe of yet more honours came towards him but he did not even rise from his golden curule throne.* A spot of giddiness perhaps? It was rumoured in Rome that his ambition was to be buried within the city limits, an honour granted only to a Roman who had died in a victorious battle. Even Augustus was careful to build his mausoleum well outside the city limits. Caesar had said, had he not, that it needed a king in Rome to defeat Parthia. What did he mean?

Caesar had not wanted to attend the meeting of the Senate on 15 March, not because he listened to the apprehensions of his young (fourth) wife Calpurnia, but because he felt unwell, and he sent a message to that effect to the Curia, where the Senate was meeting on the Tiber. But they besought him to come and so he went, unescorted and unarmed. He was surrounded by a crowd of petitioners, one trying to hand him a note warning him of the plot. Then

* Only ever a very elaborate camp-stool.

they struck. Twenty-seven blows later the boldest man in history fell dead at the foot of Pompey's statue. The horses he had liberated by the Rubicon were later seen to be weeping.

The plebs saw the assassination of their hero as the patricians striking back, possibly the first of a series of *coups* to regain the authority Caesar had taken from them. They cowered in their tenements, shutters bolted; Rome cringed. Cicero had arranged a deal between the Caesareans and the Republicans whereby the assassins were to be amnestied and Caesar's will and acts were to be honoured. In the breathing space thus gained, Brutus and Cassius, the assassins, dined with Mark Antony on the Capitoline Hill. The will, which embittered Mark Antony in naming Octavian as his heir, gave every citizen 300 *sesterces* and his gardens on the other bank of the Tiber to the people of Rome. Mark Antony's oration for Caesar has come down to us in a number of different versions apart from Shakespeare's. Suetonius says it was short, Dio long. Whatever happened, the mob's reaction was such that Brutus and Cassius had to leave Rome.

The most famous assassination in history was also the vaguest. The conspirators may have wanted to restore the shaky institutions of the Republic; all they had done was set the scene for the next civil war, whose victor would finally anaesthetize them, prior to a kindly death.

✦ AUGUSTUS ✦

Caesar's great-nephew, his sister's grandson, was in Illyria (modern Albania) when he heard the news of the great event in Rome. He was studying rhetoric and undergoing military training for the proposed war in Parthia. He was eighteen. With his classmate, M. Vipsanius Agrippa, the son of an Italian farmer, who became his number two for life, he crossed to Brindisi, and there learned he was Caesar's principal heir and adopted son. Adoption was an honoured and frequent practice in Rome where the ladies were not philoprogenitive, disliking the rigours of childbirth; their husbands did not complain because the greater the number of children, the greater the diminishment of the family estate (primogeniture was unknown). Adult sons of good birth, therefore, were a rare enough commodity for it to be easy for a father with more than two of them to find a richer and more powerful parent. Henceforth C. Julius Caesar Octavianus, as he called himself now, always referred to Julius Caesar, deified two years later in 42 BC, as 'my father' and to himself as 'son of the divine Caesar'. He entered quickly and eagerly upon his inheritance.

At first his name appeared to be his only asset, but with Caesar's legacies he was able to lure Mark Antony's legions to his side (Crassus always used to say that no one could call himself rich in Rome if he could not afford to keep an army).

Cicero was mad about the boy, suggesting to the Senate that he would be a counter to the ambitions of Antony. Two battles followed immediately which Antony lost. He fled to Gaul. Octavian was now in charge of eight legions but the Senate refused to make him consul so he marched on Rome. He was nineteen. Then on a small island near Bologna he met his rivals, Antony and Lepidus; they left their legions behind them, but had with them their kitchen cabinets. Octavian's now consisted of one Q. Rufus, Maecenas (an elegant Etrurian prince) and Agrippa; they were all the same age. The first was a disappointment, made trouble and was obliged to commit suicide. Agrippa became his commander-in-chief, minister of works, son-in-law and stayed with him all his life, as did Maecenas, who was put in charge of propaganda and the arts. From this encounter emerged the second Triumvirate, official unlike the first, and recognized by the assembly in November. The deal was that Antony kept Gaul, Lepidus Spain, Octavian Africa, Sicily and Sardinia. The Triumvirate needed money for its forty-five legions and land. The speediest resource was through proscription of their enemies and the language of the edict was as savage as the action. Informers were promised rewards and no one was safe. According to Plutarch, Octavian argued for two days to try and save Cicero, top of Antony's hit-list in revenge for Cicero's pillorying of him in the Philippics, but he failed and the head and right arm of the great orator were displayed on the rostra in the forum. Cicero died because he had no army, no *gens*, no fortune to protect him. Faced with force his talents failed him – the fate of intellectuals throughout the ages.

The civil war continued. Brutus rampaged in Greece and Cassius in Asia Minor. The Triumvirate defeated them. The chaos of the times – even contemporary historians did not know exactly what was happening – suited the temperament of Octavian, who was perfectly willing to wade through slaughter to the throne, though he did not himself like the sight of blood. Octavian had Brutus decapitated and sent the head to Rome to be thrown at the foot of Caesar's statue. At the fall of Perusia in 41 BC he had 300 high-ranking prisoners sacrificed on the Ides of March at the altar of the God Julius, his 'father'. The bloodthirsty and cowardly Octavian was later unrecognizable in the benign Emperor Augustus, a change of personality which Roman historians, accustomed to categorize their people into good and bad, found difficult to accommodate.

Sextus Pompeius, son of the great Pompey, entered the ring ironically as a sort of pirate king,* and to the military were added some marital musical chairs, for the day Octavian's wife, Scribonia, a relative of Sextus, bore him a daughter, Julia, of whom much more anon, he divorced her. Octavian had fallen in love – with Livia, the nineteen-year-old wife of one Tiberius Claudius Nero, who though he bore the names of three emperors was only the father of one, Tiberius. With Livia, quickly divorced though pregnant at the time, Octavian – Augustus – lived happily ever after for fifty years. The connection was socially and politically important to him like the marriage of the Cornet William Pitt to the Grenvilles, for, though Augustus' father was now a God, his actual father was a provincial banker. Livia's provenance was of the best and from 38 BC the Patriciate began to move towards Augustus. Over the years the love between them cooled but Augustus always found his wife useful, if only as the provider of virgins for his bed.

---

* His father had cleared the Mediterranean of pirates.

In the next five years, Agrippa subdued Pompey junior, whose legions the triumvir Lepidus tried to turn against Octavian. Smarter with his tongue than with his sword, Octavian talked the legions round and preserved Lepidus in a seaside town for the rest of his life, occasionally dragging him up to Rome for public spectacles. Octavian loathed him but dared not have him put down because at some point he had become Pontifex Maximus.

By 33 BC, the contest for the Roman world was between the brothers-in-law Octavian and Antony. Antony had married his rival's sister, always described as the 'virtuous' Octavia, but was now psychologically and financially dependent on the extraordinary Cleopatra, who had totally ensnared him. When the scene shifts to the court of the Queen of Egypt, Roman history becomes grand opera. Cleopatra had enchanted Julius Caesar, scared Herod the Great, and had now become the mistress of Mark Antony, through whom she hoped to be mistress of the world.

In late 34 BC, Antony celebrated a Roman-style Triumph for his victory over the Armenians, which became known as the 'Donations of Alexandria'. Plutarch describes the occasion:

Antony also aroused great resentment because of the division of his inheritance which he carried out in Alexandria in favour of his children. People regarded this as an arrogant and theatrical gesture which seemed to indicate a hatred for his own country. Nevertheless, he assembled a great multitude in the athletic arena there, and had two thrones of gold, one for himself and one for Cleopatra, placed on a dais of silver, with smaller thrones for his children. First, he proclaimed Cleopatra Queen of Eygpt, Cyprus, Libya and Syria and named Caesarion as her consort. This youth was believed to be a son of Julius Caesar, who had left Cleopatra pregnant. Next he proclaimed his own sons by Cleopatra to be Kings of Kings. To Alexander he gave Armenia, Media and Parthia, as soon as he should have conquered it, and to Ptolemy, Phoenicia, Syria and Cilicia. At the same time he presented his sons to the people, Alexander in a Median costume which was crowned by a tiara, and Ptolemy in boots, a short cloak and a broad-brimmed hat encircled by a diadem. The latter wore Macedonian dress like the kings who succeeded Alexander the Great, and the former the dress of the Medes and Armenians. After the children had embraced their parents, the one was given a guard of honour of Armenians and the other of Macedonians. Cleopatra, not only on this but on other public occasions, wore a robe which is sacred to Isis, and she was addressed as the New Isis.

Octavius Caesar reported these actions to the Senate, and by repeatedly denouncing Antony in public he did his utmost to rouse the Roman people's anger against him.

('Antony' in Plutarch's *Lives,* Penguin, pp. 54–5)

With Maecenas as his Goebbels, Octavian stepped up his hate campaign against Antony, who, in proclaiming Caesarion as Caesar's son by Cleopatra, implied that Caesarion was a potential usurper. There being no libel laws in Ancient Rome, nor any rules of evidence in courts of law, character assassination was invoked to harness public opinion, to which men in power were so sensitive. They could not avoid the evidence of public opinion by roaring through the streets in bullet-proof cars, or disappear in helicopters. Every citizen could make himself heard in courts of law or at the Games or in the streets. Julius Caesar had disdained protection but none of the five emperors descending from him were successfully protected by their guards from the anger of the Roman people, fomented by professionals.

Octavian defeated Antony with propaganda long before the battle of Actium. The message was simple. Antony, once an upright servant of the state, to whom Octavian had been so well disposed that he gave him his own sister in marriage, who had been twice consul and many times *imperator*, had become the slave of a queen of a people who worshipped reptiles, a queen with the insolence to look forward to issuing her decrees from the steps of the Capitol in Rome. He could prove it. Octavian took Antony's will from the temple of the Vestal Virgins, where important people lodged their wills for safekeeping, and read it to the Senate. Antony's will acknowledged Caesarion, provided for his children by Cleopatra, and stipulated that he was to be buried next to her – i.e., so propaganda ran, the capital was to be transferred to Alexandria. One hundred thousand copies – before the invention of printing – were distributed throughout the Roman world denouncing Cleopatra as a *fatale monstrum*, Horace's expression. Throughout Italy communities took oaths of allegiance to Octavian personally, later seen as another nail in the coffin of the Republic. Octavian declared a just war on Cleopatra and advanced to Greece.

The war was not religious, political, ethnic or ideological, as so many were to be in Europe and in the Balkans, where the battles of the Roman civil war were often fought; it was a fight between rival gangs for dominance but the gangsters' 'manor', with Virgil to record the outcome, was the dawn of the Augustan Age. In terms of force, naval and military, they were evenly matched, but Antony was handicapped by what we would call today the 'Cleopatra factor', and equally Octavian was boosted by the Caesar connection. Before, during and after the battle, Romans deserted Antony. The naval battle at Actium was lost by Antony more than won by Octavian, who may have passed the time lying on his back on a hill overlooking the bay, gazing into the sky; but Agrippa was there. According to Dio, Cleopatra, impatient, anxious at anchor with her treasure (in ancient times one never left the family silver at home), very much a woman, decided to return to Egypt; or did Antony signal her to retreat? Agrippa's sailors, with no sails on board to unfurl, had anticipated a naval battle, a hand-to-hand business in those days, grappling, ramming, catapulting and stoning. They won.

Actium was not a glorious finish to the civil war, but it was the end or almost the end of 100 years of conflict between Romans. The entire Senate and equestrian order turned up in Brindisi to acknowledge Octavian, whose forty-year tenure of power had now emphatically begun. Antony and Cleopatra were back in Egypt and Octavian pursued them in August of the next year. As he approached they sent him presents, which he kept, and pleas, which he ignored. Antony pathetically reminded Octavian of their happy times in Rome together, an odd note to strike as there were some twenty years between them and Octavian had never been a gadabout. Cleopatra threatened to destroy herself and *her treasure* but Octavian would not listen to her. He sent a smooth-tongued freedman to suggest that he was already in love with her at a distance, and that the distance between them would soon vanish. As Octavian approached, Antony's soldiers left him; told that Cleopatra was dead, he tried to kill himself; told she was not, he had enough strength to drag himself to her chamber and die in her arms.

The set was now clear for Cleopatra's interview with the new ruler of the world. When Octavian entered her apartment, she rose from the richly ornamented chaise-longue where she had carefully and carelessly arranged herself, her asses' milk complexion enhanced by her mourning, and cried out, 'Greetings my lord, for the Gods have given supremacy to you, and taken it from me.' Her apartment had been filled with busts and memorabilia of Julius Caesar and she had stuffed her bosom with his letters, which she read out in a soft, plaintive, musical voice. Octavian was unmoved. Then she threw herself on her knees and begged to be allowed to die. Octavian was still unmoved. Perhaps he was considering her part in his procession down the Via Sacra; she would add gloss to his Triumph so he wanted her alive. Accordingly, he arranged for her food to be monitored. It was a possibility, though, that her extraordinary presence might backfire. Mobs could be fickle . . . (When the executioner of Charlotte Corday, who murdered Marat in his bath, took her guillotined head by the hair and punched it in the face, he was fined for misconduct.)

Cleopatra fooled him. She did not want a bit part in someone else's Triumph. She knew, from experiments on live human beings – no problem in the ancient world – that asps work. The asp is a small, poisonous, hooded snake, endemic to Egypt and Libya, and its fatal sting guaranteed, according to Cleopatra's advisers, deification. In the literature of the world, the asp is only referred to in connection with Cleopatra. She took two. Dio, from whom this account is taken, says that Octavian was shaken by Cleopatra's death and tried to have her revived. At least he was able to compensate himself with her treasure. He could also do what he liked with Egypt.

From this moment on, Octavian became benign, lenient, forgiving – he was only horrid to his own daughter. He let go the children of Antony and Cleopatra, the pretentiously styled Helios (sun) and Selene (moon), and they were brought up by their ever-virtuous stepmother, Octavia. Antyllus,

Antony's son by his first wife, Fulvia, and Caesarion, being too dangerous to be left alive, were killed.* Egypt was annexed as the possession of the Emperor and administered by a prefect. The Donations of Alexandria were naturally cancelled but the arrangements made by Antony in Asia remained unchanged. All this, together with amnesties and pardons, was announced to the Egyptians by Octavian in a speech in Greek. He visited the corpse of Alexander the Great and may have knocked off his nose by mistake. There was enough money in Cleopatra's treasury, carefully collected from her temples, to give every soldier a year's pay. On 11 January 29 BC, the gates of the temple of Janus (the God of War) in Rome were closed. 'The Republic and liberty had gone, and men turned gratefully to their new saviour.'**

Octavian was careful to preserve the physical appearance of the Republic. Like a taxidermist, he extracted the vital organs from the dead beast, replacing them with stuffing without damaging the skin. His autocracy came from a series of powers voted to him but never seized, such as the proconsular power and the tribunician power. As Mr Carter explains, 'The brilliance of this arrangement lies in its dissociation of the powers of an office.' Augustus, which he became in 27 BC and which we shall now call him, was granted the imperium for ten years (renewable); he had all the powers of officers of state without the bore, uncertainty and expense of elections. He wanted to be called Romulus, but this had echoes of kingship distasteful to Romans, and he was dissuaded. After 19 BC, he had 'the power of the consul without

---

* John Carter, in the Penguin edition of Dio Cassius' *Roman History*, comments that they paid the penalty of being adult sons of their father.
** *From the Gracchi to Nero, A History of Rome from 133 BC to AD 68*, H.H. Scullard, Methuen, 1959.

being a consul, the power of a tribune without being a tribune, and the power of a proconsul without being a proconsul, for it was his *legati* who occupied that position on his behalf'. Through a series of conjuring and confidence tricks (deplored by Gibbon), Augustus, who had the Senate, the people, the army of Rome and the bourgeoisie of Italy in the palm of his hand, seemed set fair to be Princeps, first amongst equals, for the rest of his natural life.

Dio Cassius treats us to imaginary monologues from Octavian's two lieutenants, Agrippa and Maecenas, on how to handle himself from this – 29 BC – moment on. Agrippa, the man of action, waffles on but after a résumé of his achievements warns his master against becoming a monarch, for if Romans suspected such an intention, he would be doomed like his 'father', Julius Caesar. Maecenas, the think-tank, is more subtle: Octavian should become a monarch in all but name, he should not allow images of himself or temples in his honour, but should build images in the hearts of men; he should appoint magistrates and appear to listen to their advice in Rome but the provinces, and therefore the armies, he should control absolutely himself; he should spare no expense in making the capital beautiful, and, for his own safety, should create *two* prefects to command the Praetorian Guard; finally horse-races should be confined to Rome so as not to deprive the cavalry of good animals.* Knights, Maecenas went on, should be trained from childhood to run the treasury, state property should be privatized, senators if they misbehave (even towards you, Octavian) should be judged by their peers, but rebellious army commanders should be condemned as public enemies.

* Napoleon was the first ruler to categorize horses into race, cavalry and artillery.

Augustus did not heed this advice, though in his own tactful and duplicitous way he seems to have followed it. He was particularly respectful of the Senate, subsidizing senators who had lost out in the civil wars, rather like the Duke of Newcastle's dole to peers in the reign of George III, and he helped old families to keep up their obligations to the temples. Publicly Augustus was in favour of old-fashioned family virtues and put a telling tax on childless couples. We must also remember that, like all Emperors, he was as rich privately as the Roman state.

On embarking on his seventh consulship he read a speech beginning, 'I know very well, Conscript Fathers, that I shall appear to you to have made an incredible choice. I lay down my office in its entirety and return to you all authority absolutely, authority over the laws, the army and the provinces, not only those territories which you entrusted to me but those which I later secured for you . . . I restore to you your freedom and the Republic.' It was all completely untrue. But few noticed, fewer cared, and even fewer Romans dared to do anything against the regime. The conspirators against Augustus throughout his reign were rare and inept and were dealt with by him with a leniency which was almost humiliating. In the case of Gnaeus Cornelius Cinna Magnus, the grandson of Pompey the Great, Dio has Livia his wife give Augustus such a convincing (and lengthy) lecture on the quality of mercy that he releases all the conspirators and makes the man a consul. Livia was less concerned with mercy in her husband's behaviour towards his own immediate family, particularly his only child, Julia. Like Caligula, she could plead (if she could have been bothered) in justification of her madness and badness, a traumatic childhood and broken homes due to her father's manipulation of her life and children, but Julia, arrogant, stubborn, insolent, defiant, libidinous and deeply tricky, was not inclined to plead. Augustus' hard treatment of his daughter began on the day she was born when he divorced her mother, as we have seen. He expected his daughter to inherit his own almost inhuman self-control. He exposed her to the high life of Rome but allowed her no freedom. He married her off three times without consulting her and, being without male heirs himself, deprived her legally of her first two sons, by Agrippa, the golden boys Gaius and Lucius, whom he brought up as his own (one of the most beautiful buildings in the world, the Maison Carrée, in Nîmes, currently being done up, is dedicated to them). In revenge Julia tried to outrage him, by sleeping around – but usually when pregnant by her husbands. Her young lovers bore the great names of Rome, Antonius, Pulcher, Gracchus, Scipio. With them she plotted parricide at a bacchic orgy in the middle of the night in the middle of the Forum. It was a serious orgy but not much of a conspiracy and Augustus only executed Julius Antonius, Mark Antony's son, who had been a consul and should have known better, and banished the rest. He exiled his daughter Julia for the rest of her life, making sure she never had another drop of wine.

He was equally callous towards his granddaughter, the younger Julia, banished when pregnant in AD 8, obviously through pressure from Livia, who wanted no obstacle to the inheritance of her son, Tiberius. When the child was born it was declared illegitimate and, on the ancient authority of a Roman *paterfamilias,* starved to death.

At the same time, for reasons unknown, the poet Ovid (famous for his amorous advice – but not a serious plotter, it was thought) was exiled to a freezing port at the mouth of the Danube on the Black Sea. Ovid, in his autobiography, never says why, but blames 'the treachery of friends and malice of servants'. That Augustus was able, out of pique, to banish from Rome, without explanation or protest, its most popular poet shows the extent of his power.

Augustus over-promoted and spoilt rotten his grandchildren, alienating his stepson Tiberius, the other candidate for the succession, who withdrew sulkily to Rhodes for seven years in 6 BC. Augustus, expecting much from these boys to whom so much had been given, received, as was his wont, nothing in return; in fact they died on him, Lucius in Marseilles of an illness in AD 2, and Gaius of melancholy after being wounded in Armenia in AD 4. So the ageing and increasingly embittered Emperor had to overcome his distaste for Tiberius – he could not bear the way he chewed his food – and wrote him artificially jocular letters.

He had outlived his own friends, his buddies (but never quite his equals) Agrippa, Maecenas, Horace and Virgil, all of whom left him their fortunes; but he needed their presence and not their presents, for he was not a greedy man. He spent his time watching the pretty little boys sent to him from all corners of the Empire playing their games in his modest house. He liked being asked out to dinner and offered and expected little in the way of lavish entertainment, except of course for political purposes. Once when returning from a particularly unpretentious dinner he was heard to mutter, 'I did not know I knew him *that* well'; on another occasion, when he was dining with Pollio, who was proud of his collection of crystal, a slave broke a piece and was about to be thrown to his master's lampreys for their dinner, when Augustus ordered the man to be given his freedom and all the crystal to be smashed. He did not like other people to play the tyrant. However, this did not deter Pollio, a terrible snob, from leaving him a beautiful beach-house.

His own house on the Capitoline Hill was as different from his official palace as his private from his public persona. The first had been bought from the estate of the orator Hortensius in 44 BC, when Octavian was still only Caesar's presumptive heir. The house consisted of twelve rooms and was turned in on itself, being separated from the street by blank walls. A modest enough establishment, symbolic of the inner Augustus, it was known then as now as Domus Livia, and it was there he lived for forty years, sleeping in the same room. The Emperor's adjoining palace had been built after a fire in 3 BC from a public subscription which exacted no more than one denarius from each citizen and one gold coin from each municipality. (Augustus was genuinely popular with his subjects.) At home he was a randy little man – five foot five in his stockinged feet – who suffered from the cold, enjoyed practical jokes, wore simple clothes woven by his own household (like the Emperor of Japan), ate peasant food and nibbled a dried apple or fig between meals. He was not in the least pompous, often made fun of himself and allowed others to do so. 'The ruler of the world looked very sheepish when, on going to meet a curtained litter that he had sent to collect a lady of easy virtue, he saw his old tutor Athenodorus leap out of it. Athenodorus had sent the woman packing and taken her place, and now started to lecture Augustus on his incontinence.'*

He was never very healthy and nearly died twice, the first time in Cantabria (northern Spain), where he endured a *crise de foie* – and indeed *de foi* for it was there that he became a Stoic. His doctor** and oculist were never far away and some

---

* From *Augustus and Nero* by Professor Gilbert Charles Picard, Phoenix House, 1966.

** A Greek called Antonius Musa, who cured his kidney infection with cold baths, the only remedy which had worked for George III. A grateful and perhaps obsequious Senate erected a statue to him in the temple of Asclepius. One did not have to wait to be dead to have a statue of oneself in Rome.

of their medicines and artefacts are reproduced in the Museum at Eur. He suffered from gallstones all his life. His body was covered with blotches, which his flatterers declared were in the configuration of the Great Bear but which were in fact the marks of endogynous discoid eczema, not contagious and caused, quite simply, by nerves; underneath the armour of a faultless political machine was the body of a frightened little man. (He was constantly accused of cowardice, notably by Mark Antony, and certainly was terrified of thunder and lightning, putting on a sealskin coat for protection.)

But on parade as Emperor, Augustus was dazzling. No one stood near him so in his imperial toga or imperial armour (and with his lifts) he walked tall, and no one could resist the glare from his grey eyes, which were set in a sea of white, like kernels of a sun. When he moved from his inner home to the sanctuary surrounding it he became the High Priest (Pontifex Maximus), the Father of his People (Pater Patriae, an official title in 2 BC), Commander-in-Chief (Imperator), and on New Year's Day and at great festivals when he wore the dress and insignia of a triumphant commander (which his adoptive father had been allowed to wear *every* day) the purple toga, embroidered in gold, a crown of golden laurel and a long ivory sceptre – Augustus must have looked every inch ruler of the world.

When he died, he had been that for forty-two years and had visited every corner of the Empire, except Sardinia – the Romans did not like Sardinia – and if Romans no longer felt free, at least there was no outcry in the streets and the arts bloomed in the peace and prosperity of what even then became known as the Augustan Age. The *ara pacis,* a four-sided frieze, can be seen in its huge glass case by the river Tiber, next to his mausoleum. The pastoral idyll there in relief is as if the Pastoral Symphony of Beethoven were frozen in white marble and the Imperial family floats serenely through wreaths and garlands.

As *princeps* in Rome, Augustus believed in extending the hegemony of the Senate and People, but his two humiliating defeats, both in Germany, decided him at the end of his life that enough was enough and that the frontiers should stay as they were. Varus, a stumblebum of a general, had lost three legions, massacred through trickery in a forest in AD 9, and this disaster remained the daymare of Augustus' life towards its end. When nobody (he thought) was watching he would bang his head on the wall of his little house on the Hill and cry, 'Varus, Varus, give me back my legions.'*

Augustus' apotheosis happened in a way designed, by chance, to appeal to his modest, frugal spirit. He was *en route* to his villa in Sorrento when the crew of a ship from Alexandria, dressed in white, carrying wreaths of flowers and swinging censers, courted him, singing: 'Through him we live, through him we sail the seas, through him we enjoy freedom and riches'. This sentiment would have been echoed by the whole of the new middle class and the bureaucracy he had created, at the expense, if it mattered, of the old families of the Republic, which he had married into but of which he had never been a part. This memory sweetened the last few months of what had become a lonely and unhappy existence. Almost his last words were: 'Well, I performed quite well, didn't I?'

---

* A tenth of the Roman army.

✤ TIBERIUS ✤

In a television film the Empress Livia, announcing to her son Tiberius that the Emperor has just died, is made to say, in an aside, 'and by the way, don't touch the pears'. But she had no reason to want to poison her husband. Their relations had cooled over fifty years of marriage but he was more use to her alive than dead and she didn't hate him. Augustus had never liked his stepson, son-in-law and, *faute de mieux*, heir to the imperial throne he had consciously (dissembling heavily the while) created, and Tiberius' succession was not in his mind a foregone conclusion. Indeed, towards the end of his life he amused himself with guessing games, out loud, as to the identity of the next emperor – who was able and willing, who was willing and not able, who was just greedy for power – and the name of Tiberius was not mentioned. Tiberius, of course, heard of this and the names of the other candidates were lodged in his savagely retentive memory.

Further, at the death of each Emperor of the Julio-Claudian line – Tiberius brought in the *gens Claudia,* prouder and grander than the Julians – patrician Romans persistently fancied that the Senate might take the opportunity to re-establish consular government with the republican system of checks and balances and its attendant perks and jobs for the boys.

Finally, did Tiberius really want total authority?

He appeared before the Senate, emphasized his own

unpretentiousness, compared to the *gloire* of the instantly deified Augustus, and proposed power-sharing with others. Tiberius was genuinely modest, hating crowds, fuss, pomp, 'fearing freedom but hating flattery more'. He was also prone to say the opposite of what he meant. At the end of the debate, however, stung in a sensitive part of his psyche, perhaps the only one, by Gallus, who had married his beloved former wife, Vipsania, and by another senator, Arruntius, whom Augustus had admired, who both implied he was evading responsibility, he yielded and accepted the throne. Tiberius was consistent only in being contrary, but was in fact the best candidate, trained for the job, a successful and economical commander in the field, having served as Augustus' number two for years and shared his tribunicial and proconsular powers. In the event, he ruled impeccably, if without charm or panache, until his unchecked misanthropy turned him into the sadistic and paranoid old tyrant on Capri – in which role he is, unfairly, mostly remembered.

Livia had always been determined that her son should succeed, but not to the point of disposing of the grandsons or of her husband. Neither action had been necessary. She lived to a great age and was rewarded by Tiberius with dislike, his standard response, salted with respect, for he had loved one person only in his life – Vipsania. She was the daughter of Augustus' favourite man of action, Marcus Vipsanius Agrippa, and Tiberius' marriage to her had been in the nature of a political alliance; but he had loved her, and when told to divorce her and marry Augustus' only child, Julia, for a closer, dynastic bond, what heart Tiberius had was broken and never mended. Suetonius tells how seeing Vipsania by chance in Rome he 'followed her with tears in his eyes and intense unhappiness written on his face; arrangements were made so that he never saw her again'. Tiberius became the dutiful son-in-law, trying to like Julia, but when their child died he turned to loathing her, to war and bibulous evenings in the mess.

His first campaign was against the Cantabrii, a resourceful and dangerous tribe (the Basques?) which Julius Caesar thought he had subdued by sending their men of military age into slavery; but six years later they had simultaneously murdered their masters and reconvened for another rebellion, and they had to be attended to. Then Tiberius crowned a king in Armenia, recovered the standards lost by poor, or rather rich, old Crassus in Parthia, commanded armies in Pannonia (Dalmatia) and in Germany, where he marched to the Elbe and back, taking 40,000 prisoners-of-war to colonize Alsace.*

Although a young man Tiberius became a workhorse of a general and was appropriately honoured, being elected quaestor, praetor and consul before he was really eligible, due to his lack of years. At this point, on the crest of a spectacular career, Tiberius announced his intention to retire to the island of Rhodes, as a private citizen. This cold, gaunt, bitter man, never loved and never understood, with a strong sense of justice and responsibility, was also impulsive, and, as has been said, contrary. He longed to be accepted by men of learning and this was his reason for choosing Rhodes, a beautiful place favoured by Greek scholars, which was for Romans what Florence became for the English, somewhere to imbibe an older and superior culture. The Romans, to whom he had not bothered to say goodbye, said that his self-exile was to avoid his appalling wife and to remove himself from the

---

* Then much of northern Europe was still empty. When the Romans left Brittany the place was vacant until rediscovered by Irish priests in coracles, centuries later.

competition of his stepsons, Gaius and Lucius, then considered by their grandfather, the Emperor, and the Empire most likely to succeed. In Rhodes Tiberius played the modest scholar, wandering round the forum chatting, dressed like an ordinary citizen; but his astrologer, Thrasyllus, was also there, reminding him he could not avoid his destiny. (This all-knowing fellow knew his employer's mind so well that when asked once why he looked so gloomy, admitted apprehensions that Tiberius wanted him out of the way. He was forgiven.)

Tiberius' stock in Rome was falling. Like Louis XIV (their only similarity), Augustus did not like absentees. It was assumed that 'the exile', as he became known, must be into some kind of conspiracy. He wasn't, and when Gaius visited nearby Samos, Tiberius attended his court to throw himself at the feet of his stepson and protest he wasn't. Suspicion still increased and Tiberius, realizing he had been out in the cold long enough, wrote to his mother asking her to plead with the Emperor that he be welcomed home. Augustus never liked Tiberius and after the death of the grandsons, when Tiberius had become his heir, forced himself, for reasons of state, to be civil, even intimate, but his letters to Tiberius glow with insincerity. Augustus was exceedingly vain, as his *Res Gestae,* the account of his achievements, dictated by himself and engraved on an enormous tablet for all to applaud, clearly and precisely shows. Not an aqueduct or temple built or restored, not a benefaction, not a province conquered or a law initiated is omitted from this self-satisfied recital. But he was anxious to be loved as well as revered by posterity. Like many cruel men he was sentimental. Suetonius suggests that one reason for Augustus' choice of Tiberius was that his stepson was so unpleasant that his own reign would be remembered with even greater affection.

In his early days as Emperor, Tiberius was circumspect. He consulted the Senate on every matter, encouraging debate. Not he but Augustus or Livia had arranged for his possible rival, Agrippa Postumus, Julia's remaining son who was regarded by all as a bad hat, to be put to death. He obeyed Augustus' instructions – he left a lot – in naming Germanicus (the nephew of whom he was jealous, popular son of a popular father) his heir, and while this young man and his mother were alive Tiberius behaved well. Indeed during these years, described by Tacitus as *mitia tempora*, Italy and the Empire prospered, conscientiously monitored by an Emperor who respected the laws and the constitution, rose in the presence of consuls, gave way to them in the streets, kept a modest household with few slaves, spent no money on himself (or anybody else), refused grandiose titles and deferred to the Senate, whose judicial powers were increased at the expense of the popular assembly. These good years, which were a blessing, did not last. Tiberius despised senators for their deference towards him. 'Oh you lot, fit only for servitude', he was heard to mutter, in Greek, after one session.*

The first bleak sign of tyranny – of the kind of tyranny Caligula was later to enjoy with such zest and caprice – was the re-establishment, in dangerously undefined terms, of the law of treason; originally designed to protect the Republic from subversion, by making *maiestas (lèse majesté)* a crime against the state, it became an excuse for the *princeps,* or anybody who wished to ingratiate themselves with him, to punish those who had offended him, however trivially. There was no public prosecutor in Rome and any citizen could bring a charge, so a whole new profession was born, the *delatores,*

---

* cf. Abraham Lincoln: 'Senators are hogs and should be beaten like hogs.'

denouncers or informers. (Romans had a nomenclature for everybody; legacy hunters were *captatores.*) At first Tiberius resisted their uncongenial activities. The first accused was a knight, for allowing an actor (a synonym, as we have observed, for a male tart) to join the worshippers of a cult of Augustus and for selling, along with a garden property, a statue of the god, his predecessor. Tiberius reacted with scratchy propriety, writing to the consuls that Augustus had not been made divine in order to ruin Roman citizens, that the actor in question had been taken to Games given in honour of Augustus by his mother Augusta (Livia had been belatedly elevated to this honorific) and that selling a statue was not a sacrilege. So that was that.

Next, a governor of Bithynia was accused by his assistant and colleague, a man who 'created a career which was to be made notorious by the villainous products of subsequent gloomy years'. 'Needy, obscure and restless he wormed his way by secret reports into the grim Emperor's confidence. 'Then anyone of any eminence was in danger from him,' wrote Tacitus of this early McCarthy. The charge was that the governor had bad-mouthed the Emperor, telling stories about his meanness, his fondness for wine, his dislike of his mother – stories serious (and accurate) enough to warrant a conviction. Tacitus continues that 'the Emperor "lost his temper" and, voluble for once, exclaimed that he personally would vote, openly and on oath . . . Gnaeus Calpurnius Piso asked: "Caesar, will you vote first or last? If first, I shall have your lead to follow; if last, I am afraid of inadvertently voting against you." This struck home . . . Tiberius voted for acquittal.' (Tacitus, *The Annals of Ancient Rome,* tr. Michael Grant, Penguin.)

The new métier of *delator* appealed to an increasingly suspicious and sensitive Emperor, especially after his retreat from

Rome to Capri, and his dependence on men without scruples is epitomized by the rise and fall of the favourite Sejanus, with whom the morale and morality of Rome hit a distressful low.

Caprae (Capri) was and is an enchanting island, opposite Baiae (Naples), where Augustus had built a villa, having exchanged it with the municipality for Ischia. The climate is balmy, the sea crystal and though tiny the landscape is varied. (Anacapri, where Axel Munthe lived at San Michele, has a feeling quite different from Capri, its inhabitants being still visibly of Greek descent.) The views are splendid and the dawn touching the cliffs between the twin rocks of the Faraglione – which Tiberius, from one of his twelve houses, must have seen often – is one of nature's great polychromatic shows. More to the point, he could see who was approaching from afar and relished the economy of the small number of guards needed for his protection. The Emperor did not like unexpected callers – as the fisherman, who scaled the cliffs to present him with a mullet, found out; a *langouste* was rubbed in his face and he was thrown back into the sea.

From this natural fortress, where, it was hoped, he had gone to die, Tiberius ruled the Empire for the last eleven years of his life, the first five through Sejanus, who had talked him into this voluntary exile and had further strengthened his hold on the Emperor by saving his life when a grotto, in which they were dining on the journey south, had collapsed. Sejanus was the first adventurer to effect a (sort of) *coup d'état* in Rome without an army, for Augustus had succeeded in removing this opportunity from generals by regulating their commands and paying their troops direct. Power therefore was now centred on the imperial palace and the Praetorian Guard, which Sejanus had regrouped in one barracks under his sole command. People who mistrust everybody often trust one person too much.

Sejanus' weapons were slander, intrigue and poison and his strength was his access to Tiberius, who trusted him and called him 'the partner of my labours'. He was the son of a knight, who became a prefect of the Praetorian Guard and had made some money in his youth, it was said, out of a rich old queen, before joining the staff of Gaius, Augustus' grandson and putative heir. He was strong, tireless and hard-working. A quiet exterior concealed implacable and indeed outrageous ambition, but Tiberius only noticed and applauded his conscientiousness – to such an extent that Tiberius' son was once provoked to engage him in fisticuffs. That there were many legitimate heirs between him and the imperial purple did not daunt Sejanus. He began by seducing Drusus' wife Livilla, sister of Germanicus, promising her a share in the Empire which one day would surely be his, and the death of her husband, who was a bad-tempered bully. In AD 23 Drusus suddenly died and everyone, except the grieving father, Tiberius, suspected poison. He leaned harder on Sejanus, who had divorced his own wife, but would not let him marry Livilla until some time later. He did listen, however, to his tales of conspiracy against him by his niece Agrippina, whose children now looked like his heirs. There were too many of them and they were too protected, or so it seemed, until Livia died, aged eighty-six, and Tiberius left Rome. In that year, through the influence of Sejanus, Agrippina and her son Nero (not the future Emperor) were banished and the other boy, another Drusus, imprisoned.

To Romans, Sejanus with his pride and power seemed to be Emperor, Tiberius a mere island potentate. He was poised to marry into the imperial family now that he had permission – his friends controlled the crucial provinces, he, the Praetorian Guard. In AD 31 he became consul with Tiberius and there seemed no limit to his ambition.

At last Tiberius, prompted perhaps by a warning letter from Antonia, widow of his brother Drusus and mother of Germanicus, stirred. He moved carefully, testing and muddying the waters. He sent for his young great-nephew Gaius (the future Emperor Caligula), whose brother Nero had died and who had been living neglected in Rome. He sent conflicting signals to Sejanus, that he was on the point of death, that he was well and coming to Rome, that Sejanus could be a priest with Gaius; and then, noticing how well this went down with the soldiery, who loved the memory of Gaius' father, Germanicus, hinted that he might make Gaius his successor. The Emperor went on to support an enemy of Sejanus, blocking a prosecution, and referred to Sejanus in an offhand way in a letter to the Senate; he forbade sacrifices in honour of any human being, including Sejanus, whom he was reported as alternately praising and denouncing. Sejanus was rattled, wishing he had struck when he had been consul – but he still could, because he still had the Praetorian Guard.

Romans began to cut Sejanus. The crowd seeking favours at his doors thinned, and when this was reported back to Tiberius he decided to set his plan in motion. No conspirator moved more cunningly and, now, more swiftly than the Emperor in the destruction of his former favourite. First, to quieten him, he let it be known that he intended for Sejanus the tribunician power, that authority which guaranteed immunity from arrest. Then he wrote a long letter of denunciation to be read out to the Senate, which he entrusted to Naevius Sertorius Macro, the new confidant he had made commander of the bodyguard. (We now know from an inscription that he had once been a prefect of the Vigiles, so he was a good choice.) Macro entered the city at night, briefed one of the consuls – the other being on Sejanus' side – and confided in the commander of the Night Watch. At dawn he climbed up the Palatine Hill to the Temple of Apollo, where the Senate was to meet.

Macro saw Sejanus pacing up and down outside, worried that he had no message from Tiberius. Macro told him (in the strictest confidence) that the Emperor had decided to give him the tribunician power, at which news Sejanus bounded happily into the Senate. Macro was then able to order the Praetorians (Sejanus' men) to return to their barracks, having sweetened them with Tiberius' promises of donatives. They were replaced by men from the Night Watch. At times of crisis, control of the guards outside the Senate was more important than the majority inside the chamber. Then the admirably efficient Macro hurried off to the camp to prevent any uprising, having handed over Tiberius' letter to the consuls.

Tacitus tells how, as this tortuous and finally damning document was read out, the senators at first cheered Sejanus, believing, as *he* did, that more authority was to be given him, but as the tone changed and the intention of Tiberius to unmask him became clear, the senators seated near him moved away and *praetors* and tribunes moved in to prevent his leaving the chamber and creating trouble. But Sejanus stayed in his seat, unable to believe his ears. Once, twice, thrice the consul Regulus, pointing to him, summoned him. 'Who, me?' answered Sejanus, unaccustomed to being addressed in this way. Finally he stood up and was joined by the commander of the Night Watch, Laco. At the conclusion of what Juvenal described seventy years later (for the downfall of the tyrant became legendary) as 'the long and wordy letter from Capri', Regulus asked one senator if he thought there was any reason why Sejanus should not be imprisoned. When the answer was no, Laco led him off.

Each movement in this affair had been choreographed by the fearful old man on Capri; in one day, a figure who had been honoured as second only to the Emperor saw his images overturned and was reduced to having his face beaten as if he were a runaway slave, as he was led to his execution. His body was abused by the mob then thrown into the river and his children were put to death, his daughter being first betrothed then violated, for a virgin could not be executed – a convention still honoured, if that is the word, in some parts of the world to this day. The episode did *not* honour the Senate and People of Rome, even if the Emperor's chief appetite, revenge, had been temporarily satisfied. The evil that Sejanus did lived long after his humiliating death. His first wife wrote to Tiberius how Sejanus had poisoned Drusus, slowly, over the years. Tiberius spared the second wife, Livilla, out of consideration for her mother, Antonia, who then starved her daughter to death.

Rome, thinking the Sejanus chapter was closed, breathed a sigh of relief, hoping for a balmier breeze from the sweet isle of Capri; it was not to be. For Tiberius the 'conspiracy' – there had not been one, as we have seen – was an opportunity for private revenge. He was quite selective,* executing another twenty of Sejanus' followers in AD 33 before amnestying the rest. That year is better known for the crucifixion of Jesus of Nazareth under Pontius Pilate, Procurator or Prefect of Judaea.

Tiberius, with no need to justify himself militarily as Emperor, followed the injunction of Augustus about freezing the frontiers of Rome. He had only three small local difficulties in Thrace, Gaul and Africa (Libya and Tunisia) to deal with. His handling of the provinces was so sensible –

---

* In the twenty-two years of his reign Tiberius only executed seventy-three of his enemies (cf. Claudius, Caligula or indeed Augustus).

'You should shear my sheep, not flay them', was his rebuke to a greedy governor – that under him the Empire was peaceful. He chose intelligent governors like L. Vitellius, legate for Syria, into which province Palestine was subsumed. By the standards of the day, modern historians have judged Pilate to be 'below average' (*vide* H.H. Scullard quoted above) and even discounting the complaints against him from the Jews (who, alone of his clan, Tiberius had not favoured), the fact that his superior Vitellius sent him to Rome to stand trial for, amongst other offences, the unnecessary massacre of some Samaritans, suggests that the reputation of Pilate as a just man is more biblical than historical. The story that he reported the punishment of Jesus to Tiberius is equally untrue.

Tiberius' resignation to a vicious old age on Capri was compounded by the death of his mother, his nephew Germanicus and his son Drusus, but when it was revealed to him that Sejanus, whom he had so trusted, had conspired with his daughter-in-law to poison his son, Tiberius collapsed and for nine months did not leave his villa. However, he never abandoned his duties – although these were less amply recorded than his debaucheries, because all Roman historians were nearer in spirit to *Confidential* and the *News of the World* than to the *Wall Street Journal* or the *Economist*. Details of public administration or private industry bored them. Tacitus, says Professor Reid (Professor of Ancient History at Cambridge), used as a (poisoned) source for his accounts of Tiberius' sexual depravity and his ingenious, sadistic and, presumably usually unsuccessful, attempts to achieve orgasm the memoirs of the younger Agrippina. One can tell from the epigrams of Martial and the satires of Juvenal and even the letters of Cicero that Romans gossiped, lied and exaggerated a lot about each other's private lives and especially about their Emperors. Tiberius, they said, used to boast about his 'minnows' who fellated him under water. One wonders how.* He is also supposed to have obliged the noble youths of Rome to become his catamites. None of them, however, came to any serious harm, and one, Galba, became Emperor. It amused him to have people flogged – a constant Roman pastime but in his case often just for crossing his path and once a newborn babe, removed from its mother's breast, for crying. This behaviour was rooted in hate, unleashed in the form of sadism, when there was no one left alive to restrain him. Professor Reid wrote of Tiberius: 'It is a question whether he ever liked or was liked by a single being.' The answer must be no, save for his first wife, Vipsania of course, whom he was forced to exchange for Augustus' daughter Julia. Apart from the sexual, his consistent pleasure was in the company of what he would have called his fellow intellectuals, lawyers and men of letters whom he put up in his villas on Capri and who put up with him. Their continued, voluntary, presence suggests that Tiberius cannot have been totally, as he was often described, uncongenial, all the time and to everybody. He was the most unkindly represented of all our Emperors but his real crime was to have been depressed and depressing. Conscientious in the matter of bread for the people, mean over circuses, secretive, devious, calculating and lonely – and finally, like Hitler in his bunker, loathing his own people – he was, like Hitler, dangerous and powerful till his dying day.

His problem, *solus et senex,* alone and old, was the succession. His grandson Gemellus, the son of Drusus, was too young and his nephew Claudius was generally, but as we

---

* A professor I met at the British School in Rome, who will remain anonymous, assured me it is possible if children are trained early enough.

shall see, wrongly, thought to be feeble-minded, so the next Emperor had to be Gaius, nicknamed 'Caligula', from the soldiers' leggings he had worn when displayed as an infant to the mutinous Roman army on the Rhine by his mother Agrippina. This young man, untrained, except in the art of dissimulation – and was there not a saying, 'Who cannot dissemble will never be king'? – was recognized by Tiberius, with satisfaction, as a 'serpent' (his phrase) and as such the appropriate legacy to bequeath to an ungrateful Rome. He therefore made Caligula co-heir with Gemellus – at one moment taking that little boy in his arms and, with tears in his eyes, indicating Caligula and saying, 'He will kill you.'

Tiberius' later actions were worthy of the administrator who had always done the right thing. He solved a financial crisis with an interest-free loan to debtors, he paid for the restoration of buildings damaged by fire on the Aventine out of his own pocket, he reduced the sales tax and when he died there was a surplus of 2,700 million sesterces in the public treasury.

The manner of Tiberius' death was characteristically tricky. Since the age of thirty he had disdained doctors and so issued his own bulletins as to his state of health. His ability to dissimulate was the last of his senses to go. On 16 March AD 37 he ceased to breathe, and Gaius began to breathe freely. Then suddenly he called out for something to eat. There was a general panic. Gaius was stunned. Nobody answered his call and Macro, the man he had trusted since the death of Sejanus, ordered him to be smothered with his own bedclothes and left alone. When the news reached Rome the people went wild with joy. 'Tiberius to the Tiber!' was the cry. But Tiberius had his revenge. He had left them Caligula.

✦ CALIGULA ✦

Gaius Julius Caesar Germanicus, Caligula ('little leggings') as he became known to posterity, but never to his contemporaries, was, as he liked to point out, the most royal of Emperors. He reached the purple at the age of twenty-four to the acclaim and high hopes of the Senate and People of Rome, who imagined that nobody could be as bad as the late Emperor Tiberius. He was descended, separately, from both Augustus and the Empress Livia and, through his grandmother Antonia, from Mark Antony, and both his father and grandfather, Germanicus and Drusus, had been famous and well-loved generals. An early memory was of riding in the chariot of his papa, to the cheers of the populace, and another was of being shown off, dressed as a little soldier, to the mutinous army on the Rhine by his theatrically inclined mama, Agrippina.

One of Caligula's fantasies was of himself as conquering hero, but he never seriously went to war. In AD 39 he had to crush a revolt in a camp in Upper Germany, promoted by Aemilius Lepidus, son of the triumvir of the same name* who had given so much trouble to Augustus. This man's

---

* Almost exactly the same names recur in Roman history. For instance in Nero's paternal family there are three L. Domitius Ahenobarbuses and two Gn. Domitius Ahenobarbuses within five generations.

pretensions were based on his proximity to Caligula as the widower of his adored sister Drusilla, and the lover of another sister, Agrippina. The two main conspirators were executed and two other sisters banished.

Then Caligula had to think how to occupy and impress his armies. He made some raids across the Rhône assisted by Vespasian, then a *praetor*, and Galba, who had been interfered with as a youth on Capri (both of whom were to become Emperors). He wintered in Lugdunum (Lyons) and received a goodwill delegation from the Senate, which included his uncle Claudius, whom he is said to have ducked in the river Rhône. This is very much Caligula's style for he had organized a speaking contest and the local punishment for a poor performance was exactly that. Uncle Claudius had a speech impediment. He also conduced an auction of imperial property, obliging those who attended to pay crazy prices; a pattern was beginning to emerge. For his German Triumph, Gallic slaves were produced with their hair dyed red and trained to mutter German. The next year, AD 40, in the spring, Caligula assembled an army at Boulogne for an invasion of Britain, but the operation was cancelled on the grounds that the exiled son of the British king Cunobellinus (Cymbeline) had crossed the Channel to offer submission to the power of Rome. The truth was that the troops, fearful of an expedition across the 'ocean' to what they regarded as the end of the world, to conquer an island which had not fallen to the great Julius Caesar, where the possibility of loot was minimal and which was inhabited by a barbaric people who painted their skin blue and sacrificed children at the start of battles (a habit of the Druids), refused to budge. Caligula ordered them to collect sea-shells, *musculi,* by the sea-shore, or was this a misinterpretation of a command to the engineers to pack up their huts, also *musculi*? Certainly he decreed decimation – one in ten of the soldiers to be killed – certainly this order was ignored. Thus ended Caligula's military pranks.

The reign had begun so well. The Roman people welcomed the untainted scion of a popular family (on his father's side) and the survivor of an imperial house where violent and premature death had been the norm with an outburst of *joie de vivre*. (Inscriptions discovered in Lusitania and Asia of oaths of allegiance show that the accession of young Gaius was popular throughout the Empire.) The Senate, mobbed by enthusiastic citizens, voted him all the powers Augustus had accumulated and some which Tiberius had declined. Romans celebrated in the way they most enjoyed, slaughtering 160,000 animals. Caligula responded piously and generously. He buried the late Emperor with an expensive funeral, which would have shocked the deceased, and wept during his own funeral oration. He sailed over in rough weather to collect the remains of his mother and brother. He changed the name of the month of September to 'Germanicus',* heaped as many honours on his grandmother Antonia as Livia had received in a lifetime, upgraded his stumbling, bumbling uncle Claudius from mere knight to fellow consul, adopted (yet another) Tiberius, recalled all exiles, abolished censorship and, to ensure that he would be loved in the provinces, restored client kings and gave them their back taxes. Twice he gave

* This appellation did not stick (unlike July, after Caesar, and August, after Augustus) due to the obloquy attached to Caligula's name subsequent to his death. The Roman months from September to December remain intact in their numeracy (the Julian Calendar began in March), and will surely be so till the end of time, for while the Romans ran the world and could do this sort of thing, any such change of nomenclature would be difficult in our time. Perhaps the Mother Teresa or Gandhi lobby might take up the challenge?

banquets for all the knights and senators and soon, of course, he had blued his inheritance.

One folly must have cost a pretty *denarius* or two. He assembled a bunch of merchant ships, bracketed them in pairs at anchor in a lane about three miles long between Baiae and the new port of Puteoli, covering them with earth and planks to make a sort of artificial Appian Way, and drove up and down it for two days in a chariot, wearing the breastplate of Alexander the Great. After this story Suetonius remarks: 'So much for Gaius the Emperor, now for Gaius the monster.'

In October of the year of his accession Caligula became seriously ill and the people feared for the life of their new benign young prince and prayed for him. He recovered. Historians have tried to find clinical evidence of insanity in Caligula from his behaviour, which could be explained, it was thought, only in this way, but his two most recent biographers* do not agree. Professor Ferrill, paraphrasing Acton in a manner Caligula himself would have enjoyed, writes: 'Power corrupts but absolute power is more exciting.' Caligula is best understood as an *enfant* allowed to be infinitely *terrible* by an obsequious Senate and subject to no restraint or authority, until stopped in his tracks by the daggers of the inevitable assassins. He is surely the classic example of a man dominated by 'the child within'. After the death of his sister Drusilla, with whom he had a passionate and enduring affair, and who was thought to have been a restraining influence, Caligula was utterly alone in the world; although he

---

* *Caligula, The Corruption of Power* by Anthony A. Barrett, Batsford, 1989, and *Caligula, Emperor of Rome* by Arthur Ferrill, Thames and Hudson, 1991. Nor, though obviously friendly, do they agree with each other, the former regarding their subject as rational, the latter as a monster.

had been one of seven children, four sons and three daughters, the others were all now dead or banished.

He was a murderous child star with a licence to kill. His nearest relations had been murdered and his last relationship had been with a vicious old man, convoluted by hate and mistrust, his moral tutor. His only playmate and friend was Herod Agrippa, a charming but feckless young man whose ancestor was the greatest family murderer and torturer of them all, Herod the Great. Caligula was a (very) sick comedian, playing the ultimate in practical jokes, rather than a criminal madman; nor was he an idiot, otherwise he could not have ruled in Rome. His targets were only ever from the upper class and the toll was not as high as posterity has imagined.* It was observed at the time that the home lives of the Emperors only affected those unfortunate or ambitious enough to be close to them. The horrors and high jinks at the courts of Caligula and Nero occurred in isolation and during both their reigns the people prospered, and both were popular with the plebs. (Caligula restored to the assembly powers carefully withdrawn from them by Augustus.) The Roman Empire ran on automatic pilot.

Caligula was a terrible tease – which was his undoing – and he used his caprice to amuse and terrorize his court. But he never made his horse a consul; though he said he could. And he never had any of his guests at his dinner parties killed; though he said he could. He pushed outrage to the edge of reality, dressing up – he loved dressing up – with the insignia

---

* Professor Barrett has done a tot of the victims, viz. two humiliations, nine driven to suicide, eleven executed, a friend of Seneca and an actress tortured, Sextus Pompeius – whom he forbade the use of the family cognomen 'Magnus' (the Great) – starved to death, Columbus, a gladiator, poisoned, and one senator, hacked to death by his fellows.

of a god and setting up a shrine to the Egyptian goddess Isis as a certain way of offending Roman sensibility. (Echoes of the dreaded Cleopatra.) As a revenue raiser (he said) he converted part of the palace into a brothel, with Roman matrons and their daughters as the personnel. He conducted auctions, and once a rich old knight nodded off during the proceedings and woke to find he had bought a clutch of gladiators for 9 million sesterces. One can imagine his planning these complicated tricks with a satanic giggle, but more dangerous was his pitiless pursuit of legacies and New Year gifts (hence the suicides). When one man, thought to be rich, harried to his death by the Emperor, turned out to have left no money, Caligula commented: 'Oh dear, he died in vain'. This sort of remark, repeated, as he had intended, in the taverns of Rome, endeared him to the masses, who saw him as an ally in a sort of class war.

Like many rich, spoilt young Romans he indulged in *nostalgie de la boue,* playing hookey with his guards, rampaging, in disguise, with his cronies in squalid parts of the city till the early hours, occasionally ending up in a prison. If Caligula was a danger to himself, he was death not only to his imagined enemies but also to his obvious allies. One man who had vowed to sacrifice his life for the Emperor's recovery was forced to do just that, in public; another had promised to fight a gladiator, Caligula made him do so. Of course, as Tiberius had predicted he had his co-heir, Gemellus, done away with* but he also forced his father-in-law and the faithful

---

* Gemellus, Tiberius' grandson, saw the danger to his own life clearly. Apparently Gemellus drank a cough medicine that Caligula, smelling it on the young man's breath, mistook for an antidote to poison. Gemellus, when accused offered a famous reply: 'Antidote – how can one take an antidote against Caesar?' (from Professor Ferrill).

Macro into suicide. The latter had only tried to help the young Emperor, whose accession he had organized, with advice, perhaps with too much advice, which irritated Caligula. Philo the Jew, a contemporary witness, relates how Caligula remarked on Macro's approach, 'Here comes the teacher of one who no longer needs to learn . . . who holds that an Emperor should obey his subjects, who rates himself versed in the art of government and an instructor therein . . . And then does anyone dare to teach me, who even while in the womb, that workshop of nature, was modelled as an Emperor . . . ?' Thus the authentic voice of tyranny, yes, but of madness . . . Caligula gave the downfall of Macro a typical twist, having had an affair with his wife, he accused him of being her pimp.

Caligula's cruelty was not wanton or casual like that of Tiberius, but planned, even painstaking, outrageous and, to him, enjoyable . . . His cruelty was political – 'Let them hate me as long as they fear me' – and never far from his thinking even with his lovers – 'You'll lose this beautiful head whenever I decide' – as he kissed them on the neck. Suetonius also tells how he forced parents to attend the executions of their children and once made a father come to dinner immediately afterwards, joking throughout the meal.* He gloated over the deaths of his victims, requiring the torturers to take

---

* The son's offence, for which he was imprisoned at first, was to be too well dressed and coiffed. The father had made the mistake of pleading for his life. After the first dinner he was made to return the day of the funeral when he behaved as if nothing had happened. Seneca, who tells this story and himself was nearly executed for making too good a speech in Caligula's presence, explains that the father had another son, whose future he did not want to imperil.

their time – 'Strike so he may feel he is dying'. His capacity for horror appeared to be limitless. He once ordered the guts and arms and legs of a senatorial victim to be stacked up in front of him.

It would be unbalanced to imply that Caligula's only activities were in the area of cruelty and outrage. He did rule – amazingly – for three years and nine months in Rome and attended to a few of the standard duties of an Emperor. He rebuilt, for instance, the burnt theatre of Pompey, removing, of course, Pompey's name from the façade. His foreign policy was quite as bizarre as his domestic, over which he had totally alienated the Senate. Apart from the absurd expedition to the north with a quarter of a million men under arms, and baggage including women and actors, to construct, it seems, a lighthouse in Boulogne, still standing in the sixteenth century, and the consolidation of Mauretania (north-west Africa), which was happening anyway, his most significant move in the Empire was nearly to provoke a Jewish rebellion.

Caligula found particular pleasure in annoying the Jews, although he had honoured his friend 'Herod' (actually M. Julius) Agrippa by adding the tetrarchy of Philip to his kingdom, to the fury of his sister, Herodias. (The descendants of Herod the Great were no more fond of each other than those of his patron Augustus.) On his way to take up his new kingdom, Agrippa stopped over in Alexandria and to encourage his own people, feuding as always with the Greeks of that city, thought it would be a good idea to parade through the streets with his bodyguard. This started the first recorded pogrom, which the Roman governor made no effort to suppress. Both parties sent delegations to Rome to complain about each other and were received cordially by Caligula. The Jews, headed by the philosopher Philo, were told to come back later.* Months passed and in the meantime a Roman procurator in Jamnia, Judaea, reported to the Emperor, who had decided he was a god, at least in the East, that the Jews had destroyed an altar erected to him in that city. (The same man had arrested Agrippa for owing Tiberius a million *sesterces*.) Caligula decided the Jews should be taught a lesson and commissioned Petronius, governor of Syria, to build an enormous statue of himself, dressed as Jupiter, and to install it in the Holy of Holies in the Temple at Jerusalem, a place so special that it was entered only by the high priest, only on Yom Kippur. If necessary the governor could use two of his four legions (12,000 men) for this purpose.

This ultimate in outrage has been held as a sign, nay proof, of Caligula's insanity but we may consider, granted his previous performance in this area, that it was par for the course, for Caligula had the devilish cunning to hit not just a nerve, but *the* nerve of his Jewish subjects. Petronius did as he was told up to a point, moving his legions south to the border of Galilee, but wrote to his Emperor that the Jews were so upset that they were neglecting the harvest; i.e., a revolt was imminent with consequent loss of revenue. His only friend, Herod Agrippa, who had returned to Rome, was appalled, hearbroken, and possibly had a stroke, when he heard the

---

* Philo describes how the Emperor received the delegation while surveying the redecoration of one of his palaces, rushing from room to room while the (probably) elderly petitioners panted after him, occasionally turning round to snarl at them or snapping, 'Why don't you eat pork?' and 'Are you the god-haters who do not believe me to be a god . . . acknowledged by all other nations . . . but not by you?' The Greeks sniggered, enjoying the discomfort of the Jews. What he said to them Philo does not record. Finally Caligula was bored and dismissed them quite gently saying: 'They seem to me people unfortunate rather than wicked . . .'

news. He sent Caligula a long letter rehearsing imperial policy towards the Jews, and out of friendship Caligula counter-manded the instructions to Petronius, on the understanding that the Jews would not interfere with his new cult outside Jerusalem; but, according to Philo, he had secretly decided to renege on the deal and planned to bring the statue with him on his forthcoming trip to the East. Fortunately, he died.

Caligula was a (conscious) artist in making enemies, espe-cially out of friends. He lost Agrippa and now his freedman, Callistus, a responsible figure, turned against him, appalled at his master's political folly. But it was not this, or a high-minded conspiracy, of which there had been many, which caused his death. When a man possessed of absolute power insists publicly on immediate sexual congress with the wife of another, he offends. When after the adultery he returns and comments to the husband that his wife's per-formance was inadequate, he offends absolutely.*

Cornelius Sabinus, a tribune in the Praetorian Guard, was one of the young husbands humiliated in this way by Caligula. Another conspirator was Cassius Chaerea, a soldier of a certain age, distinguished in the Rhine mutiny of AD 14, where Caligula had been present as a little boy. Like General Patton, the American tank general in the Second World War, he had a high squeaky voice, which Caligula imitated remorselessly. He taunted him for effeminacy, and embar-rassed him by inventing the daily passwords for the palace, which were in his charge, like 'Venus' and 'Priapus'; not too much provocation for an assassination, one might think, but enough.

---

* It was this, not political misdemeanour, which caused Zulfikkar Bhutto, once president of Pakistan, to be taken from his intentionally squalid cell and hanged.

On the last day of the Palatine Games, 24 January AD 41, the Emperor, while sacrificing a flamingo, spilled some blood on his toga. He had a hangover that morning and perhaps his hand was unsteady. Persuaded to adjourn for lunch, around one o'clock, by the Senator Asprenas, he was being carried up to the palace via an underground tunnel in his litter, when he stopped to talk to a group of young aristocrats from Asia who were practising a Trojan war dance they were to perform for him later that night. (They had been 'planted'.) In the confines of the tunnel and unprotected by his German guards the Emperor was temporarily vulnerable . . .

Chaerea struck the first blow, Sabinus the second, in the chest, then again and again – thirty times – he was stabbed by the patrician assassins, finally in the genitals, surely by Sabinus? His litter-bearers tried to defend him with their poles – he was not the only bad man to be loved by his servants – but they were no match for his determined killers. The Germans arrived too late to save him but killed a few of his assassins, Asprenas and another senator among the bystanders for good measure. They also killed one conspirator who could not resist looking at his dead body, 'for the sheer pleasure of it'. A praetorian tribune killed his wife Caesonia* and then their little daughter, Julia Drusilla, was

---

* His fourth and last wife, seven years older and married already five times, nevertheless towards whom he was affectionate, uxorious and monogamous. In his early days, on Capri, Caligula was reported to be both a prude and, indulged by Tiberius to calm his savagery, licentious. On gaining power, though he first expelled known perverts, he became sexually omnivorous, bedding everybody near him including the actor Mnester, his brother-in-law, various hostages and, of course, his sisters. His earlier marriages are not well documented, and do not appear to have counted for much, except for one to Pollia, who had a lot of money.

picked up by her feet and had her brains dashed out against a wall.

'On this day,' wrote the historian Dio Cassius, 'Caligula learned by experience that he was not a god.'

Caesonia had been found weeping over the dead body of her husband. She was the only person in Rome who wept. Caligula was the first Roman Emperor not to receive a state funeral. His legacy was nil, though dramatists and film-makers have been attracted to his extravagant life. A movie has been made about Caligula, so salacious that the egregious Gore Vidal, not known for his sensitivity in this regard, had his name removed from the credits. Malcolm McDowell, the actor, is better-looking than Caligula, but the manic laugh, the exaggerated grief for his sister, the violent changes of mood and costume are authentic and likely. The erotic scenes are juicy. The sets glitter with convincing replicas of marble, gilt and porphyry, the floors are spattered with stage blood and the entrails of the tortured. In the palaces of Caligula the blood and the spunk and the shrieks of pain were real.

✦ CLAUDIUS ✦

Claudius had more than one reason for keeping out of the way when he heard that his nephew, the Emperor Caligula, had been assassinated, just after one o'clock on 24 January AD 41.

He had left the Games to go to lunch, before Caligula, with two senators who may or may not have been in the plot, and would have heard the rumpus below. If he had been complicit – and historians still disagree – Claudius might have been in danger from the Emperor's enraged German body-guard, if not, from the assassins, young nobs with no clear plan, save that the death of an Emperor was always, in the patrician mind, an opportunity to restore the Republic. So Claudius, who never pretended to be a hero, hid himself, but not very successfully. Maybe the Praetorian who spotted an expensive pair of sandals peeping from behind a curtain and discovered him – crying, 'I have found a Germanicus!' – did not have to search too hard. This officer, one Gratus, was a member of an élite, whose high pay and perquisites would be at risk were there not an Emperor in Rome, so he held on to this gibbering middle-aged man, comforted him, saluted him *imperator* and ordered a litter to convey him to the safety of the Praetorian barracks about three kilometres away.

There Claudius stayed, a 'captive' he said, but willing to be drafted, using a technique described by his most recent biographer as 'disreputable, essentially infantile, but useful and adopted by others – by Henry II [of England for the murder of Beckett] and Elizabeth I [for the execution of Mary Queen of Scots] against internal threats (1170 and 1587) and by Reagan in the USA against Iran and Nicaragua – which consisted of allowing others to act or engineering them into it, while the principle remains "ignorant" of what is going on. Thus servants or subordinates have to take responsibility, eschewing the defence of superior orders.' This process, which sounds so complicated, was invoked by Claudius, considered so simple-minded, in a matter of hours to make himself Emperor. However it happened, and the main authorities have different versions – to Suetonius he remains an idiot, to Josephus, inept and manipulated by that great family friend, Herod Agrippa (who had buried Caligula in a shallow grave) – it *did* happen, and forty-eight hours after he had been taken off to the barracks, the same Praetorians escorted him to the Palatine Hill, where he was invested with all the powers accorded to his predecessors.

The night of the assassination, chatting in the mess over a jar or two – if Claudius remained sober, it was the only night of his life, including his last, that he had – Claudius had promised a donative of 15,000 to 20,000 *sesterces* per guardsman and pro-rata for the officers. This enormous and unpredecented sum riveted the Praetorian Guard to his side. Each needed the other, the Praetorians had to have an Emperor and though Claudius was not the natural heir of Caligula, if anyone cared, he was the nephew of Germanicus and so linked to the founder, Augustus, for which connection many Romans did care. This gave him a lineal edge on his rivals: M. Vinicius, Caligula's brother-in-law; V. Asiaticus, a rich man from Vienne near Lyons, of whom more will be heard; and Galba, in command of the legions in the Upper Rhine, who heard too late about the death of Caligula to make a move. From the barracks, therefore, Claudius had been able to send a message to the Senate, 'that he had not sought power but he would not renege on an offer he had accepted, that he of all people understood the dangers of tyranny, that his rule would be just and allow room for all in his administration if he were accepted, vengeful if he were not'. The Senate had collapsed. Claudius knew his history – had he not written forty books about Rome? – he knew that force, sharply applied, was the best weapon in politics.

So, in his fifties, Claudius entered on what few could have thought ever would be his inheritance. He had always been the runt of the family; historians used to attribute his feebleness to polio but now cerebral palsy, coupled with slight spasticity, is thought to be the cause of his symptoms, which were a dragging right leg, a cracked raucous voice and, when excited, a running nose and an uncontrollable laugh. His hands shook slightly and he occasionally stuttered, the result perhaps, as with the late George VI, of a stupid nurse having bound his left hand, the one he preferred to use, behind his back. He performed better when seated, and since he stopped suffering from stomach cramps after his accession, part of his trouble must have been psychosomatic.

Awareness of his condition came to Rome with his coming of age, the assumption of the *toga virilis* at fourteen, before which a young Roman did not really count. In the case of a prince of the imperial house this ceremony was an occasion for a public party, as if, as it were, a prince of the House of Windsor were to be *bar-mitzvahed* in Trafalgar Square.* (The

---

* Not so fanciful a notion as at first it seems. The humanist historian Gore Vidal, who has so many skills, maintains that Constantine's conversion to Christianity was not inevitable. If the zealous, energetic, peripatetic

wretched young Tiberius Claudius Nero Germanicus was given his *toga virilis* in the dead of night, muffled in a blanket, so apprehensive were the family of his public appearance.)

Concern or compassion for the disabled is a modern phenomenon. The Romans, sensitive to physical beauty and outward perfection, showed only distaste for the 'ill-met knight', which was all at first Claudius ever became. His mother referred to him as a 'monstrosity of a human being, one that Nature began and never finished'. Seneca, particularly, sneered. His grandmother Livia could not bear to look him in the face. His great-uncle Augustus was more circumspect and Suetonius quotes three letters between them about how to deal with Claudius and his problem. In the first, Augustus worries whether he is in full possession of his faculties and if he might make a fool of himself (and the family) if allowed into the imperial box at the Games; in the second he says he will ask young Tiberius Claudius to dine every afternoon rather than leave him to his tutors all the time, and in the third he is amazed that he can speak so well in public. Nevertheless Augustus gave him no serious position and no serious money, naming him in his will 'an heir of the third degree'. During his years in the shadows Claudius endured social and political frustration, aggravated by poverty and illness. Though hailed cheerfully by the crowd at the Games, as a Germanicus, he was mocked and snubbed by his equals, who amused themselves by throwing date and olive stones at him at Caligula's dinner parties, even when he shared a consulship with their host, and when he fell asleep they put slippers on his hands, so that he rubbed his eyes with them when he woke up. He was made a member of two

and convincing Saul of Tarsus had remained a Pharisee and talked the Roman élite into Judaism. . .

down-market priesthoods and once picked up a perquisite of forty gold coins, which the family considered quite enough. Twice Tiberius refused his request for a minor magistracy but did leave him a small interest in his will.

Claudius spent his time scribbling at his histories; for recreation he pursued women and indulged in a lot of food, wine and gambling, convinced he could beat the system. (He wrote a book about that too.) Like Caesar and Caligula, Claudius was married four times; first to one Plautia Urgulanilla, by whom he had two children. He divorced her in AD 24 for adultery and, unbelievably, suspicion of murder. Then there was a non-starter who died on her wedding day but whose brother emerged later as a minor conspirator against him. Next was Aelia Paetina, relation of Sejanus, the favourite of Tiberius, and obviously selected by him. He was not important enough to have played any part in the downfall of his wife's relative and simply kept his head down, pretending to be, as he explained to the Senate, during the reign of Caligula, a fool. Once Emperor, he became successively the sexual target of the two most notorious women in Roman history, Messalina and Agrippina. Alone of the five rulers in this book, not the faintest whiff of homosexuality attaches to his name.*

---

* Charles Laughton, convincing as a Roman emperor, played Claudius, perhaps unintentionally, as a homosexual, in a movie which was never made. A series of 'takes' shows him fluffing his lines just when he is supposed to condemn a good-looking young man (Sabinus?) to death for taking part in the assassination of his precessor, Caligula. The episode, though touching, is historically unsafe since the real Claudius actually spared Sabinus (who, tactfully, later committed suicide) and easily consigned Chaerea and co. to execution, with that limp wave of the wrist which was to become so notorious, on the grounds that such men could become a nuisance to himself.

Of all the Emperors so far, Claudius was the most insecure. Augustus, who invented the role, accumulated the necessary powers but his titles, 'Augustus' and 'Father of the Country', had been voted to him and were expressions of his popularity, constantly renewed. Tiberius had been designated by Augustus, Caligula was nothing if not of the imperial blood, but Claudius was almost an alien, a usurper inducted by a massively bribed Praetorian Guard, which he paid with gold coins, struck again and again, one depicting him shaking hands with a guardsman and another with the barracks as a background. Nevertheless Claudius has been called by modern historians the 'first Roman Emperor' because for the first time the public and private personae of the *princeps* were fused into one man – an Emperor. Tiberius referred to himself as: 'master of his slaves, *imperator* of the armies and *princeps* among senators' and observed these distinctions. In the reigns of Caligula and Claudius their power increased, and, worse, was increasingly unquestioned. 'The Conscript Fathers', the senators, guardians of governmental propriety, had become obsequious, terrified and, because they had less and less to do, bored. The manner of the accession of Caligula and Claudius had demonstrated that only the supreme post in Rome *had* to be filled. Any autocrat prefers his own creatures to do his bidding, so Emperors chose their own men, not their equals, for positions of authority. A freedman was – this was the rule – dependent, therefore dependable, unlike knights and senators who might consider themselves, in their hearts, as competent as an Emperor to rule.

At first a champion of the equestrian order, to which he had for so long belonged, Claudius quickly became alienated from them and, suspecting their ambitions, connived at or engineered their executions. He was the paradigm of a man 'willing to wound and yet afraid to strike' – or to do the striking himself. His final tot was chilling – thirty-five senators and 321 knights. He was abetted in this grisly exercise in self-defence by his third wife, who started as a well-connected nymphet of fifteen and galloped into becoming a bloodthirsty, power-crazy nymphomaniac, who finally had to be put down.

Messalina married Claudius in AD 39, when he was fifty. She was the great-great-granddaughter of Augustus' sister, the patient Octavia, and also his first cousin once removed. Her mission in her (short) life was to ensure that her son, born Tiberius Claudius Caesar Germanicus, later Britannicus, should become Emperor. She had a good chance. Coins were struck at his birth with the legend *spes augusta* – the hope of the dynasty – but because her husband might not survive for her child's majority, she had to eliminate the opposition; so she embarked on a policy of murder. Her first victim was Julia Livilla, exiled sister of Caligula, married to M. Vinicius, a candidate for the principate (so why not again?). She then pursued another Julia, daughter of Tiberius' son Drusus (poisoned by Sejanus), a blameless lady who nevertheless was guilty of having a son and was therefore a contender. She was accused by Messalina of immorality (!). Then she destroyed a prefect of the guard who was about to report her sexual goings-on to Claudius and at the same time created a vacancy for one of her favourites.

Because of her husband's doubtful title to the throne, many were the claimants to Messalina's vengeful and often lethal attention, not just from the family but from the descendants of the famous names of the Republic, like Sulla, Pompey and Crassus, who, precisely because they were not related, imagined they could offer Rome a fresh start. At first Claudius tried to conciliate them with high office but over the years these high-born grandees were destroyed, usually through the indirect technique at which Claudius became so adept and his wife so co-operative.

No conspiracy can have been so unreal, bizarre and revealing of this infernal couple as that of Appius Silanus. One night, Claudius revealed to the Senate, his freedman Narcissus burst into his bedroom and announced he had just had a dream in which Silanus had decided to assassinate him. The distinguished nobleman, summoned to the palace in the early hours, admitted his intentions and had been duly executed. Claudius presented Narcissus' dream as cut-and-dried evidence of a plot. It was said that Messalina was piqued because Silanus had refused her sexual advances and had put up Narcissus to this murderous farce. The episode shows the easy access of private, and therefore now public, servants to the Emperor, and that the closer they were to the royal person, like the grooms of the bedchamber of Henry VIII or Louis XIV, the greater their influence. The secret and unjustifiable execution of Silanus provoked a revolt by the Governor of Dalmatia, put down in five days but giving Messalina the opportunity of her most notorious killing, of the husband of her best friend in childhood, who had been an associate of Silanus, with the words: 'It doesn't hurt, Paetus.' Getting rid of her stepson-in-law, who had married Claudius' daughter and was therefore a possible rival, was no problem. He was killed, *in flagrante delicto* with a male lover.

Messalina's most ambitious *coup* was to engineer the death of Valerius Asiaticus, the rich and bumptious Gaul* who had married into the Roman patriciate and considered himself to be imperial material. His wife had had an affair with Caligula

* His tribe, the Allobroges, had prospered through collaboration with Julius Caesar.

and her sister, famous for her emeralds, had briefly married him. Asiaticus was quite a figure in Rome; his family had entertained every important Roman touring Gaul over the years, including the Emperor's mother, which may be why Claudius was reluctant to execute him. But Messalina was implacable. Asiaticus owned the gardens of Lucullus, the successful general and stylish gourmet, and she coveted them. Asiaticus was brought to the palace in chains and charged with homosexuality, a charge invoked in the absence of any other. Claudius had a mind to acquit, so a compromise was reached. Asiaticus was allowed to choose the manner of his death.

The prefect who arrested him was given one and a half million *sesterces* and made up to *praetor*. Again, the trial had been *intra cubiculum*, behind closed doors in the privacy of the palace, and the victim was not just a wealthy Gaul who was disliked for his extravagance – he spent too much on Games – but the son-in-law of a powerful family, one of whose members was found at a morning levee with a sword hidden in his toga. Under torture, which Claudius had once forsworn, he revealed nothing, but his attempt showed the extent of the alienation of Rome's upper classes. Messalina's downfall, according to Tacitus, was due to her own madness -*furor.* She fell in love – she was only in her early twenties – with a handsome young consul-designate, Silius, swamped him with presents, and 'married' him at the *vendange* of AD 48 in a bacchic ceremony. All Rome knew and Narcissus and his clique of freedmen decided that so should the Emperor, both out of loyalty and because they thought Messalina capable of setting up her lover as *princeps,* and replacing them.

The idea of such a *coup* might have entered her pretty head on noticing the popular favour shown to Agrippina,

Caligula's surviving sister, and her charming ten-year-old son, at the Trojan Games of AD 47. Since the already socially dextrous lad became the Emperor Nero, she may have had a point, but it was not one she lived to make. For once, Claudius reacted directly and fast. He saw the danger to his *dignitas* – we would say credibility – in his wife's repudiation of himself and, since there were few officials in Rome he could trust to arrest her, he rushed up from Ostia and conferred with Narcissus, who took command of the Praetorian Guard for one day. With him, Vitellius and a consular who was a good friend of the Germanicus family, he proceeded to the house of Silius when Messalina intercepted their carriage. She played her ace – the children. Claudius trumped it with a list of her lovers.* The carriage rolled on. Then it was stopped by the senior Vestal Virgin, demanding, as Rome's leading feminist, a hearing for the Empress. Narcissus pushed her away with promises. The party checked out Silius' house, was astonished by the number of imperial heirlooms Messalina had given her lover, and drove to the Praetorian barracks, Claudius' ultimate 'safe house', where a drumhead court martial was convened. Silius was brought in and asked only for a speedy death. Messalina was found in the gardens of Lucullus and stabbed to death.

Claudius, for some reason, had told the Praetorians that they should kill him if he married again, but the execution of an Empress created a vacancy in the state which had to be filled. Factions at court fought for their candidates. Narcissus proposed Aelia Paetina, who was harmless and had once before been married to Claudius; Callistus suggested Lollia Paullina, very rich and briefly one of Caligula's wives; but

---

* This brilliant if anachronistic description is from *Claudius* by Barbara Levick, Batsford, 1990.

the favourite, and the choice of Pallas, the rising star among the Emperor's freedmen, was Agrippina, daughter of the fondly remembered Germanicus and Vipsania, the beloved wife of Tiberius. That she was Claudius' niece by blood, the daughter of his brother, was a modest drawback compared to the number of brownie points a shaky Emperor could pick from such a splendid connection. Claudius' friend Vitellius assured him the choice would be welcomed by the people and canvassed his fellow senators, who removed the inhibition and recommended the match. The marriage, took place on 1 January AD 49. Claudius had been a widower for three months.

Agrippina was thirty-three, more adroit politically than Messalina and equally ruthless and determined that *her* son should succeed as Emperor. She moved fast. Claudius agreed that her ten-year-old Nero should be co-heir with his own son of seven, Britannicus; there were predecents. She wanted to marry her son to Octavia, Britannicus' sister, his cousin; there were predecents here, too. She detached Octavia from her betrothed by accusing him of incest. She had Seneca recalled from exile and made him Nero's tutor. She procured for herself the title of Augusta. All this within one year. By AD 51 Agrippina appeared to be wearing the trousers, as it were, at the palace – actually it was a military cloak, threaded with gold, in which she greeted ambassadors. Her face appeared on coins and, since she successfully advanced her own son at the expense of Britannicus, she was, as the mother of the future Emperor, the most powerful woman Rome had ever known.

In the power games at court, played with such ferocity by his women, against whom he railed quietly as he grew older, Claudius appeared to be something of a patsy, but in the areas of justice (where he was often eccentric), finance, legislation and administration of his Empire, Claudius was conscientious, efficient, innovative and powerful. He was an intelligent man who had studied Roman history and, when his own survival was not in question, he was just, tactful and considerate. His reforms were unpopular with his own class because he preferred procurators, his own people, to prefects, the Senate's. His contribution to the streamlining of the imperial administration was not recognized until well after his death, though he was promptly deified. Because of his ailments he was interested in medicine and prone to give his subjects much homely advice, extolling the benefits, for instance, of farting. His almost daily attendance at court was deplored by the legal profession because his judgements were capricious, emotional and inconsistent. Once an exasperated advocate threw a briefcase at him. He did not mind. Then a superstitious orator, a knight from Gaul, let fall from his toga a snake's egg, a Druidic good luck token. Claudius, terrified that the magic might affect him, waved him away to be executed. He panicked easily but his decisions were always sound if there was time for consideration.

Juvenal invented the phrase 'bread and circuses' as the basic needs of the Roman populace, but it also expected public works from its rulers. Cicero distinguished between the useful and the decorative, the docks, aqueducts and walls, and the theatres, colonnades and temples (preferred, of course, by Caligula). Claudius obliged in the useful categories and added another of his own – maintenance – the *sine qua non* of civilization.

He turned Ostia, where he was working when the Messalina scandal broke, into a grain port with a lighthouse and a flood barrage. His most macro-economic project, still unfinished after eleven years and 30,000 navvies, was the draining of the Fucine Lake to recover farmland eighty-five

kilometres from Rome. Like the Mahaveli Dam in Sri Lanka*
it was not a total success. He had trouble finding (doomed)
players for the sea battle he wanted to stage, and the sluice
gates the spectacle was designed to celebrate failed to sluice.
Claudius repaired the aqueduct of Agrippa, which still supplies the fountain of the Trevi, and built two aqueducts, one
eighty-seven kilometres long.

He strove with these public works to become, early in his
reign (and remain), a 'populist' Emperor. He practised
'walkabouts' and picnicked with the plebs; as we have seen,
he told them how to make vintage wine (a Roman skill which
disappeared from Europe till the early eighteenth century)
but he had not yet attempted the traditional imperial role,
that of conqueror, and Rome was surprised when their
fifty-three-year-old Emperor, a scholar with a dragging foot,
a trembling hand and a wobbly tongue, decided to go to war.

Ignoring the advice, respected by Tiberius, of the dying
Augustus, that the frontiers of the Empire should not be
extended, Claudius decided to invade Britain. The south-east
of England was no longer the foreign country it was for Julius
Caesar 100 years before. Gaul, successfully Romanized (witness Asiaticus) had stronger tribal links with England than
it has now. The Catuvellauni round Herts were Belgic as were
the Atrebates in Berks and Hants, centred on Silchester,
founded by Caesar's once favourite Gaul, Commius. These
tribes had a king, Cunobelinus (Cymbeline), who paid tribute to Rome, but when he died his sons did not, and one of
them attacked a Roman ally who fled to Claudius for help.
This was the excuse.

---

* The original waterworks there were functioning in the first century
AD during the Anaradhapura kingdom, and the Sinhalese, who used trigo-
nometry in their hydraulic engineering, were invited to Rome by Tiberius
for his coronation.

Four legions, from the Rhine and Pannonia, were assembled, topped up with auxiliaries and stiffened with a cohort from the Praetorian Guard. To impress the barbarians a few elephants were added to this force of 40,000 men which nevertheless, giving the usual reasons (*vide* Caligula), refused to embark. (Roman troops, we must remind ourselves, had to be convinced, as well as inspired, to go into action.) Claudius summoned Narcissus, the first freedman to address an army, who made them laugh, making unnecessary the exemplary executions planned by the generals.

Within a month, with Plautius as Commander-in-Chief, they had landed at Richborough and, after some fierce fighting in the Medway, had captured London and were able to send for Claudius, waiting in Boulogne. The Emperor, accompanied by a glittering entourage of powerful patricians he thought unsafe to leave in Rome – the Frugi, Silanus, Asiaticus and Vinicius, who all later became victims of Messalina – crossed the Channel and headed for Camulodunum, where he held a sort of 'durbar'. There he received the submission of the local chiefs (including a queen, Cartimandua, who controlled twelve tribes in the north). It was a long time before the inhabitants of Colchester saw another elephant.

Claudius only spent sixteen days in Britain, but he had been away from Rome, where the trusty Vitellius had been keeping watch, for five months and was determined on his return that the Roman world should know of his success. It did. Plautius was given a (rare) Triumph and in every city and town of the Empire peasants coming to market would see some sort of representation of Britannia, who became the symbol of that hitherto remote and unknown island. A marble relief has been recently discovered in Aphrodisias showing Claudius subduing her, and coins were struck with his new cognomen, 'Britannicus'. As Barbara Levick writes:

'The impact of the conquest throughout the Empire was considerable ... a stroke of elegance and power for a new and underestimated Emperor, and its effects on the minds of his subjects, as its fame washed through the Empire and rippled even into its remotest provinces, incalculable.'

In fact the victory was celebrated ahead of the conquest, because that required the military talent of Vespasian, who had particular difficulty in netting Caratacus (finally betrayed by his fellow monarch, the queen in the north). Claudius kept Caratacus for another celebration of the conquest of Britain in Rome in AD 51 when he made a splendid speech which earned him and Claudius, who pardoned him, much applause and which Tacitus records: 'Had my lineage and rank been accompanied by only moderate success, I should have come to this city as a friend rather than as a prisoner ... As it is, humiliation is my lot, glory yours. I had horses, men, arms, wealth. Are you surprised I am sorry to lose them? If you want to rule the world does it follow that everyone welcomes enslavement?' Caratacus was as famous an enemy to the Romans as Vercingetorix, and just as eloquent, but thanks to Claudius he kept his life.

Claudius declared St Albans the capital of the new province – a province that later became a place to retire to, because of the low land-values and the amiability of the local servants. The Romans built roads – stretches of Watling Street and Ermine Street still survive – and thus enabled King Harold, 1,000 years later, to make his dash from Stamford Bridge in Yorkshire to Hastings. The Romans mined lead in the Mendips and later pearls, hunting dogs were exported, and 40,000 British prisoners-of-war were used to build the network of roads in Gaul, but finally the cost of monitoring the island was greater than the benefit to the Empire. Nero even considered withdrawal.

A Roman Emperor, like a President of the United States, was both commander-in-chief of the armies and in charge of foreign policy. Apart from the British expedition, Claudius did not visit his Empire, preferring to pad around Italy, but he was a passionate builder of roads (notably the 525-kilometre route over the Brenner Pass), and his vision of himself as ruler and pacifier of a world he wanted to be Roman – everyone should wear a toga, he said – was near to the truth.

He was less successful on the home front. Agrippina now had Nero's aunt, Domitia Lepida, in her sights. Once beautiful, always rich, now ancient and depraved, she had had Nero to stay with her for two years while his mother, Agrippina, was in exile. She might therefore exert a rival influence, if and when *(when?)* Nero became Emperor. Domitia was charged with magic and letting her shepherd slaves run amok in Calabria, where she had huge estates. Nero had been persuaded that she favoured his cousin Britannicus, her grandson, and he actually appeared as a prosecution witness against his doting aunt. The Emperor sentenced her to death, despite the contrary advice of Narcissus.

All Roman historians describe the death of Claudius and accuse his wife of murder. (A modern historian has diagnosed a heart attack.) Here is a précis of Tacitus' version, the most lively and likely. Agrippina employed an expert, one Locusta, 'recently sentenced for poisoning but with a long career of imperial service ahead of her'. The Emperor's taster, the eunuch Halotus, and his doctor Xenophon were also brought into the act. The poison was sprinkled on some mushrooms Claudius particularly liked and he consumed them happily. At first nothing happened – Claudius was either torpid or drunk – then he evacuated his bowels. Agrippina was aghast, but under the pretence of making him vomit, the doctor tickled his patient's throat with a feather dipped in a quick-acting poison. ('Xenophon knew that major crimes, though hazardous to undertake, are profitable to achieve.') The Empress clung on to Britannicus, ostensibly for comfort but actually to prevent his leaving the room. She also detained the sisters. No announcement was made. The dead man was put under wraps and it was pretended the Emperor was very ill. Then at midday on 13 October, the propitious moment according to the astrologers, the palace gates were opened and there was Burrus, commander of the Praetorian Guard, well-primed ally of Agrippina, with a battalion, ready to acclaim Nero the new Emperor. A few Praetorians were heard to wonder where Britannicus might be, but Agrippina's operation was too well oiled to be halted now, and Nero was conveyed to the Praetorian camp in a litter where he promised the usual donatives and was hailed Emperor; the Senate and the provinces followed suit. Agrippina had achieved her ambition, to secure the imperial throne for her son and have him accept her advisers, Burrus her strong man and Seneca her think-tank, as his own. Through him and them she would be able to rule the world for a time. When Nero was born, the astrologer had said: 'He will be king and he will kill his mother.' The first part of the prediction had come true.

❧ NERO ❧

When Nero's father, Gnaeus Domitius Ahenobarbus, was congratulated on the birth of a son, he replied that the fruit of any union between his family and Messalina could only be a disaster.

The *gens Domitia* had furnished Rome for 200 years with consuls and generals, famous for their brutality. They were rich men, partly because they never had daughters to dower, and Nero's great-great-grandfather had raised money for Pompey's army through pledging lands. Despite being on the wrong side, there was still plenty left.

Nero's father was a violent man. He tore out an equestrian's eye in the Forum and once ran over a child on the Appian Way for fun. He had been rebuked by Augustus for the cruelty of his Games and he was even prosecuted. He would have been a terrible father to have around but he obliged Nero by dying of dropsy when the child was three. His mother, Agrippina, was ruthless and murderous, as we have seen; her behaviour was explained, as in the case of Caligula, but not excused, by a traumatic childhood. Her grandmother had been the dissolute Julia, Augustus' only child, and her mother, Agrippina the elder, had been beaten up by a centurion before her eyes and then starved to death – as had her two elder brothers – on the orders of Tiberius. (One of them tried to survive by eating the stuffing of his mattress.) When Agrippina's (mad?) brother Caligula became Emperor she had to watch his excesses and was then exiled, leaving her little boy in the care of a barber and a dancer. She survived Messalina's regime and, marrying her uncle the Emperor, successfully promoted her son, whom she later, possibly, seduced. With such an upbringing Nero's sexual behaviour – rating a chapter of its own in Hirschfeld's catalogue of anomalies and perversions – as a sodomite, catamite, sadist, masochist and bestialist can be understood.

He inherited the defects of both sides of the family and a geneticist would be hard put to it to find an ancestral gene for the visionary, romantic streak in Nero, dominant in this most misunderstood man ever, whom history has damned and caricatured for his almost accidental persecution of the Christians. His infamy deepened as their influence increased, yet, to contemporaries, his decision to harass this tiny Jewish sect was both understandable and insignificant. The first five years of his reign constituted, by common accord, a mini golden age. (His abdication to the Senate of powers held by his predecessors is illustrated on coinage from AD 55 to 64, which refers to Nero simply as Emperor, without indicating other offices of state. Later he became an enthusiastic and bossy numismatologist.) Under the tutelage of Burrus and Seneca, with his mother nagging but tactfully sidestepped, Nero showed generosity, kindness and accessibility – *liberalitas, clementia et civilitas* – bywords designed by Seneca for his accession speech to the Senate in the autumn of AD 54.

Both his predecessors had made the same promises in the same speech, but Nero was true to his, for nearly eight years. An immediate bonus was a return to the old Roman ideal that advocates should not receive fees, based on the notion that the right of justice, free of bribery and influence, should be the duty and concern of every Roman gentleman. Two of Nero's better *dicta* date from these halcyon days – on signing a death warrant, 'Oh how I wish I had never learned to write!' and in reply to a vote of thanks from the Senate, 'I will accept when I deserve it.'

His mentors complemented each other. Burrus, originally an accountant, had been made, through Agrippina's influence, sole commander of the Praetorian Guard and had master-minded the accession. He was a straightforward brusque fellow and, though not a soldier, bristled with officer-like qualities, firm, fair but not familiar, and was respected by his men. He was also loyal, first to Agrippina and then, when Nero had her murdered, to her son.

Seneca was an altogether more devious figure, multi faceted and complex. Born into a rich and educated family of Italians who had emigrated to Andalucia at the turn of the century, 1 AD, he was brought up in Rome by his doting daddy, the elder Seneca, who lived to be ninety. His two elder brothers were both in the *cursus honorum – la grande carrière*. The brothers were all bronchial, which saved Seneca's life because Caligula, irritated by his suave oratory, wanted to frame him for alleged involvement in a conspiracy, but banished him to Corsica instead, because one of his mistresses persuaded him that he had not long to live. He was a protégé of Agrippina, who was eventually able to recall him after eight humiliating years in Corsica and fixed him up with a praetorship. During his exile, Seneca had been writing – treatises 'On Natural Science' (including earthquakes), 'On Sympathy', 'On Anger', On Anything, for he was a polymath and *encyclopédiste,* like Voltaire. On paper Seneca was exemplary, the darling of Classics masters down the ages, for his sweet reasonableness and for the dignified manner of his suicide. His Stoicism, imbued with gloom and a sense of duty, also appealed to nineteenth-century moralists and he was so well regarded by the early Christian Church that a correspondence was invented between him and St Paul in the fifth century AD. In fact Seneca was a hypocrite.

His compassion was muted by greed. Though one of the few to disapprove of slavery, he did not even attend the debate in the Senate which agonized all night about whether to execute the 400 household slaves of the murdered prefect of police, Pedanius. (They were all led off to their deaths, the troops pushing back a hostile crowd.) Seneca spent much of his time lending money – cf. Proust's daily communications with his stockbroker – and through this occupation became one of the richest men in Rome, with over 100 citrus wood and ivory tables (*one* of which was a status symbol in ancient Rome), yet Plutarch describes his lecturing Nero on the virtue of true poverty.

With Burrus, his partner in power, Seneca became a friend of the Emperor, *amicus Principi,* in an autocracy more important than any official position. Their immediate concern was the Emperor's mother, still implacable, whose need to rule was disruptive. 'They both,' wrote Tacitus, 'waged a crusade against Agrippina's ferocity.' Her first move, advancing in public session to sit beside her son on the imperial dais, was deflected by Nero, rising to greet his mother and escorting her to another *curule*. Subsequently she would hide behind curtains to observe proceedings. Then the partners told Acte, a freedwoman mistress they had provided, to explain to the Emperor that his mother's boasting of her influence was alienating the soldiery. Nero, alone of his line, was naive. However, he reacted by depriving his mother of her personal Praetorian Guard and by firing Pallas,* Claudius' freedman, and so a creature of Agrippina, from his position of financial controller, thus honouring his pledge to keep palace influence out of public affairs.

Roman historians make the death of young Britannicus the crime of Agrippina, as consistent with her policy of removing any obstacle (including and especially her husband's son) to her son's enjoyment of power; but Nero's latest biographer, Miriam Griffin,** has her in a panic, switching sides and deciding to support Britannicus as the rightful heir in a move to unnerve Nero and force him into submission. It did not work. Britannicus was poisoned at a children's party at the palace during the holidays and much later many famous children claimed to have had tummy troubles from the same cakes. A reconciliation between Nero and his mother in AD 55 did not last.

Nero grew irritated at the failure of his advisers (who, he was beginning to reflect, had been hers) to suggest a method of ridding him of this turbulent mother, and asked help of his old mentor, the ingenious Anicetus, now Prefect of the Fleet at Misenum.

Like George IV, who installed the first gaslight system in England, at the Pavilion in Brighton, and turned the apparatus on himself, with the courtiers standing well back, Nero, also an extravagant builder, encouraged inventors. He imported a team of mechanical engineers from Alexandria (who had previously come to the notice of Julius Caesar and who had invented amongst other extraordinary artefacts, a toy

---

* Pallas lived on for another seven years on his enormous estate, but his wealth was too great for the then greedy Emperor to endure and he was quietly poisoned.

** *Nero,* Batsford, 1984.

steam-engine). He employed them to realize his dream of the Golden House, of which more anon, and they may well have conceived the collapsible boat, seen by Nero on stage and used in an attempt to drown his mother. (The roof descended automatically as the hull let in water.) The Empress Mother was induced to embark at Baiae in this strange vessel, imagining a nautical promenade in her honour. The devilish machinery performed as advertised, but, in front of a large crowd, Agrippina swam safely to the shore. Nero was terrified. He appealed to Burrus, who told him to do his own dirty work. He ordered a military tribune to kill her and when the moment came Agrippina was not surprised – the second half of the astrologer's prediction had to come to pass – and simply directed that the first blow be to her womb, whence the Emperor had (with difficulty) once emerged. Seneca, ready as always with the quill, composed a letter to the Senate describing how the Empress had been discovered in a plot against her son and the farcical, seedy matricide was in this way converted to a sick little triumph of deliverance.

Liberation from his mother (but not from nightmares about her death, which caused him to avoid numinous places like Delphi and Eleusis with their attendant Furies) triggered the release of Nero's inhibitions. He began his *nostalgie de la boue* trips, in disguise, like Caligula, to the seedy parts of the city, beating up passers-by in the way of rich bored young men in pursuit of kicks throughout the ages (cf. the 'Mohawks' in the twenties in London). Oddly Nero was a private but not a public sadist and his Hellenism revolted against the Ancient Roman pleasure in the Games, which he tried to suppress in favour of mock gladiatorial combats among the patriciate. Of course he failed here, but he persisted till the end – and it *was* his end – in conceiving his mission as the re-education of the Roman people. If only his fellow human beings were as committed to the arts as he, as talented, as extravagant, as gifted, as generous and as peaceable as he – the world would surely be a better place! He was a genuinely naive artist and once proposed to appear before an enemy host and cry.

The first indicator of his ethics and aesthetics was his reception of Tiridates, the client king, the Roman general Corbulo, of whom Claudius had been so jealous, had imposed on Armenia, as part of a deal with the Parthians. The first day passed in the traditional way, as practised by Augustus, and the king knelt in homage to the Emperor seated on the rostrum in front of an army parade. On the second day, Nero, who was for centuries after his death acknowledged on medallions as the world's greatest ever party-giver, had the whole of Pompey's theatre gilded (in twenty-four hours) and an awning stretched over the auditorium depicting the heavenly orbs with the sun at their centre, and in the centre of the sun, his face. (For Nero saw himself as Apollo, the Sun King, a conceit emulated by Louis XIV, imitating that god by playing the zither and driving a chariot with two white horses.) King Tiridates prostrated himself before the Emperor, reciting a Persian prayer of oriental adulation which would have embarrassed the Roman audience had they understood it. Some scholars have solemnly dated and stated Nero's conversion to Mithraism from this event, and certainly Tiridates was well paid for his performance, with an 800,000 *sesterces per diem* expense allowance and 100 million *sesterces* 'take home', but Suetonius denies Nero any serious religious belief and, knowing as we now do from excavations of the Domus Aurea – the Golden House – about Nero's taste, it is more likely to have been an expression of his pleasure in the very high camp.

This enormous, breathtaking, environmentally unfriendly – because, with its dimensions of 2,000 by 1,000 metres, it took up so much of other people's environment – complex of palaces and pavilions, disliked as much by his contemporaries as George IV's miniature at Brighton was by his, was revolutionary in concept, design, decoration and even construction; for a technique of combining rubble with cement to create vaulted domes was used for the first time, models for Hadrian's revised Pantheon and many churches of the Renaissance, and was as significant architecturally as the discovery of reinforced concrete.

Nero was a science buff. In the middle of the Vindex revolt he insisted on taking a day to show the consuls and *praetors* a new hydraulic organ from the 'polytechnic'* in Alexandria which he proudly dismantled and reassembled himself. The wonder of the Golden House was a revolving dome which turned day and night in harmony with the stars. No Roman historian has bothered to tell us how it worked, but it must have been powered by a flow of water, like the 'machine' which produced such a heavenly show for Louis XIV in the gardens of his pet palace at Marly.

The *magistri et machinatores,* master workmen and engineers, must have been thrilled to be employed by an autocrat (cf. Speer and Hitler) on grand and glamorous enterprises, quickly decided, quickly executed and quickly paid for. The Neronian team of technicians, headed by two Italians but manned by experts from Alexandria or supplied, at a price, by Tiridates, 'were clever, and bold enough,' explains Tacitus,

---

* The personnel of this originally Ptolemaic institution also invented weapons of war and were therefore encouraged to emigrate to Rome, rather than to Parthia, like German scientists before the Second World War going to the USA rather than the USSR.

'to use technical means to overcome Nature itself, and make light of the requirements of the Prince'. The imperial *fiscus* was quickly exhausted and Nero began to raid the rich, driving them to suicide having first forced them to make him their substantial heir. One man, seeking to protect his grandchildren, slit his own, his mother's and his daughter's wrists in the same bath, having manumitted and tipped all his slaves, rather than comply.

The style of the Golden House, as well as the depredations necessary to create it, offended the older and richer of Roman society. The traditional *domus* of a good family in Rome was modest, introvert, familial and severe, like the Domus Livia where Augustus lived and died, symmetrical and, in every sense, square. Nero's dream palace was vast and open, yet at the same time secretive, curved, carved, despotic, more of a harem than a house, designed to impress and even terrify. The person of the patron was represented by a bronze statue, 100 feet high, impressive enough to be left standing until the Goths captured Rome. The swamp where the Colosseum was later built became a lake with an imitation port, surrounded by artificial meadows, plenished with wild animals and beeches designed to look like forests. Within, according to eighteenth-century reproductions like Tiepolo's, the ceilings and walls were heavily ornamented and decorated – the work of one Fabullus, a correct, middle-aged Roman gentleman, who wore his toga as he executed the bizarre romantic frescoes. The Golden House, still unfinished at Nero's death, ruined the treasury, and, more than any other extravagance, the reputation of its builder. At first his successors tried to finish it, but finally Trajan, contemptuous, buried it. However, the chance discovery, intact, of some parts of this fantasy in cement, 1,500 years later, astonished and inspired architects and artists of the Renaissance like d'Udine and Caravaggio, who went underground to scratch, in admiration, their names on Nero's gilt.

All in the Julio-Claudian clan were skilled in the deployment of their Latin tongue, which became as crucial an element of conquest in the Roman Empire as English, or perhaps really American, after the Second World War.* They were the most literate rulers the world has ever known – Charlemagne could not read or write – and rejoiced in the Latin language, that most pungent, vivid, versatile vehicle for human expression, writing their own speeches (except for Nero, who had Seneca, but then who has a thoroughbred dog and barks himself?). Unselfconsciously, and for pleasure, they practised all forms of *belles lettres.* Caesar the military historian and master of the soundbite, wrote a play, suppressed, it was said, out of kindness. Augustus wrote long letters to Horace and Virgil and had a sharp line in obscene epigrams (pornography being considered a legitimate art form). Tiberius wrote Greek and Latin verse. He also wrote his memoirs, as did Agrippina hers, both suppressed by their alarmed descendants. Caligula was an impressive orator but threatened to remove the works of Virgil from the public libraries simply because they bored him. Claudius wrote volumes of history, eight of them in Greek, and gave public lectures, but Nero was the most lavish, effective and genuine patron of them all. 'Olympian Muses, daughters of Zeus!' wrote Lucillius, the epigrammatist, 'I would be finished, had not Nero Caesar given me cash.'

Nero's phil-Hellenism was such that he fell for a Chatterton-style forgery, buying the translation of a diary

---

* Before which the language of physics, for instance, was German; now, an Italian, lecturing to an audience in Milan in that discipline, must speak in English if he wishes to be reported in learned journals.

of the Trojan War, written in Punic, allegedly discovered in a collapsed tomb in Crete. Troy obviously fascinated him. The biggest mural in the Domus Aurea depicted the wooden horse arriving within the walls of Troy at night and just after the fire of Rome – he did not start it, he was not there, he did not fiddle – he sang about the capture and fire of Troy in his private theatre, or so the rumours ran. He had, all agreed, an agreeable voice.

His first 'Neronia', a literary festival, was in AD 60, and at the second, in AD 65, he recited (part of) his epic *Troica,* whose hero was, typically, not the macho figure Hector, but the soft-skinned androgynous Paris. Quite a bunch of talent, some found by Seneca, assembled at Nero's literary 'academies', at whose 'working' dinners Nero was accepted as a fellow, and though Tacitus was bitchy* about them, even he allowed that Nero could be considered a serious poet. Nero patronized wildly the young and the unknown but his most famous protégé was Petronius, whose *Satyricon,* coruscating with charm, corruption and subversion, is a constant world-seller. The satire is set in Puteoli, a new city, encouraged by Nero, in the Bay of Naples; the characters are culled from the lower classes and the richest; Trimalchio, who gives the dinner party where a sow is revealed to be stuffed with live partridges, is a fabulously vulgar freedman. The love interest is homosexual.

Those of the figures round Nero's literary dinners who were knights and senators were his only link with the upper classes of Rome, but even this was broken when in AD 65–6 they joined Seneca's nephew in the conspiracy of Piso, also a

---

* So was Nero. He wrote a poem about the effeminacy of one Afranius Quintianus which so offended the subject that he joined the conspiracy of Piso (see p. 142).

poet. Indeed Miriam Griffin thinks they joined the political opposition out of literary pique towards the Emperor, who had become aggressively jealous of their success.

'Music,' a headmaster of Eton once observed, 'is the least dangerous of the arts',* but it was the stage performances of the Emperor which caused his downfall. The acting profession was not esteemed in Ancient Rome. Actors, as we have seen, were synonymous with male tarts and it was often proposed, for one reason or another, that they be flogged. Nero began quietly, performing as a charioteer and actor in his private circus and private theatre, but he craved awards and public applause, accepting the former before a contest and organizing the latter. (Vespasian once fell asleep during a performance by the Emperor and was sharply nudged by an attentive freedman.)

He chose Naples, more Grecian and lax than Rome, for his big part. The Senate, ashamed of the offence he would cause, offered him crowns for his singing and oratory, hoping he would neither sing nor orate, but Nero wanted the real thing and brought to Naples his Praetorians and a claque of 5,000. Those who did not listen in silence and applaud noisily were reported and rebuked, giving a special twist to the phrase 'captive audience'. On this occasion, Nature intervened with a small earthquake, collapsing the theatre but causing no deaths (for it was empty) and therefore being interpreted by Nero as a sign of divine approval, an excuse for a poem and yet another celebration. Although Roman historians have lingered on the monstrous aspects of his personality, he was full of gaiety and *bonhomie* and genuinely hurt that Romans did not recognize his ability. 'The Greeks

---

* I am indebted to a former Provost, Lord Charteris, for this remark by the late Claude Aurelius Elliot.

alone,' he said, 'appreciate me and my art.' So to Greece (where he could be sure that if he brought his lyre to a party, everyone would ask him to play) he went – on an elaborate tour, city by city. Nobody in Rome recorded his successes. When he returned via Puteoli, Naples, Antium and Alba Longa, with processions in each, imitating the Triumph of a conquering general, riding in the chariot designed by Augustus for such occasions, borne before him were banners with the titles of his victorious songs, as if they were the names of the cities he had captured for Rome. Such was Nero's Triumph, Rome's indignity.

Enter Poppaea. Poppaea was a rich girl from Pompeii, where the family owned five houses and sponsored Games. Her father had been a friend of Sejanus, Tiberius's disgraced number two, and she had adopted the name of her grandfather, a consul and governor for twenty-four years of Moesia in the Balkans. She was beautiful, ambitious, enchanting and, compared to Messalina or Agrippina, only mildly wicked, and Nero fell and remained in love with her till the end – hers. She became his mistress when he was still married to Octavia, whom he feared to divorce because she was so popular. Octavia was a gentle, blameless lady, but Nero accused her of adultery (which her maid, under torture, denied). She was taken to an island and her wrists were cut in pretence of suicide; the charge that she had tried to seduce Anicetus and subvert the fleet convinced no one and increased the distaste felt at her murder. Octavia's death provoked the same reaction in the plebs as that of George IV's daughter Charlotte, also rumoured to be murder, provoked in the British public, both monarchs being considered by their subjects capable of any wickedness, on account of their jealousy.

One of Nero's friends was Otho, a young man-about-town of odd appearance, for he was knock-kneed, flat-footed, prematurely bald and supposed to shave his body hair.* He must have developed characteristics which overrode these defects, because he did become an Emperor, but at this moment in time, he is simply a good enough friend of Nero to oblige by marrying his newly beloved, to tide her over an awkward divorce and keep her warm in his house, until the right moment, or such was the plan. According to Suetonius, Otho also fell for the enchanting Poppaea and, when the Emperor's people came to claim her, he locked his doors and refused to give her up. Then Nero himself went to Otho's house and made a scene, enjoyed by passers-by, alternately begging him to deliver her and threatening punishment if he would not. The punishment for the twenty-six-year-old quaestor was the governorship of Lusitania (Portugal), where he took to religion – the cult of Isis – and ruled admirably.

Poppaea became Empress and queen of extravagant fashion – the Eugénie of Rome. Her carriage mules were shod in gold and the milk of 500, yes 500, wild asses was needed for her daily bath, so important for her complexion. She was not, like the last two Empresses, politically inclined, though she so favoured Jews at court, she might have been a proselyte, and protected them from persecution after the fire of Rome but together with the new man Ofonius Tigellinus, who had replaced the old reliables, Seneca and Burrus, her influence on the Emperor was disastrous.

Tigellinus was a handsome two-way stud, who had had affairs with the husbands and wives of two grand Roman households before graduating to Agrippina and her sister which had earned him a spell out of Rome. He bred horses in Calabria and met Nero when young and encouraged his

* Not uncommon in the ancient world; besides, the pose of 'heroic nudity' in statues only allows a little tuft of hair above the genitalia.

interest in racing. He was made prefect of police, then of the Praetorian Guard, where he uncovered the conspiracy of Piso.

This was a miserable affair compared with the boldness and despatch of the groups of assassins who killed Julius Caesar and Caligula. Tyrannicide was an Ancient Roman tradition and the personnel were always patrician, but these conspirators were different in that they invited one of their number, C. Calpurnius Piso, to become Emperor, showing how deeply the imperial concept had sunk into the psyche of the once republican Roman upper class. The conspirators were shopped by a disloyal freedman and Piso himself developed cold feet at the last moment. Nero was shaken by the numbers of the patriciate involved. He did not know he was so disliked. He reacted moderately, forgiving some and forgetting others, but by AD 65, affected by the death of Poppaea and his unborn child – had he lost his temper and kicked her in the belly? – he began to hound important senators on the usual trumped-up charges of treason.

Poppaea, too beautiful to become ashes, was, unusually, embalmed and her obsequies cost a fortune. He proved, to himself, his undying devotion to her by having a freedman, Sporus, a lookalike of Poppaea, castrated and 'marrying' him in Greece.

Nero, this madman as people have said, was Emperor in Rome for fourteen years and though he contrived to alienate every section of his sophisticated contemporaries in that city, including and perhaps especially the Stoics, he never lost the affection of the populace and was respected in the provinces, particularly in the East. He accepted and discharged the then traditional basic duties of an Emperor to provide bread, water and circuses, the last considered even by the sage Seneca to be as important as military successes. In his foreign policy

Nero was effective, choosing governors and procurators wisely – perhaps the success of his old companion Otho was not entirely by chance? – and behaving, even according to Tacitus, rationally in the face of military disaster.

He was imaginative – sending a couple of centurions to look for the source of the Nile, dreaming of the Corinth Canal and driving in the first golden spike, invoking the glories of Rome, without, it was noticed, mentioning the Senate – but the provincial event of his reign has to be the revolt of Boadicea (Boudicca or Biudica). Nero never liked the idea of Britain and would have withdrawn from that relatively cold and unproductive island were it not for the memory of his father. Britons were quarrelsome and violent and it was said that it was only for their own country that they did not know how to die. This was not true of Boadicea, who also 'had uncommon intelligence for a woman' (Dio Cassius). She was the daughter of a client king of the Iceni (Suffolk), to which tribe Romans had lent a lot of money for the fur-bishing of their homes with curtains and other luxuries. Seneca, attracted by the high rate of interest, had lent 40 million *sesterces* and when a governor was imposed in replacement of the royal family, 'called it in at once and not very gently' (Dio Cassius). The strong-arm Roman soldiers looted the palace, raped her daughters and flogged the queen herself. When she recovered, Boadicea raised the flag of revolt and with an army of 120,000 razed two Roman cities.

'Every kind of atrocity was inflicted upon their captives . . . they hung up the noblest and best-looking women naked, cutting off their breasts and stitching them to their mouths, so that the women appeared to be eating them and after this they impaled them on sharp stakes, run up the body' (Dio Cassius). Tacitus describes how she repeated the performance in Verulamium (St Albans) and Camulodunum (Colchester), killing 80,000, 'taking no prisoners, sold no captives as slaves and went in for none of the usual trading of war. They wasted no time in getting down to the bloody business of hanging, burning and crucifying.' (This last technique Boadicea must have picked up from her enemies, though the Romans did not adopt hers, of attaching the blades of scythes to the wheels of her chariots – as shown in her statue on the Embankment, Westminster – because, for the Romans, the chariot was a sporting vehicle.)

The rebellion was squashed by Nero's freedman Polyclitus, at the head of a vast army – to the astonishment of the snobbish Britons – and he not only reconciled the warring Roman governor and procurator, but was tactful enough to play down his own role in the pacification. (Nero appreciated the talents of freedmen, who were recruited from all over the Empire to serve, without passing Foreign Office examinations, in high office at the centre of power. He promoted Claudius Etruscus, who died at the age of eighty loaded with wealth and honour, a former slave from Smyrna who worked for ten emperors, six of whom died under him, to be controller of finance, in place of Pallas.) After the failure of the rebellion, successive governors, including Tacitus' father-in-law, Agricola, attempted to Romanize Britain, favouring the sons of the élite with a Roman education, building baths, assembly rooms, temples, public squares and introducing the usual Roman apparatus, but the investment did not pay off, as Appian, writing under the Emperor Antoninus Pius a century later, says: 'The Romans rule the greater part of it [Britain] and have no need of the rest; in fact the part they have brings them in little money.' Nero's instinct was correct.

The great fire broke out early a.m., under a nearly full moon,

on 19 July AD 64, in some shops round the Circus Maximus.
It lasted six days, levelled totally three of the fourteen
regions into which Augustus had divided the capital, and
damaged another seven. The grandest houses in the heart of
the city were destroyed and the rumour that the Emperor
was the arsonist might have begun with their owners. In fact,
though Nero flung himself with zest into the town planning
necessary after the event, with his new palace as its crowning feature, he had no interest in starting the fire himself.
Great fires, like that of London 1,600 years later, for which
an apprentice French baker was hastily hanged, aren't started
by anybody; they happen; but sinister persons have to be
found to take the blame.

Nero, deflected by Poppaea from the Jews, chose to blame
the Christians 'on account of their sullen hatred of the whole
human race. They were put to death with exquisite cruelty
... and many were lighted up, when the day declined, to
serve as torches during the night.' This is the first reference
in history to the sect, not yet named, whose members were
forced to wear a *tunica modesta* (a leather jerkin) smeared
with tar and set on fire, to illuminate the parties in the gardens which the Emperor opened for those made homeless
by the fire. Tacitus adds that they behaved so bravely that
'humanity relented in their favour'. It was also the first time
in history that a distinction was made between Jews and
Christians, a distinction, ironically, laboured for by St Paul.
The last verse of the Acts of the Apostles reads: 'And there
[Rome] he stayed for two full years at his own expense with
a welcome for all who came to him, practising without let or
hindrance the gospel of the Lord Jesus Christ.'

St Paul was in Rome under house arrest, waiting to
appear 'before Caesar', in AD 62. In fact he would not have
been tried by Nero himself but by the consular who dealt

with Syrian affairs, but he could have been still in Rome during the fire and would surely have been broken-hearted – perhaps unto death? – at the decision of the Roman authorities, whom he had spent his life trying to conciliate, to persecute his new religion. Boadicea, Nero and St Paul were, oddly, exact contemporaries – with Seneca as the loose connection.

Towards the end of his short life – thirty-two years – but relatively long reign – fourteen years – Nero lost touch with the real world. The palace was run by freedmen, the senatorial and equestrian ranks having become suspect to the Emperor, whose greed had made the profession of *delator* (denouncer) the surest route to a fortune – a quarter of the victim's property was the reward. Seneca, trembling in a remote corner of his palace before the imperial jealousy had finally and grandly and stagily made him do away with himself, manumitted his slaves, and so Nero had been left to the care of his freedmen, two of whom, Sporus and Pythagoras, he had 'married', with public simulation of the bridal nights. Then he decided, at quite the wrong time, to leave Rome, with his freedman Helius in charge of life, death and confiscation.

Julius Vindex, a governor in Gaul, had been circulating his colleagues, proposing an uprising, and they had obligingly forwarded the letters on to the Emperor, who reacted sluggishly. Galba and Otho, governors in Spain and Portugal and both to attain the purple briefly in the year of the four Emperors which followed Nero's death, were in revolt. Nero was dragged back from Greece by Helius, who went to fetch him. Vindex was defeated and committed suicide but the successful troops wanted to make their commander Emperor. He refused on the grounds that this was a decision for the Senate and People of Rome, but the feeling in the air, shared gloomily by Nero himself, was that the present

Emperor had to go. The trouble was, where? Even the Prefect of Egypt, the imperial province, was not necessarily sound. Then the Praetorian Guard declared for Galba, the Senate outlawed him and Nero did not have quite enough time to stab himself properly, before the horsemen cantered up to the villa where he was hiding . . . '*Qualis artifex pereo!*' ('What an artist dies with me!') were his determined last words, and they promised not to mutilate his body. He was buried by the faithful freedwoman Acte, who had been the first of so many to share his couch, and for years afterwards there were flowers on his grave in the spring.

ROME

✦ THE CITYSCAPE ✦

After Augustus had marblized Rome, during his long reign (31 BC–AD 14), the city must have looked like a cross between the Lower East Side of Manhattan, before the fire regulations, and a stately if garish Disneyland. Most of Rome's two million inhabitants lived in 46,000 *insulae,* or tenements, parading the splendid public parts of the city in the day and retreating to their private squalor only for sleep.

A rich family in their *domus* (of which there were some 1,700) or owning the ground floor of an *insula,* could be connected (sometimes illicitly) to an aqueduct for water, have a lavatory attached to a sewer and enjoy hot-air heating, but most of Rome had to carry its water upstairs and bring its excrement down, or throw it into the street, often no wider than a man's outstretched arms. (This was so commonplace that lawyers specialized in the detection and prosecution of such offenders.) Owners of apartment blocks rented the spaces giving on to the broader streets as shops *(tabernae)* and often subcontracted the management of the upper storeys, dangerous not only because these consisted of light wooden partitions, liable to collapse, but also because of the nature of their tenants – thieves, gangsters and prostitutes. No regulations inhibited the avarice and irresponsibility of the speculators and jerry builders who put up these buildings, often financed by magnates, senators and 'new men' like Cicero.

Indeed, that great moralist was a typical property-owner, earning 80,000 *sesterces* a year from tenements. In a letter about him to Atticus, we have the story:

Two of Cicero's tenements had completely collapsed and the rest were in such imminent danger of doing likewise that not only had the tenants abandoned the place in terror of their lives but even the mice were leaving. Cicero, clearly, had had no repairs done. It was only when the two tenements had fallen down and the other inhabitants had fled, that is, when his income had been cut off, that he instructed the architect Chrysippus to effect the necessary repairs. Chrysippus, however, produced an estimate of costs. Cicero was appalled that he would have to spend good money in this way. He consulted one Vestorius, who combined the profession of banker with that of an instructor of building workers. He in some way enabled Cicero to turn his feared loss into an actual profit. The details of this remarkable manoeuvre Cicero, unfortunately, did not disclose.*

Cicero was, in his acquisition of villas (no less than eight, and four lodges), typical of his age; he borrowed the money, which was easy for a man of his repute.

Like the orator Hortensius, whose modest house Augustus bought (modest that is for an Emperor), Cicero lived in a chic enclave on the Palatine Hill, the Hampstead of Rome, near to Mark Antony, the dictator Sulla, Crassus and the rival

---

* Nor does his most recent biographer. I owe this slice of high-republican Roman mores to Donald Earl in *The Age of Augustus*, Elek, 1968.

demagogues Clodius (Caesar's man) and Milo (his opponent). So did Chrysogonus, Rome's first really rich freedman, who had made a fortune out of Sulla's proscriptions, with his silver, his curtains, his ivory-clad tables, his statues, his jewels and his automatic cooker (purchased for the price of an entire estate) – not that automation in Ancient Rome was anything but an eccentric foible, domestics being both plentiful and skilled. We know from the execution of the entire household of 400 slaves of the prefect Pedanius Secundus, under (but not on account of) Nero, how many they could be, helping a rich man to near autonomy in his style of life and, from pastrycooks to firemen, providing him with every service.

The story of Crassus, who didn't care how he made his money, offering to buy a house on fire, and putting it out only when the price had been agreed, is not apocryphal, and the poor were justifiably scared of perishing in a blaze from which they were not protected. The great fire of 50 BC, as damaging as Nero's in AD 64, had been succeeded by others every few years and still no precautions were taken or town-planning considered. One politician made his career out of fire-fighting, using his own slaves. Quite simply the poor did not count and were not counted. (The figure of two million for the population of Rome is an intelligent guess, not official.) Rome had grown in 100 years to become the greatest power on earth but her city officials were too busy administering an Empire (more profitable) to attend to their own dirty backyard.

Finally Augustus decided to sort Rome out. He lectured the Senate by reading a dissertation on the maximum height of buildings; he organized public slaves, under aediles, into fire brigades; he set in motion an imperial concern with town-planning (which did not become effective until Nero, but he started it); he established, at last, a police force – *vigiles*

– under a prefect (the unfortunate Pedanius, murdered by a slave or slaves unknown, was one such). He was justified in his boast of 'finding Rome built of sun-dried bricks and leaving her clad in marble'. (In fact there never was one brick wall in Ancient Rome, nor are there any sun-dried bricks extant; bricks, like marble, were used for cladding and facing buildings which were made of concrete, a mixture of tufa, volcanic rock, travertine and broken bits and pieces from the mason's yard.) Although personally permanently under-housed, to use a pretentious phrase from the 1980s – Augustus used to go and stay with Maecenas when he was ill – his public works were opulent and showy and his guide was the architect Vitruvius, who wrote ten books around the subject, including one on sundials and another on water mechanics. (Even he failed to design an efficient clock.) Vitruvius preached the grand concepts of harmony, dignity and utility but he was a practical man too; here he is on 'Doors and Windows in Baths and Elsewhere': 'Also there will be natural seemliness if light is taken from the east for bedrooms and libraries; for baths and winter apartments from the win-try sunset; for picture galleries and the apartments which need a steady light, from the north, because that quarter of the heavens in neither illumined nor darkened by the sun's course but is fixed unchangeable through the day.'

Basically Rome was built out of concrete *(opus caementicum),* poured into wooden slats as it is today, travertine, a creamy white stone, laid horizontally (laid ver-tically it collapsed) and tufa, which could not stand fire. Roads were paved with silex, a dark grey volcanic rock from the Alban Hills. For fine buildings these materials were coated with stucco and nine different marbles – yellow, orange and pink from Libya and Euboea, blood red, brilliant green, onyx and porphyry from the Nile. Like all conquerors – they were the first – Romans decorated their capital with artefacts from the defeated; bought and looted. They worshipped, sometimes literally, statues from fifth-century-BC Athens and there is a catalogue of seventy-four great works of this period by sculptors of genius like Praxiteles. (Rome was full of antiques *and* fakes. The reproduction of famous statues by Greek artisans was an industry and the genuine article had to have been made 'without wax' (sine cera), hence our word 'sincere'.)

Augustus built a forum, 'narrow because he could not bring himself to evict the existing tenants' (Suetonius), with temples for the avenging Mars, Jupiter and Apollo. These great buildings were not single-purpose affairs like our churches because worship of a cult was irregular, but they served as places of assembly, for the selection of juries and as archives and libraries. The temple of Saturn was the state treasury. The *Curia,* where the Senate met, was burnt at the funeral of Clodius in 52 BC, rebuilt by Caesar, then burnt down again and this time restored by Augustus. Therefore it often happened, during our period, that the Senate was convened in a temple.

Augustus encouraged his family, especially his wife, Livia, and his daughter, Julia – though he pulled down her country villa saying it was too grand – his rich friends and protégés to build and embellish. His nephew Marcellus built a theatre, much of which is still standing (near the nineteenth-century synagogue by the Tiber), designed to accommodate an audience of 17,000 but the first stone theatre had been put up by Pompey, who called himself 'Magnus' (the Great), at the age of twenty-two. Alas, the quality of the entertainment did not match the grandeur of the surroundings; it consisted mainly of the frothy plays of Plautus and vaudeville acts, variously obscene; Rome produced no great drama – for the stage. Agrippa, Augustus' friend, ally and son-in-law, built the original Pantheon,* possibly the most beautiful classical building in Rome, nominally for the gods, but of course the real motive for all these magnificent constructions was the greater glory of Rome and her rulers.

The public parts of the city glittered, the public baths and lavatories were clean, warm and well maintained by public slaves, often manumitted for their service. The aqueducts never lacked cool, clear water, more appetizing, Augustus often insisted, than the free wine. The ordinary Roman citizen, with access to libraries and the frequent distractions of the Games, could not feel deprived – until he went home . . . The luxury of private houses was hidden from his view; Augustus even had a (fireproof) wall built round the Forum, hiding the stinking suburb of Subura from the patrician gaze. Triumphal arches, thirty-six by the end, were a particularly Roman invention, adopted but barely adapted by the vainglorious in succeeding centuries. Functional but massively adorned with bas-reliefs and sculptures, they marked the entrances of forums and bracketed important roads. One of the few still more or less intact, that of the Emperor Titus at the summit of the Via Sacra down which the Triumphs processed, is still awesome, especially to the pious Jew, whose law forbids him to pass under it but who must surely blench at the clear representation of the golden *menorah* (candlestick) and other treasures from Herod's Temple in Jerusalem being carried into Rome by the cowed high priests.

The money, men and materials, the time and the effort, spent on Rome's grandest construction, the Colosseum,

---

* The building we see today is the creation of the Emperor Hadrian, a greater builder even than Augustus, who modestly had it inscribed M. AGRIPPA COS. TERTIUM FECIT.

properly the Flavian amphitheatre, is a monument to the persistence and consistency of Roman Emperors. Although strictly outside our scope, to omit it would make any description of public Rome lightweight and deficient, though its function, as grandiose space for watching the slaughter of men (never actually Christians) and beasts, was deplorable, and, indeed, deplored. Blocks of seventy cubic feet of stone, each weighing five tons, formed the base of its pillars and 50,000 wagonloads of travertine were transported between its inception under the Emperor Vespasian in AD 72 to its opening by his son Titus eight years later. It was not fully finished until the reign of Diocletian. The raising of the canopy, the *velarium,* to shield the 50,000 spectators from the sun was a performance as spectacular as the show in the arena below. A thousand sailors levered the canopy on 160 winches to the beating of drums, against which the action of the wind, which had to be calculated, the roar from the famished wild beasts in the caves and the excitement of the spectators in the crowded four-storey auditorium created a unique cacophony. In its first 100 days the Colosseum consumed 9,000 animals and 2,000 gladiators.

✦ DOMUS, THE TOWNHOUSE ✦

Knights and below lived in ground-or first-floor apartments in *insulae,* but patricians of senatorial rank traditionally operated – because theirs was a powerhouse too – from a *domus,* an ancestral town house, often sited on one of the Seven Hills of Rome. (We have seen how Caesar rejoiced at being able to abandon his in the Subura, which had become a slum.) Like townhouses in eighteenth-century London, graded from I to III, they varied in scale but all were designed to the same pattern. None was as grand as the houses of the rich in Park Lane, Park Avenue or the Champs-Elysées, although they would have needed more servants to function, for in a pre-mechanical age, a patrician with his resident barber and hairdresser for his wife also had to have messengers, stokers for the furnace, pole-bearers for the litters and the sedan chairs, a *brigade* as extensive as a London hotel's for his chef – all slaves of course, and even an individual to announce the time of day. A resident poet laureate, might, engagingly, form part of the establishment.

In a large *domus* husband and wife slept in separate, barely furnished bedrooms, and the staff were crammed, sometimes locked, into basement rooms so small they were virtually cells. The regular *domus* was built as one rectangular floor, all rooms being lit from within, with no outside views, whether free-standing or part of a street; shops were let into the outside walls. If there was an upper floor it would not cover the whole building and the rooms would be small. Augustus, in the modest house he lived in for forty years which was *sans* mosaics, *sans* marble, *sans* anything much,* retreated to an upper room he called 'Syracuse' for secret discussions. During the construction of the embankment for the Tiber, remains were found of five-storey houses with vaulted domes built into the rock, but these were as unusual as, say, the Countess of Seafield's house on the south-east corner of Belgrave Square, or the Frick Mansion in Manhattan.

The *domus* was entered by a vestibule, where visitors waited (and were kept waiting unless you tipped the usher) looking at the statues and trophies of the ancestors of the owner, or indeed of the previous owner, since they were integral to the house. Giant double folding doors, ornate with bronze and ivory, faced the visitor (though the family could slip into the main part of the house via a side entrance, above which there would be an inscription or a parrot in a cage trained to say 'Good luck' in Greek). The doors gave on to a large rectangular reception hall where the wealth and style of the owner, in the shape of statues, brilliant – nay, garish – murals, mosaics and marble everywhere, especially for the basin and fountain which was in the middle of this space under the open skylight. It was a room designed for showing off. Seneca, with little right since he too was a self-indulgent millionaire, complains of the *nouveau riche:*

---

* Suetonius comments: 'His simple taste in fittings and furniture is apparent in the couches and tables that are still preserved, most of which hardly reach the standard of elegance to be expected from a private person.'

'He seems to himself poor and mean unless the walls shine with great costly slabs, unless marbles of Alexandria are picked out with reliefs of Numidian stone, unless the whole ceiling is elaborately worked with all the variety of a painting, unless Thracian stone encloses the swimming-baths, unless the water is poured out from silver taps . . .' Prominent was the strong box, secured to the floor by an iron rod, which held the family silver and money not lodged with a banker and which accompanied them on their travels. The private rooms opening off the hall through tall doors consisted of the dining-room, *triclinium,* (quite small because only three couches surrounded a table), bedrooms, the library (with up to 3,000 scrolls stored in pigeon-holes) and a picture gallery. Another room would be filled with family treasures and the wax death-masks of ancestors, which were trotted out for funerals and which, like much in Rome, could be bought by parvenus wanting instant lineage, just as 'family' portraits could be acquired by war profiteers – often what they were – in the twenties in England. Beyond the hall was the parlour where the master of the house would transact business and beyond that a window – the Romans used glass – with a view into the peristyle and garden, where the family could dine outside in the summer.

In winter, portable charcoal-burning braziers and a central-heating system from the furnace in the basement circulated hot air through ducts in the floors and walls. Lavatories were cued into the public sewers and water tapped from an aqueduct. (The Roman equivalent, for an ambitious maiden, of a 'breakfast-eating Brooks Brothers guy' was a man with a library and a private loo.) Furniture was scanty, consisting of couches and beds (without sheets and blankets but with a few cushions), chests and wardrobes, tripods, backless chairs and folding stools, all, like the kitchen utensils, beautifully made, with carved lamps burning olive oil. Investing in elaborate drinking vessels of crystal, gold and silver, encrusted with jewels, was a favourite way of spending money for Emperors (especially Nero) and subjects alike.

All in all, apart from the fact that a master or mistress could, in our period, have a slave crucified in the garden, the *domus* was a cosy place compared to the palaces of the rich in the capitals of later Empires.

❧ RELIGION ❧

No single, revealed religion dominated Ancient Rome.

Jews believe that Moses showed them the one God through his Law, Christians that Jesus is the way of the same one true Lord, Muslims that Mahomet interpreted the will of Allah, Lord of the Faithful, and with each of these monotheistic beliefs goes, as it were, a handbook whose assertions its believers would die for – the Torah, the Gospels and the Koran.

That the Romans had no one God, no one moral text, does not mean they had no religion. Not even the sophisticated, like Cicero, who had an opinion on everything, believed in the possibility of a Supreme Being directing the universe, be he like Robespierre's short-lived invention motivated by Reason, or like the latter-day Jupiter, grumpily omnipotent; but gods they had a-plenty.

Our Romans were exposed to, and curious about, religious cults from the East – they detested what they knew about the Druids from Gaul, Germany and its think-tank, Britain – particularly Judaism, with which a few flirted, notably Poppaea, Nero's extravagant lady, but it was two and a half centuries before an Emperor nailed the Cross, that unlikely symbol, to the standards of his soldiers. In the meantime Romans lived with, but never had to die for, their own gods.

They honoured, celebrated and sacrificed to, rather than regularly worshipped, a variety of gods including some who had been human, like Caesar and all our Emperors except Caligula and Nero. (Seneca wrote a satire about the reception of Claudius in the next world which was not kind.) The major Gods, Jupiter, Mars, Venus, Saturn and Apollo, who alone kept his name, had been taken over from the Greeks and had splendid temples in the Forum, maintained by the state, while lesser deities were the responsibility of patrician families, who competed for the prestigious and occasionally profitable priesthoods, and the duties, mostly occasional and ceremonial, which went with them. Julius Caesar, who claimed for his *gens Julia* descent from Venus, was not best pleased when Marius, the First Man in Rome, his uncle by marriage, made him as a young man *flamen dialis,* priest of the cult of Jupiter, which honourable but invidious appointment debarred him from riding a horse, bearing arms and enjoying most delicacies. It was a malicious act. The awful old man, as he had then become, had spotted the boy's talent and was jealous. Of course Caesar cheated, galloping his horse, Bucephalus, on the other side of the Tiber at dawn, but he had to wait for Marius' replacement by his erstwhile protégé Sulla, the first dictator in Rome, to be released from his vows. Sulla, the least superstitious and most cynical of men, who nevertheless kept a little statuette of Apollo which he kissed in moments of crisis, arranged the affair through the technicality of Caesar's child-bride (aged eleven) not being truly Roman by birth. (He had earlier refused the dictator's demand that he divorce her on political grounds.) This episode shows how seriously Romans observed the *form* of their religion, however indifferent they were to the spirit.

Roman historians do not describe religious ceremonies any more than Macaulay retails the coronation of his hero,

William III, and one would search Trollope in vain for an account of the liturgical activities of *his* ecclesiasts. In Rome they were an assumed part of life, unnecessary to record, but we do know that sacrifice of animals, in propitiation of the god, was a *sine qua non* of any service, the prize offering being a milk-white bull and the least a tray of cakes. (No Orthodox Jew could quarrel with this practice, since six pages of his current morning prayers detail the exact procedure for the slaughtering of animals and the sprinkling of blood on the altar, abandoned only after the destruction of the Temple in Jerusalem and one day, he must hope, with the Temple, to be restored.)

Births, marriages and deaths, obviously, were celebrated by invoking the gods, but also various gods were separately appealed to for special effects. The danger of crop failure through blight, there being (happily, some would say) no pesticide in the ancient world, was a nightmare which had to be prevented by propitiating Robigo, the power of rust. Ovid writes how, returning to Rome one April, 'a white-robed crowd blocked my path./A Priest was passing to the grave of ancient Robigo/to offer on the altar entrails of dog and sheep/I went straight to him, wishing to understand the rite.' Ovid puts these words into his mouth:

Be merciful I pray, take your scabby hands off the harvest.
Do no harm; be content with the power.
Set your grasp on hard iron not on pliant crops;
destroy the destroyer.
You'll have better results from swords and lethal weapons;
no need for them, the world's at peace.

This gentle poem, infused with the spirit of the Augustan Age, tenderly idealizing bucolic procedures, like the Emperor's altar, winsome and only half-reverent, is typical of a sophisticated Roman's attitude to religion. All are happy, except a reddish brown dog which has its throat slit.

The Emperor Augustus was not himself particularly moral in his private behaviour, but publicly he was a prig. He was, like all Romans, superstitious, but he was not religious. However, he regarded the approval of the gods, as did the humbler of his subjects, as crucial to the safety and wellbeing of the state and would have nodded at Marx's dictum that religion was the opiate of the people. He dosed them heavily. He revived the national day of prayer to the goddess Salus (Greek, Hygeia) and for the Festival of the Century, a well-documented affair, commissioned Horace to compose 'a carefully scripted and well-composed hymn' to be sung by choirs of twenty-seven boys and twenty-seven girls, all of whose parents had to be alive. It was a grand affair, lasting three days in a wooden theatre specially built on the banks of the Tiber, but everybody had to stand up, including 110 wives of free citizens and the Council of Fifteen, the high flyers of Rome, the relations and 'friends of the Emperor', descendants or ascendants of the consuls, generals and governors who had ruled, or would rule, the world. Augustus' prayer was direct. 'O Moirae [the Fates], I pray and beseech you to increase the power of the citizens, the people of Rome, in war and peace ... grant for all time safety, victory and might to the citizens, the people of Rome ... look with kindly grace ... on me, my family and household, and that you may receive this sacrifice of nine ewe lambs and nine she-goats ...' and so on; for three days in June the blood flowed for the gods, and the flat cakes and pastry cakes and cup cakes were dutifully burnt. The Fates must have been listening. Augustus reigned for half a century and his dynasty supplied another four Emperors. M. Agrippa picked up the tab for the chariot races.

Augustus repaired eighty-two temples in Rome but never imposed any Roman cult, not even of his great-uncle Julius Caesar, on the provinces or on a defeated enemy. Trade, sometimes in the shape of carpet-baggers, followed the standards of the legions; missionaries never. There were no wars of religion in the ancient world; genocide (or 'ethnic cleansing') was unknown; controlled massacres occurred *in extremis* – for political or military reasons in Gaul, for instance, by Julius Caesar – but the motives were never religious.

Indeed part of the success of the Romans as imperialists was their tolerance, acceptance and even takeover of the gods of their enemies. Shrines to those of Carthage were erected in Rome after its destruction; the cult of Isis was condemned from time to time, banished by the austere Tiberius, restored by the exotic Caligula, and especially frowned on when Augustus had been propagating the line that his rival Mark Antony was a nice Roman boy seduced by the wiles of the Egyptian Queen Cleopatra. But did not Antinous, much later, the beloved of Hadrian, drown himself in the Nile, as a sacrifice to the goddess, to protect the Emperor, or was he just losing his looks? The cult of Isis had been brought back by Roman soldiers from their Eastern campaigns and an illustration of there being one religion for the rich – essentially a belief in the divinity of the power of Rome – and many for the peasants, the proletariat, the rank and file of the army, is the story of the Consul Aemilius Paullus, who had to throw off his toga and take an axe to destroy a temple of Isis because no workmen could be found prepared to execute the decree.

Mithras was the focus of another seductive cult whose priests were adept at special effects and produced a textbook describing the mysterious power of rushing water in subterranean tunnels with mechanical contrivances opening and shutting doors. A more home-grown diversion, practised by some cults, was the propitiation of the god through the flogging of naked boys laid on the altar (the thick red line of the lash being, as it were, the logo of Ancient Rome).

Two systems of philosophy from fourth-century-BC Athens attracted the Roman élite, both so all-embracing that they encompassed religion. The Stoics, so called from the *stoa*, a painted corridor off the market-place in Athens, were inspired by Zeno, a Cypriot, who propounded views on every aspect of human thought from physics to epistemology (the theory of knowledge). Their like of abstract discussion was too highfalutin for Roman taste, which also failed to take to the equally influential Plato and regarded Greek thinking as unsuitable for the young; but Stoicism, modified by the grandee Seneca, Nero's tutor and one of the richest men in Rome, and by the slave Epictetus, whose motto was 'bear and forbear', hit a chord in Rome because it seemed to answer the uncertainty and danger of the times. The Stoic message was gloomy. Men are weak and miserable in the face of evil, outward calamity is an instrument of divine training to be met with dignity and the contemplation of death (possibly by one's own hand), self-discipline and respect for the dignity of the individual. Seneca at least practised what he preached in this respect (in other ways being far from moral), disapproving publicly of slavery and committing suicide in the classic manner.

Epicurus was a contemporary of Zeno, less ambitious and less passionate, whose gospel was salvation by common sense (and nothing else). This philosophy, at first shunned in Rome, was promoted by an amiable figure called Lucretius, of whom little is known, save that he did not die by his own hand after taking a love potion, as immortalized by Tennyson. In 55 BC he published a long poem, *On the Nature of the*

Universe, which everybody read, especially Cicero. He dismissed divine providence and the immortal soul as illusions, sacrifices as absurd, maintained that all our knowledge comes from our senses and the world is fun as it is. The universe, he said, is boundless, nothing is created out of nothing, atoms are indestructible, but man, through greed, is exhausting the resources of the planet. (This was BC. Lucretius was a very early 'Green'.) We must enjoy and rejoice in the manifold bounties of Nature, which we must study though we may never completely know. Who has ever heard the footfall of a midge?

Lucretius was a poet but he was also practical, warning against the use of dangerous beasts in warfare – 'wild boars can turn on their employers' – and the hazards of intense love between human beings. Here he is on sex (translated brilliantly by Ronald Latham, Penguin): 'So, when a man is pierced by the shafts of Venus, whether they are launched by a lad with womanish limbs or a woman radiating love from her whole body, he strives towards the source of the wound and craves to be united with it and to transmit something of his own substance from body to body. His speechless yearning is a presentiment of bliss.' The results of love are disastrous '. . . a hard-won patrimony is metamorphosed into bonnets and tiaras . . . entertainments, perfumes, garlands . . . to no purpose.' Never mind, it will end badly '. . . perhaps he thinks she is rolling her eyes too freely and turning them upon another, or he catches in her face a hint of mockery'. One is reminded of Lord Chesterfield, a truly Roman figure, and his view of love-making: 'The pleasure is momentary, the position ridiculous, and the expense enormous.'

Romans took to religions from the East but they detested that of the Druids. As we have seen, Claudius panicked at the sight of a Druidic charm, a snake's egg, in court; his troops, about to engage an army in Anglesey, were literally sickened at the sight of Druid priests sacrificing children to appease their gods before the battle – but they went on to win. That the Romans finally adopted Christianity, the most aggressive of the revealed religions, whose God came from one of their least respected provinces, with a Church of career priests, is one of the oddities of history.

✢ ROMAN FOOD ✢

Julius Caesar as a priest of Jupiter, an appointment forced on him by Marius to prevent his taking up a military career as a young man, was also, as part of the vocation, denied delicacies, and remained a moderate and fussy eater. Augustus, for political reasons a fair and generous host, preferred the diet of the common people – coarse bread, whitebait, goat cheese and dried figs – and, too impatient to wait for mealtimes, often snacked. Tiberius seemed to prefer wine to food, enjoyed fish but, as we have seen, did not like surprise deliveries. Caligula gave exotic banquets, which the guests were sometimes too terrified to enjoy, but accepted payment for invitations. Claudius drank himself into a stupor every night and was fatally fond of a particular mushroom. Nero was an extravagant gourmet and spent fortunes on jewelled crystal goblets.

Dormice in honey, peacocks' tongues, garum, lolling, vomitoria and Petronius' account of Trimalchio's Feast – all of which, more anon – it was not only thus. The food consumed by most Romans, most days, for hundreds of years was frugal, coarse and nasty. The excesses, fun and games and much quoted feasts and extraordinary dishes, were only 'enjoyed' by a few.

At the beginning, when Rome was a tiny Etruscan village with few resources or outlets, the *populus* ate figs, olives, oil, barley (with which they made porridge) and hard wheat (which they ground to a paste). They drank goat's and sheep's milk

and made a simple cheese. But this village was on an important salt road where the locals exchanged their few products
for precious salt. Salt underpinned Rome's position.

It took Romans 200 years to conquer all the various tribes
who peopled the Italian peninsula and they didn't have anything resembling bread till the sixth century after the founding
of Rome. André Simon says: 'The Romans were greater eaters
than the Greeks, but not such great talkers. They also loved
feasts and banquets, large quantities of food and wine, rare, exotic and costly fare which was sought more for the sake of ostentation than of its gastronomic excellence. It was not always
thus: it might even be said that the greatness of Rome was built
on porridge and austerity.' But austerity for the rich and ambitious was replaced by gluttony and swank, despite sumptuary
laws, as the Roman armies conquered in Africa and in the East.

The three Punic Wars – the first 264–241 BC and the last
149–146 BC – secured for Rome a vast granary and useful coast-
line. They ended up with all the Carthaginian territory – North
Africa, Sicily (whence the best cooks), Corsica and Spain. They
destroyed Carthage but they did not destroy her wheatfields.
Nor did they ignore the usefulness of the Phoenicians, Arabs
from the Syrian coast, who were indeed the founders of
Carthage; through the Phoenicians the early Romans learned
about the vines of Persia and the spoils of the East.

Ali Bab, the nineteenth-century French cookbook guru,
is moved to quote Flaubert's *Salomé* to illustrate the sort of
feast the Romans would have learned about after their successive conquests:

> *Le festin donné dans les jardins d'Hamilcar pour célébrer
> l'anniversaire de la bataille d'Eryx.*
>
> *Les cuisines d'Hamilcar n'étant pas suffisantes, le conseil
> leur avait envoyé des esclaves, de la vaisselle, des lits; et*

l'on voyait au milieu du jardin, comme sur un champ de bataille quand on brûle les morts, des grands feux clairs où rôtissaient les boeufs. Les pains saupoudrés d'anis alternaient avec les gros fromages plus lourds que des disques et les cratères pleins de vin, et les canthères pleins d'eau auprès des corbeilles en filigrane d'or qui contenaient des fleurs. La joie de pouvoir enfin se gorger à l'aise dilatait tous les yeux; çà et là les chansons commençaient.

D'abord on leur servit des oiseaux à la sauce verte, dans des assiettes d'argile rouge rehaussée de dessins noirs, puis toutes les espèces de coquillages que l'on ramasse sur les côtes puniques, des bouillies de froment, de fève de d'orge et des escargots au cumin, sur des plats d'ambre jaune.

Ensuite les tables furent couvertes de viandes: antilopes avec leurs cornes, paons avec leurs plumes, moutons entiers cuits au vin doux, gigots de chamelles et de buffles, hérissons au garum, cigales frites et leurs confits. Dans des gamelles en bois de Tamrapanni flottaient, au milieu de saffran, de grands morceaux de graisse. Tout débordait de saumure, de truffes et d'asa foetida. Les pyramides de fruits s'éboulaient sur les gâteaux de miel et l'on n'avait pas oublié quelques-uns de ces petites chiens à gros ventre et à soies rose que l'on engraissait avec du mare d'olives, mets carthaginois, en abomination aux autres peuples.

Flaubert wasn't exaggerating, too much; it was initially from the Carthaginians that the Romans got the taste for huge, crazy meals.

Meanwhile, it was during the wars against Samnium, finally destroyed by Sulla, that the Romans became aware of real culinary skills; they came across the Greeks.

The Romans were never great sailors, so used the Phoenicians' knowledge, trading skills and seafaring abilities to widen their booty network. The Phoenicians sailed to China, Malaysia, Indonesia, India and Sri Lanka and brought back precious metals and spices – notably pepper, nutmeg, ginger, cardamom and cinnamon *(cassia)*. The Romans got hold of exotic birds like pheasants and flamingos; pretty fruits, like peaches, cherries, apricots and, most likely guavas, mangoes and quinces, as many Roman dishes seem to show a penchant for 'sweet and sour'; and asparagus, since Pliny wrote that the asparagus from Ravenna each weighed a third of a pound, but remember that the Roman pound was and is only about thirteen ounces. And before the introduction of the heavy asparagus, a forebear of the chunky white Italian, French and now Californian variety, the Romans called the tender tips of all green vegetables asparagus.

As the Roman world expanded, so did the numbers of slaves, prisoners and itinerants who arrived in the city of Rome itself. The authorities had therefore to keep them fed, and quiet. The *annona* or grain and later bread dole was a fact of life and a topic of politics which obsessed Rome from about 200 BC till the fourth century AD. Rome had been troubled by serious famines and shortages as far back as the sixth century BC; in 123 BC Gaius Gracchus, seeing the cost of living was staggeringly high, allowed all citizens to buy from public granaries at a hugely subsidized price; by 71 BC, free grain was being dispensed to 40,000 male citizens of Rome. In the decades that followed, the number of people receiving grain increased so greatly that Julius Caesar felt he had done terribly well to reduce the dole queue to a mere 150,000. Augustus let the queue creep up again to 320,000 – just under a third of the total estimated population of Rome. At one point food was so short that extravagance just had to be curbed and the Fannian Law was introduced – according to this presumably impossible law, it was an offence to entertain more than three guests to a meal apart from members of the household; except on market days, when five guests were allowed. There were three market days per month. And the same law made it illegal to spend more than two drachmas and a half on provisions, or to serve at any one meal more than one hen – unfattened (they got round this through castration).

Of course, politics played a huge part in the *annona* system. Look at today's welfare system. In the third century AD, Septimius Severus made himself popular with the Roman plebs and with the people of his native Leptis Magna in North Africa, who were suffering from some terrible trade setback, by buying up all the North Africans' oil for free distribution in Rome. A few years later, Septimius Severus decreed that cooked bread should be distributed instead of grain. Less trouble, less danger of fire, less wastage, less indigestion? Aurelian increased the daily ration to a pound and a half and added pork fat to the list of free goodies, and, in order to use up the wine ponds on his hands paid as taxes in kind from the wine growers, he shoved wine in too . . . When he mooted that all this should be expected permanently by *annona* takers, a horrified official exclaimed: 'Before we know where we are, we'll be giving them chickens and geese as well!' But as the Empire got into hotter financial waters towards its close, money became tight all round and free distribution stopped, many basic foodstuffs remaining available, but at an exorbitant price.

As to the quantities – at the time of Augustus, it has been estimated it was necessary to import 14 million bushels of grain a year, the produce of several hundred square miles of wheatfields, to feed the poorer of the city of Rome alone. A third came from Egypt and most of the rest from North Africa and Sicily. Transport was efficient and rapid. A Roman cargo ship could cover 160 kilometres a day and camels about thirty-four kilometres a day. Although most import/ export merchants dealt with and through the city of Rome, or Ostia, its port at the mouth of the Tiber twenty-five kilometres from Rome, maritime, cart and camel trade routes criss-crossed the Empire. So a rich family in Britain or Germany could order silk from China, a few spices from India, or a peacock.

But the transport of grain for public distribution was subject to the strictest security. The grain was handed over in its country of origin and merchants would take it to Ostia, or, when Ostia silted up, to the neighbouring artificial harbour of Portus. If they put in anywhere on the way it was under the pain of death or deportation. Everyone in Rome knew when the grain ships were due in. If late, there was panic. When they reached port hundreds of barges ferried the grain, checked and weighed, up river to Rome, a journey which took three days.

The Greeks were great bakers. The list of breads and cakes they confected at the bakery, at home, for everyday use and for special occasions is exhaustive but it would seem that the Romans took a leaf from the Greeks' cookbook and gave bakers a special union status, mid-Republic. When the Romans took an interest in baking in the eighth or seventh century BC, a sort of flat bread was baked at home and in the embers; this new-fangled scone was disapproved of by Cato (who was still used to his pottage) and was called *maza*. And for centuries the purists like Cato forbade the offering of bread as a sacrifice in Roman religious ceremonies, thus echoing the Jewish concept of the impurity of fermented dough (and was it fermented in the early days? probably not).

Cato's ideal farinaceous sacrifice was the *libum*, a cake made of cheese and eggs – a pound of flour to two pounds of cheese and an egg, a sort of cheesecake – and note that butter hardly ever appears in Roman cooking. The cheese they would have used would have been a full fat curd cheese, either goat or sheep (probably not cow as there was so little grazing space near Rome). The curds would be pressed in a screw-top mould, according to Columella, who wrote in the first century AD a treatise on matters agricultural. Previously, they'd just put a stone on top. The compressed curds were then moulded in a basket or wooden box (*phormos* – Greek, *forma* – Latin), whence the modern French *fromage*; the English for cheese comes from the Latin *caseus,* meaning the foodstuff itself. While on cheese, the Romans used to salt, dry, smoke, mature, brine and add chopped herbs, garlic and onions to cheeses. So they must have enjoyed the equivalent of a hard Chavignol goat cheese, a *crottin* or our ubiqitous Boursin and a *feta.* Smoked mozzarella is still a great Italian speciality. Pliny, who loved cheeses, gives a long list of local specialities of the Iberian peninsula, Cisalpine and Transalpine Gaul, among them a huge sheep's milk wheel from the borders of Tuscany and Liguria; he also talks fondly of the cheeses of the Cevennes and the Auvergne, the ancestors of today's Roquefort and Cantal.

At the height of the Empire, rich Romans would have eaten cheese or curds for breakfast with milk or wine to drink; a bit like the Dutch and Germans today. Little mention is made of a cheese course at their banquets. And, when the so-called barbarians overran Rome at the end of the Empire in the fifth century AD, they proved to be great cheese lovers and eaters; but it was the Benedictine and Cistercian monks who learned and evolved the secrets of cheese-making and steathily became the new pioneers. They carried on the wine and liqueur production, fish farming, apiculture and all the careful, gentle arts the Romans had enjoyed; altogether too intellectual and finnicky for the barbarians.

Back to bread. At around 168 BC, there was an influx of craftsmen bakers from Greece. Hitherto the rich had used slaves to knead bread in their houses and had even made them wear gloves and masks to knead the dough to avoid sweat and breath getting into the bread. The Greeks had penetrated into Gaul long before the Romans arrived and had established a fine rapport with the Gauls in the bread-making (and wine-making) art. The Gauls realized that yeast from beer was a good raising agent and therefore the Greeks and the Gauls formed a good baking team. By 31 BC during the reign of Augustus there were 329 bakeries in Rome run by Greeks with Gaulish assistants. These immigrant bakers were allowed to form a *collegium* – a guild – but were subject to enormous regulations when this union became exclusive. If you were the son of a baker you had to become a baker, and you were not allowed to follow any other profession, even if you married outside. A famous baker, Vergilius Eurysaces, had a huge monument erected in his honour after his death, but his son was not allowed to enter the priesthood, the law, or even the army. A baker had to save the Republic or Empire before he could sit in the Senate; if he were to do this, he would resign from the college and make over all his possessions to the college of *pistores*. And like masons today, they had secret signs, initiatory rites and religious meetings. Interestingly, these bakers were technically well equipped and used horses to run their mills, and not slaves, and cooked the bread in a brick bakehouse. Only men shopped for bread, whether slaves or free.

Eurysaces and his confrères were the equivalent of Poilâne in Paris today; expensive, exclusive with long queues. No women were permitted to enter the bakers' college but they were admitted to the colleges of greengrocers, clothiers and tavern-keepers. The breads were usually round with tops shaped in all sorts of different ways, often a mushroom shape, like our batch loaf. The incinerated loaves found in Pompeii were shaped like eight-petalled flowers, a shape still to be found in France and Sicily. Such loaves were probably made of fine wheat flour, the *siligineus,* liked by the patricians; loaves called *plebeius* were rougher, made of unbolted flour and destined for filling plebeian stomachs (the wholemeal of today? but probably full of stones and weevils too). The Romans also had the equivalent of *pain de seigle* to eat with oysters, *ostrearius.*

The Romans had flaky pastry – no doubt copied from the Arab filo pastry – layers of pastry stretched out thin and interlaced with honey, cheese and nuts. Designed to please, these flat, layered cakes were called *placenda est;* this became *placenta,* a name we don't associate with cakes; it is the shape. They liked fritters enormously. Reay Tannahill* draws a fun analogy of the Romans and their fondness for munching their way round the town at lunchtime – not an important meal: 'In his discussion of breads ancient and modern, native and foreign, Athenaeus throws out an endless list of names for what must have been the Scotch baps, croissants, Parker House rolls, and churros of the Classical world.'

The wedding cake was a Greek institution. In Rome the cake was given to the bridal couple at the *confarreatio* (a binding and old-fashioned form of marriage), they then presented it to Jupiter Capitoline in the presence of the grand pontiff and the incumbent priest, the *flamen dialis,*** who looked after the flame on which the cake then burned. This sacrifice meant that the woman was placed under the jurisdiction of the man and bore witness to the fact that they were legally

---

* *Food in History* by Reay Tannahill, Stein & Day, New York, 1973.
** The young Julius Caesar was one.

wed. Tiberius got rid of the cake-burning custom, but in the eighteenth-century the wedding cake returned with a venegance, a colossal confection to be shared with friends and not burned.

Having established that it took centuries for the staples to be discovered, sorted out and their virtues worked out and for tastes and customs to develop, let's see who ate what and why.

Augustus was frugal, he hated huge blowouts, so did Martial:

Epigram 78

Toranius, if the prospect of a cheerless, solitary dinner
Bores you eat with me – and get thinner.
If you like appetite-whetters,
There'll be cheap Cappadocian lettuce,
Pungent leeks, and tunny-fish
Nestling in sliced eggs. Next, a black earthenware dish
(Watch out – a finger-scorcher!) of broccoli just taken
From its cool bed, pale beans with pink bacon,
And a sausage sitting in the centre
On a snow-white pudding of polenta.
If you want to try a dessert, I can offer you raisins (my own),
Pears (from Syria), and hot chestnuts (grown
In Naples, city of learning)
Roasted in a slow-burning
Fire. As for the wine, by drinking it you'll commend it.
When this great feast has ended,
If, as he well might,
Bacchus stirs up his second appetite,
You'll be reinforced by choice Picenian olives fresh from the trees,
Warm lupins and hot chick-peas . . .

(Martial tr. James Michie, Penguin)

In this one epigram Martial mentions several Roman favourites: lettuce was invariably served during the first course; leeks, tunny fish and eggs would be similar to a 'salade niçoise'; the pale beans with pink bacon would be like the French country dish of *haricots blancs aux lardons,* and the sausage sitting in polenta could appear in any trattoria. The Romans were fond of charcuterie, hams and sausages. Lupins and hot chick-peas were popular and common 'cocktail' nibbles, arriving before, after (as here) or during the meal.

Lucullus was apparently an abstemious young man, and a remarkably successful general who defeated two of the more powerful potentates of his time, Mithridates, King of Pontus, and Tigranes, King of Armenia. His campaigns made him fabulously rich and with his new-found wealth he set about procuring delicacies from all over the known world, paying no attention to his pocket, health or, presumably, figure. It was from Pontus, Cappadocia, that he brought back the cherry tree. He sent couriers all over the then known world combing for rare and fine fare – oysters from Colchester, flamingos from the Nile, peacocks from Persia. He paid his carvers thousands of pounds, as it were. He had three villas in the Bay of Naples where he built *vivaria* – fish tanks – some fed by fresh water, others by salt water. For raising exotic fowl he constructed aviaries, the size of houses to ensure plenty ... Lucullus had a private dining-room set up in an aviary so that he could enjoy a roast thrush while its friends flew around. As well as the thrushes, nightingales and larks there were cranes, whose eyes were put out before they were fattened, parrots and bustards. Ostriches were eaten but proved very tough even after a severe boiling. (The Emperor Heliogabalus, a real nutter, whose short reign was not mourned, served 600 ostrich heads at a banquet, considering the brains the only digestible part. (He was probably right.) He also fed his dogs foie gras. Why? Why not ...

Such was the scale on which Lucullus operated that he drove pipes and aqueducts through a chain of mountains in order to source his freshwater ponds. Following the example of Fulvius Lepinus, who started rearing game at Tarquinii, Lucullus, Varro and Petronius added game parks to their estates where fallow deer, antelopes, gazelles and moufflons, imported from abroad, were plumped for their chefs and banquets. Wild boar didn't become popular till the beginning of the Empire as it was considered a common menace, uprooting the countryside around Rome. Once in fashion, a whole roast wild boar was a must at every smart banquet. Hare was believed to preserve beauty, and the Emperor Septimius Severus ate it every day. Lucullus' substantial garden in the centre of Rome was coveted by Messalina, and she did characteristically manage to get her hands on it before she met her end, indeed dying there from stab wounds on the orders of the Emperor Claudius, her husband.

Lucullus would spend vast sums on a single meal, and soon others began to follow his ruinous and gluttonous example. Dinner started about four in the afternoon, the ninth hour, and was a lengthy performance in three acts – the *gustatio,* hors d'oeuvre, the *fercula,* meaning the 'dishes which are carried' (from the kitchen), and the *mensae secundae,* the dessert courses. The usual layout of the dining area was three sofas arranged in a U shape on which the guest lolled; the open side was used by the servants to fetch and carry the food, often changing the middle table after each course. They used fingers, knives and spoons but did not have forks. They drank from silver or bronze goblets, studded with precious stones if the host was exceedingly rich, and sometimes from glass or crystal; it depended on the taste and means of the host. Ausonius, the prefect-poet, writing in the fourth century AD, waxes extensively and minutely on food and manners of genteel Gallo-Romans; and he describes a wedding feast where doggy-bags were quite the order of the day. Each guest brought a *mappa,* a big napkin, and bundled up all the goodies he couldn't manage at the reception. This was expected and catered for.

At the average to posh Roman dinner, the first course consisted of tasty, light dishes, say, fritters of sheep's brains, little liver sausages, poppy seeds in honey, dressed snails, Lucrine oysters, slices of goose liver, salted sturgeon, asparagus, lettuce, radishes, eggs . . . The 'carried-on' course could run to ten dishes. Mucius Lentulus Niger entertained Julius Caesar and gave him ten starters, ten main courses and endless desserts. Ali Bab cites as crazy, show-off dishes of the greedy and competitive: sows' nipples in tuna brine; camels' heels (said to have been a favourite of Cleopatra); elephants' trunks; parrots' heads; ragout of nightingales' brains; peacocks' brains; and a pâté of tiny bird tongues – a pâté which fetched a huge price – not to mention *le porc à la Troyenne farci de becs-figues et d'huîtres* (Trojan pork with fig-pecker and oyster stuffing).

Although the dinner given by Trimalchio, the Syrian freedman, is a satire and invented by Petronius (*The Satyricon*), it still remains a perfectly vivid and amusing description of the form of an excessive Roman dinner:

MENU

GUSTATIO

White & black olives

Dormice sprinkled with honey & poppy seeds

Grilled sausages

Damsons & pomegranate seeds

Fig-peckers in spiced egg yolk

Honeyed wine

FERCULA

Foods of the Zodiac served on a round plate (over Aries the Ram, chick-peas; over Taurus the Bull, a beefsteak; on the Heavenly Twins, testicles & kidneys; over Cancer the Crab, a crown of myrtle; over Leo the Lion, an African fig; over Virgo the Virgin, a young sow's udder; over Libra the Scales, a balance with a cheesecake in one pan and a pastry in the other; over Scorpio, a sea scorpion; over Sagittarius the Archer, a sea bream with eyespots; over Capricorn, a lobster; over Aquarius the Water-carrier, a goose; over Pisces the Fishes, two red mullets).

Served with bread from silver oven by a young Egyptian slave who, singing in a sickening voice, mangled a song from the show 'The Asafoetida Man' *(Petronius' jibe)*

Roasted fattened fowls, sows' bellies, and hare
Roast whole wild boar with dates, suckled by piglets made
of cakes and stuffed with live thrushes
Boiled whole pig stuffed with sausage & black puddings

FALERNIAN
of the Opimian vintage
one hundred years old

MENSAE SECUNDAE
Fruits & cakes
Boned, fattened chickens & goose eggs
Pastries stuffed with raisins & nuts
Quince-apples & pork disguised as fowls & fish
Oysters & scallops
Snails

That's the menu in a list, but one of Petronius' guest's description is far less clinical:

Finally we took our places. Boys from Alexandria poured iced water over our hands. Others followed them and attended to our feet, removing any hangnails with great skill. But they were not quiet even during this troublesome operation: they sang away at their work ... It was more like a musical comedy than a respectable dinner party.

Some extremely elegant hors d'oeuvres were served. The dishes for the first course: an ass of Corinthian bronze with two panniers, white olives on one side and black on the other. Over the ass were two pieces of plate, with Trimalchio's name and the weight of the silver inscribed on the rims. There were some small iron frames shaped like bridges supporting dormice sprinkled with honey and poppy seed. There were steaming hot sausages too, on a silver gridiron with damsons and pomegranate seeds underneath.

Trimalchio arrives, games, swears and shows off, then a tray is brought in with a basket on it:

There sat a wooden hen, its wings spread round in the way hens are when they are broody; two slaves hurried up and as the orchestra played a tune they began searching through the straw and dug out peahen's eggs, which they distributed to the guests.

Trimalchio: 'My friends, I gave orders for that bird to sit on some peahens' eggs. I hope to goodness they are not starting to hatch. However, let's try them and see if they are still soft.

We took our spoons (weighing at least half a pound each) and cracked the eggs, which were made of rich pastry. To tell the truth, I nearly threw away my share, as the chicken seemed already formed. But I heard a guest who was an old hand say: 'There should be something good here.' So I searched the shell with my fingers and found the plumpest little fig-pecker, all covered with yolk and seasoned with pepper.

(For more see *The Satyricon* by Petronius, Penguin)

Another horror was Aulus Vitellius, Emperor for nine mind-boggling months in AD 69 – he was murdered by his successor Vespasian's allies. Suetonius has a good tale:

The most infamous of Vitellius' banquets was the dinner given by his brother to commemorate the Emperor's arrival in Rome from the provinces. They say that 2,000 of the most costly fish and 7,000 birds were served on that occasion; but Vitellius himself surpassed this with the dedication of a dish he described as 'the Shield of Minerva, the Guardian of the City' because of its colossal size: in this dish, he united the livers of wrasse, pheasants' and peacocks' brains, flamingos' tongues, and the roes of moray eels ... Because he was a man whose gluttony was not only unlimited but also untimely and sordid, he could never control himself even when offering a sacrifice to the gods from robbing the very altars of their pieces of flesh and wheat cakes, almost out of the fires themselves, and then from gulping them down on the spot.

Caligula constantly sought out the novel and bizarre in his entertainments. He invented new sorts of baths where he could soak in special oils; he also devised weird foods – he was said to have laid out loaves and meats of gold, and to have drunk pearls melted in vinegar. His settings were novel too – he had wonderful villas throughout Campania and ships so extravagantly decked out that they boasted baths and fruit trees. (The surviving vessels found at Nemi are proof of such opulence.) Those guests not too keen on sailing could join one of Caligula's picnics, which took place in a tree house in the branches of an enormous plane tree, large enough to seat fifteen!

Juvenal, Pliny and Martial were perfectly normal eaters and entertainers, and observed sumptuary laws. Juvenal would content himself by dining simply on 'a plump kid, tenderest of the flock', with 'more of milk in him than of blood', some wild asparagus and 'lordly eggs warm in their wisps of hay together with the hens that laid them' (perhaps the most memorable meal I've eaten in France lately, at Bardet in Tours, comprised one course of a lightly boiled guinea-fowl egg, served with the finest sea salt; the following course was its mother, also poached but with truffles. Bardet and Juvenal's chef share the same inclinations towards simplicity and quality). Ordinary plebeian gatherings, whether among family or friends, political colleagues or corporations, were pretty frugal and sober affairs because they mostly did not have enough money to entertain on a lavish scale as ingredients were expensive.

Rome itself was a limited space, there was no refrigeration although they knew how to make ice, but who would have got that? The rich. The ordinary people, who lived in highly inflammable and jerry-built 'high-rise' flats, often didn't dare cook due to fear of fire, the neighbours, smells, maybe even the lack of a burner. Cooking costs money. Hence, the thriving street food business, as in Asia and the Far East today – hot, tasty and cheap.

Did the Romans have spaghetti? No one can agree. Marco Polo did not bring pasta to the West. Going by eighteenth-century Italian translations of Horace's *Satires* and Martial's

Epigrams one would assume the Romans ate pasta, as *pastillas* was translated as 'little pastas'; but all translations before the fourteenth century translate the word as 'small, round cakes'. Croquettes is another rendering. Marcus Varro, first century AD, states in his encyclopedia that a *pastillum* is a bread roll; then, de Cagne, an erudite seventeenth-century Frenchman, came up with the theory that *pastillum* is a pastry stuffed with meat, a ravioli! It's possible then that the Romans had the stuffed, malleable, pudgy pastas like ravioli, gnocchi, tortelloni. Long strands of spaghetti would have been hard to eat without forks or chop sticks.

Once the Empire was nicely under way, territories enlarged and under control, the show offs showing off, it's interesting to pinpoint the spices, condiments, relishes and, to us, untasteable mixtures the Romans most cared for. The only point of view we can get is the Romans' – they knew what they wanted and thought they knew what to do with it in a sophisticated manner. The range at their disposal was vast – the Romans had the run of Gaul and they learned much from the Gauls, although Roman writers invariably cite the Gauls as noisy, rough marauders. It was probably merely one tribe, the Arvernii, ancestors of the people of the present-day Auvergne, who lived up to his uncouth, roistering image. The Gauls introduced the Romans to foie gras, oysters, barrels, mattresses (good for lolling on, having over-eaten) and shored up the wine supply at reasonable prices.

Gaulish influence coupled with that of the northern Germanic tribes was considerable – 'Westphalian' ham, sausages and, perhaps, black bread. The Romans liked smoking pork, the Greeks never liked this method of cooking/preserving, they simply boiled. And it was the people of north and central Europe who were essentially hunters, and not fancy cooks, with plenty of spindly-legged wild pigs and abundant forests, who must have invented the practical and tasty method of smoking which continues to this day especially in Germany and all countries north. Selling smoked, salted hams to the Romans also made the Germanic tribesmen a fortune. After all, 'jambon de Bayonne', 'Westphalische Schinken', 'prosciutto crudo', etc., are all expensive today. Whether hams came from the north, Gaul or Spain, Martial, Cato and others extolled their deliciousness and noticed that the secret ingredient was acorns. Spanish and Corsican hams are still loved for their acorny flavour. The Romans didn't much care for beef. It was pork, in all guises, they liked. Galen says it tasted like human flesh. A recommendation? Well, no associations seemed abhorrent to the Roman palate.

A real delicacy of a posh patrician dinner was any dish made of sows' vulvas and teats. Arguments arose as to whether the vulva of a sow who had aborted her first litter was the tops (Pliny), or whether it was those of a virgin sow. Or, were the teats of a sterile sow better than those of the sow who had just given birth and suckled her young ... the dotty Emperor Heliogabalus could eat a dish of tits ten days running.

Sausages were popular. The Romans made their own and introduced different kinds from Gaul to extend the charcutiers' range, and sausage-making hasn't, it seems, changed much either in Italy or in France for 2,000 years. They had *circelli tomacinae* and *incisia* – small chipolata-type sausages; *pendulus*, a large slicing sausage using the end of the large intestine, or caecum; *hillae*, a very thin sausage, like today's dry mountain sausage; *tuccettae*, a speciality of Cisalpine Gaul, long and a mixture of pork and beef. Faliscan sausage was like mortadella and the Gauls made something like *andouillettes* which might be smoked black puddings with milk and blood – a delicacy of the *canabae*, the settlements of Aeduan charcutiers who set up shop near Roman settlements.

Tripe, *omasum,* a completely Celtic dish, was a Roman favourite, and was made with onions and garlic, both vegetables exported in large quantities from Gaul. The Gallo-Romans and Romans at home in Rome must have liked offal: pigs' heads, strings of sausages, black puddings and the Gaulish charcutier, the *lardarius,* at work are depicted on bas-reliefs found in Narbonne, Bordeaux, Cologne and Reims.

Fatted goose- and duck-liver has been going for a long, long time. The ancient Egyptians were the first to notice the phenomenon, and appreciate the taste and, above all, texture. The Egyptians sent Agesilaus, King of Sparta, fat geese around 400 BC. Athenaeus writing in the third century BC quotes the famous cook Archestratus on foie gras: 'A liver, or rather the soul of a goose'.

The Greeks were good at cramming geese and the Romans copied. Cato, in the second century BC, explains: 'To cram hens or geese: shut up young hens beginning to lay, make pellets of moist flour or barley meal, soak in water, and put into the mouth . . . cram twice a day, and give water at noon, but do not place water before them for more than one hour. Feed a goose the same way, except that you let it drink first, and give food and water twice a day'. Columella gives the same advice in the first century AD, and Palladius, in the fourth century AD, says they should be fed on a vegetarian diet and in the warmth and dark till fat and then on rolled, pounded figs for another fifty days.

Pliny agrees that the Romans liked foie gras, the liver of the Gaulish geese (Gaul again), that arrived 'on foot all the way to Rome from Morini (Picardy); the geese that get tired are advanced to the front rank, and so all the rest drive them on by instinctively pressing forward in their rear'. Pliny goes on about foie gras. 'Stuffing the bird makes the liver grow to a great size, and also once it has been removed it is made larger by being soaked in milk sweetened with honey.' Horace thought the 'enormous liver', as Juvenal called it, should definitely come from a white, female goose . . .

Figs would have made a poor goose very sick; foie gras is in fact the liver of a severely diabetic bird. The Romans prized *iecur ficatum*, 'fig liver', above all other foie gras, and the Gauls, who loved it then as they do now, forgot about the liver bit, *iecur*, and went on with the *ficatum*. In the eighth century this became *figido*, then *fedie et feie* in the twelfth century, ending up as foie.

Juvenal says foie gras was served hot. 'Before the master is put a huge goose's liver, a capon as big as a goose, and a boar, piping hot.'

At the same dinner, given by the social climber Marcus Varro, the host amused himself by giving his guests of humble origin a paltry menu, while he had the above, followed by truffles! Lucullus loved truffles. Truffles had a special fragrance, grew in a mysterious way, and were therefore highly attractive to the Romans in their quest for expensive, rare, maybe aphrodisiac, and delicious delicacies. The Greeks and Romans didn't agree on the nature of truffles. Theophrastus, a disciple of Aristotle, thought they were born of autumn claps of thunder and especially lightning; Nicander, 100 years later, thought they were silt modified by internal heat, and Plutarch thought they were mud cooked by lightning.

No one has successfully to this day managed to grow such truffles; experiments are being carried out in the Limousin, in the Périgord, and an Israeli in California thinks he has nearly cracked the problem . . . Martial lets the truffles talk: 'We truffles that burst through the nurturing soil with our soft heads are of earth's apples second to mushrooms.' Galen prescribed truffles to his patients, amongst them admittedly Marcus Aurelius and Commodus, 'for the truffle is very nourishing, and causes general excitation, conducive to sensual pleasure'. Maybe the truffles of antiquity were not the same as the pungent black truffles of the Périgord and Strasbourg, or the distinctive white truffles of Italy familiar to us, because Pliny describes them as reddish, black or white (the Italian variety?) and Martial's come bursting through the ground like mushrooms.

The elusiveness of truffles surely lies in the fact that they spore and grow haphazardly underground and have to be sniffed out by pigs or dogs. The Romans probably enjoyed some real truffles – *tubera* – and also used the word *tuber* to cover truffles, pungent mushrooms of tubercular shape which sprout up from under the ground and are found around the Mediterranean.

Boletus mushrooms were highly esteemed. Martial again:

> To send presents of silver and gold
> Or cloaks and togas
> Is easy;
> but giving some *boleti* . . .
> That's hard.

Pliny, who in his *Natural History* gives precise descriptions of edible and poisonous mushrooms, writes rather bossily:

> Among those foods which are eaten thoughtlessly, I would justly place mushrooms. Although their flavour is excellent, mushrooms have fallen into disgrace by a shocking instance of murder: they were the means by which the Emperor Tiberius Claudius was poisoned by his wife Agrippina; and by doing this she gave to the world and to herself another poison, one worse than all the others: her own son, Nero. . .

The mushroom Agrippina gave Claudius was the 'fly agaric',

which looks like the most prized mushroom of classical times, the 'royal agaric'; the fly agaric is now commonly known as Caesar's Mushroom.

Millions of oyster shells litter Roman sites; the Romans imported them from Gaul, England having already started her own beds. The expert was Mucianus, an oyster taster, quoted by Pliny as being able to differentiate between the ten different sorts available in the fish forum – from the Sea of Marmora to the Armorican coast, including Tripolitan, Aeolian, Istrian, Latian and Asturian. Catiline's grandfather was famous for his fish ponds, *piscinae,* and he raised his gilthead bream from Lake Lucrino on oysters, opened for them day and night, which he bred in the elaborate oyster beds he had constructed. His oysters were chosen from Tarentum or Brindisi. He sold the surplus and made a fortune. The fish ponds constructed by medieval monks after the barbarian invasions were based on Roman design; it could not be beaten.

Soon after the conquest of Gaul 58–52 BC, oyster farming became one of the biggest industries. Natural oyster beds from all Gaulish coasts provided excellent specimens. The Greeks had appreciated the Gaulish oysters long before the Romans arrived. The Greek, Strabo, praises the oysters of the Etang de Berre, near Marseilles. Pliny talks about the oysters of the Médoc, then, in the fourth century, Ausonius provides fascinating oyster information. Whereas Caesar had divided Gaul into three nations, Ausonius, the prefect-poet, divides the country geographically according to the quality of its oysters! First comes the Médoc, whence the author, who came originally from Lyons and was of Greek descent, his family having been in Gaul before the Romans. Next comes Provence, including Marseilles, the Etang de Berre and Port-Vendres, whose oysters he considered on a par with those from Baiae near Naples and Lake Lucrino; still in the second category came the Saintogne and Calvados areas. Third, came Armorican oysters from the country of the Picts, La Vendée, and then Scotland and, a long way behind, Byzantium!

Certain fish were greatly revered, among them the red mullet, especially for the brains. One weighing four and a half pounds was auctioned by Tiberius; the bidding between Apicius and another rich, greedy fellow was competitive and in the end the greedy fellow won and paid 30,000 *sesterces* (about £4,000 today!). Domitian's turbot was so enormous that the Senate was convened to deliberate the best way to serve it. Gaius Hirrius was the first to invent separate fish ponds for rearing morays. He contributed 6,000 morays to the banquets at which Julius Caesar celebrated his Triumphs, but as a loan, since he was unwilling to exchange them for a price or indeed for any other kind of payment. When he sold his smallish country seat, he received 4,000,000 *sesterces*, largely on the strength of his fish ponds. It was after this that a passion for individual fish began to seize certain people. At Bacolo, in the district of Baiae, the orator Hortensius kept a fish pond in which there was a moray he so prized that it is widely believed he shed tears at its death. In the same country house, Antonia, the wife of Drusus, put earrings on a moray she loved, and some people longed to see Bacolo because of its famous fish.

Tuna, grey mullet and the abundant fish of the Mediterranean were beaten like game into the lagoon of Berre by dolphins. River fish especially from Gaul, sea anemones, still a Niçoise favourite, and salmon from the northern rivers were not to be sneezed at.

Snails and dormice were enthusiastically collected, bred and fed. It was Fulvius Lippinus who began breeding snails in the district of Tarquinii (Trachina) around 50 BC. He sorted them into four batches and gave them each their own *vivarium* – the white snails from Reate, the Illyrian snails famed for their size, the African snails known for fertility and the African sun snails known simply for quality. Lippinus fattened them with must and spelt; Apicius has a recipe for milk-fed snails. Indeed, Marcus Varro wrote that snail rearing became such a mania that a banquet snail shell could contain twenty pints.

Dormice, our fieldmice, were bred in hutches for some eighteen centuries from the Greeks to the Middle Ages. The Romans also kept them in jars and fed them on acorns, figs, walnuts and chestnuts, and when they were *à point* they cooked these delectable titbits in honey.

In AD 162 the Lex Faunia forbade the fattening of hens, to save grain, but the Romans got around this snag by castrating cockerels, thus inventing the capon – they grew to twice their size and put on a lot of weight like a eunuch. Spayed hens became fattened pullets.

The Romans, who were good at central heating and plumbing, also had steam-heated incubators for eggs. Hens were not just for consumption but for sacrifice too. The chicken, a relation of the Asian mound-bird, only reached Greece in the fifth century BC, wending its way from Malaysia to domestication in the valley of the Indus, then to Persia and thence to King Croesus in Greece. Horace thought a fowl drowned to death in wine had a particularly good taste. The Romans ate all domestic fowl we eat (save turkey, it hadn't arrived), and birds we don't – swans, ostriches, crane, bittern, stork, robins, sparrows, fig-peckers and thrushes (*vide* Trimalcio's feast), oriole, even seagulls and pelicans . . .

The only cookbook of any length extant is a fourth-century compilation, purportedly the recipes of one Apicius, a first-century gourmet, who committed suicide because he estimated he did not have enough money left to keep his gastronomic life alive. *This* Apicius was a contemporary of Tiberius. But there could have been four Apiciuses, each from a different century; let's assume the book, *De Re Coquinaria,* is from the first-century AD Apicius undoubtedly with bits added along the way. And it's only from these or other miscellaneous recipes that we can make a stab at guessing what Roman food tasted like and what sort of texture it had.

As Rome began its earliest days as a salt crossroads, they knew salt was crucial to life – Roman soldiers were partly paid in salt, hence 'salary'. There being no refrigeration, any meats or fish if not eaten fresh were salted. Spices imported from the East were inordinately precious and it seems that the more spice, herbs and pickle you could possibly stuff into a single dish the happier the host and more impressed the guests.

Pepper was the king spice. Most of Apicius' sauce recipes begin with a liberal dose of pepper. A sweet sauce for eels might consist of ground pepper, lovage, oregano, mint, onion, honey, boiled wine and fish stock. Pepper was also sprinkled or poached with pears, apples and quinces, and this was still a common practice in the Middle Ages; we sometimes pepper strawberries, and a Moroccan *tajine* of lamb, prunes and cinnamon is heavily peppered – reminiscent of Roman sweet-sour dishes which would suggest many dishes were adopted from the Far and Middle East and Greece. Pepper gives piquancy, a sensation, but not an aromatic or exotic taste or smell; nevertheless and despite its price it was used willy-nilly, and was quite indispensable to Roman gastronomy.

To get an idea of its price: in AD 390 Diocletian, in an edict, fixed the price of whole long pepper in the Roman Empire at fifteen *denarii* a pound (roughly £40), shelled pepper (round pepper?) at four *denarii* (say £14) and white pepper at seven *denarii* (£24). What a huge chunk of a medium household's income! The *honestiores,* people who didn't need state aid, certified to the *municipia,* the authorities, that they were in possession of 5,000 *sesterces'* capital, and one Jerome Carcopino (*A Rome à l'apogée de l'Empire,* Hachette, 1939), worked out that the average middle-class family with enough slaves needed 20,000 *sesterces* a year to live on! No wonder, if pepper was so expensive, and a Roman pound weight was less than ours.

Foreign monarchs who owed allegiance to the imperial city gave pepper to consuls, senators, generals and indeed any officials. When, in AD 408, Alaric, King of the Visigoths, captured Rome, he demanded 5,000 pounds of gold, 30,000 pounds of silver, and 3,000 pounds of pepper. They just couldn't have eaten it all, pepper goes mouldy. Pepper was a status symbol – mouldering gold.

If pepper came first to the cook's hand, then cinammon, cardamom and nutmeg were bracketed together as condiments used in almost every dish, rather like salt and pepper today. This mixture was used in the preparation of food and also sprinkled over cooked dishes just before they went to the table. Ginger, Indian spikenard, cloves and Indian costum were high on the list of imported spices. An indication of the Roman fever for spices by the first century AD is the fact that they accounted for forty-four out of the eighty-six classifications of goods imported from Asia and the eastern coast of Africa to the Mediterranean. (The others included elephant trainers and eunuchs, parrots and palm oil, cottons and cooks.)

Besides spices the Romans used lots of herbs and fish pickles, many of which we never use and hardly ever see today. Lovage, a green herbal plant that grows anywhere and to quite a size, crops up often and has a taste stronger and more cloying than its cousin, celery. Rue has probably, and not surprisingly, fallen from modern grace; it's bitter and smells oddly of sicky cheese (a taste they strove for, *vide* garum below). Its main use nowadays is as an insect-repellent. Brillat Savarin, in his *Psychologie du goût*, reckons that many of Apicius' recipes were disgusting to eighteenth-century palates; almost a joke, as they surely are to us, were dishes like 'stuffed wombs and udders, dormice and boiled ostriches, capons' testicles with asafoetida, and all stuffed with rue, endless rue'.

Other 'European' herbs used by the Romans, in descending order of importance (somebody reckons to have worked it out), are: coriander, cumin, oregano, celery seed, parsley seed, bay leaf, aniseed, fennel, mint, caraway, mustard seed, wormwood, chervil, colewort (rocket), saxifrage (sweet cicely), thyme, sage, pennyroyal, pellitory, elecampane, saffron and mastic . . .

But the oddest condiments are liquamen (garum) and the herb silphium or laser – strong, nasty and expensive and totally craved. Some say that garum shared responsibility for the Roman conquest of Gaul, as its manufacturing and marketing made an appreciable contribution to the prosperity of the trading posts which proliferated, from the time Greek colonists first landed on the shores of Gaul, until a whole chain had sprung up along the Ligurian (Provençal), Volcaen (Languedocian) and Iberian coastlines. The Greeks had a sauce made of fermented shrimps called *'garon'* (Greek for shrimp), and the Romans, in all walks of life, had an insatiable mania for it. Some Roman *amphoras* were recovered from shipwrecks in the *Golfe de Lion* containing crystallized deposits of the sauce and bearing the manufacturers' seals, showing there was a garum trade as early as the fifth century BC.

Phocaean, not Phoenician, Massilia (Marseilles) was an important import-export centre, and, after all, it was the people of Massilia who invited the Romans into Provence in 181 BC, providing a jumping-off-point for the entire country. Each manufacturing port had its secret recipe, and so popular was garum that the sauce was factory-produced. Pompeii, Leptis Magna and Antipolis (Antibes) were famous for a mean garum, but Bithynia on the coast of the Black Sea seems to have been *the* one. The Carthage and Cadiz brands were highly esteemed. The grandest was 'garum sociorum', 'garum of the allies', perhaps so-called because the decomposing mackerel, anchovy or (rarely) red mullet and shrimp intestines were in fact self-digesting due to the action of the fish's own intestinal microbes.

A recipe from Apicius:

It's best to take large or small sprats, or failing them take anchovies, or horse-mackerel, or mackerel, make a mixture of all and put into a baking trough. Take two pints of salt to the peck of fish and mix well to have the fish impregnated with salt. Leave it for one night, and then put it into an earthenware vessel which you place open in the sun for two or three months, stirring with a stick at intervals, then take it, cover it with a lid and store away. Some people add old wine, two pints to a pint of fish.

When the mixture had completely decomposed, carefully calculated amounts of concentrated decoctions of herbs were added; then, a fine strainer was plunged into the vessel to collect the syrupy, pale yellow, pungent, salty, fishy and, most distinctively, cheesy liquid. This was then left to mature. The residue or *alec,* something akin to *marc,* the residue of pressed grapes, was not thrown away but kept for the poor people to season their bland porridges; just as the most intense sauces in the world's repetoire – the soys of China, the curries of India and the chilli mixtures of South America – are designed, fundamentally, to perk up piles of cheap and bulky carbohydrates which both dilute and absorb the sauce. It is, however, hard to imagine what garum added to meaty dishes.

Some favoured 'sanguine garum' made of tuna blood – even stronger than the ordinary garum! The freshwater catfish found in marshes which weren't much good for eating (having thick skin and lots of bones) were pounded up and turned into a garum called *muria*. Garum diluted with water, *hydrogarum*, livened up the daily diet of the Roman soldier. Garum diluted with wine would be used to make the famous Byzantine sauce 'oenogarum', and diluted with oil it became 'oleogarum', and with vinegar 'oxygarum'. Today the nearest we can get to garum is perhaps the 'nuoc man' of Vietnam, 'tuk trey' from Cambodia or 'nam pla' from Thailand, all made from putrefying fish and yet there are no records of bacterial infection caused by eating any of these things. Indeed, Laotians put a few drops of 'nuoc man' into babies' bottles. Garum made the fortunes of the Greek and Roman trading posts and the Provençal *pissaladière*, the *pisara* of the Var and *pissala* of Nice – both fishy preserves – are its great-grandchildren.

Its price was shattering – the price of caviare is nothing by comparison; the only possible parallel is the essences used in scent-making. In Caesar's time a *congius* (about three and a quarter litres) of garum cost 500 *sesterces*, something like £4,000!

Silphium is a herb, completely unknown to us today, which was another essential in the Roman kitchen. A wild carrot is a theory. It came from the former Greek colony in Cyrene in North Africa, where the economy revolved so entirely around silphium and horses, and life was so narrow as a result, that Antiphanes the dramatist, in the fourth century, made one of his characters moan, 'I will not sail back to the place from which we were carried away, for I want to say goodbye to all – horses, silphium, chariots, silphium stalks, steeple-chasers, silphium leaves, fevers, and silphium juice!' Due to overcropping, silphium ran out in Nero's time, so the Romans had to make do with asafoetida (Persian *asa*, mastic; Latin *foetida*, stinking). It's the sap of a large, umbelliferous plant, extremely bitter, more pungent than garlic with a stench like carrion and, again, expensive. It was rubbed over plates before the food was put on to make the food taste better, by comparison. This habit would indicate that a real problem faced by Roman cooks was the danger of rancidity, so they shrouded the basic raw material in overpowering substances.

So expensive were silphium and asafoetida that Apicius suggests a way of making an ounce of silphium go further, by keeping it in a jar of pine nuts, which it impregnated like a vanilla pod flavours sugar. So when a recipe needed silphium, a few pine nuts could be used. A drop of asafoetida greatly enhances fish dishes today but we don't know how much the Romans used. Probably a strong dose. Indians have always used asafoetida under the name of *hing*, and often in such quantities that supplies have to be imported from Afghanistan. The Romans also liked an Indian plant called 'nard'; it's related to valerian and smells of decay. All these strange tastes seem to have one 'quality' in common; they all stink, are strong and bitter, and preferably evoke a cheesy, decaying whiff.

What did the Romans drink? They didn't like beer, they drank wine and preferred white wine, usually sweetened with honey. Women were not allowed wine, equated with blood, therefore suggesting figuratively adultery; wine was also thought to be an abortifacient, to bring on monsters; and as intoxication causes a form of delirium which may be prophetic, better the women didn't have the chance to be better informed. Further, the delirium of drunkenness denoted possession – divine rather than demoniac at this time – and this possession denoted violation, and a violated woman could never be regarded as pure and chaste again. The Romans did not analyse the properties of alcohol and did not, knowingly, have spirits, an Arab invention (*al-kuhl,* originally meaning a very fine powder of antimony – the kohl as in eye make-up – came by extension to mean any powder obtained by sublimation, i.e., the direct transformation of a solid into vapour, or the reverse). The rich and boozy saw nothing wrong with intoxication amongst the men and many a slave had to guide his master back from a dinner, steering him from urinal to urinal. A host could also organize extra drinking by appointing as his assistant someone whose three names contained a certain number of letters. For instance, the name Gaius Julius Caesar has seventeen letters, which meant drinking his health in seventeen cups of wine, and the capacity of a cup might be anything from one to eleven *cyathi,* depending on the capacity of the *cyathus,* the ladle. Suetonius has it that the proverbial sobriety of Augustus allowed him only three cups of wine a meal, which would have meant some litre and a half!

Not until 121 BC did the Italian vineyards take off. Earlier texts speak mainly of Greek wines. So great was the demand for white, or rather, amber wine that red wine was 'breached' with sulphur. The Greeks blended their wines; the Romans did not but they did cook some of their wines and flavour them with aromatics – a sort of sweet Dubonnet. The reduced cooked wines became *defrutum, carenum* and *sagra* – the latter being the thickest and stickiest and not greatly fermented, and all were sweetened with honey. *Mulsum* was the sweetest of all, with a ratio of ten litres of honey to thirteen litres of wine. Apicius used all these reduced wines in his cooking, plus a raisin wine called *passum* made of grapes left to shrivel to half their size on the vine – presumably *passum* would have resembled sweet white dessert wines resulting from the noble rot, or botrytis.

The wine from Alba was aged for fifteen years and from Surrentinum for twenty-five years and ended up, according to the Emperor Tiberius, as *generosum acetum* – vinegar, but magnificent and well-sweetened vinegar! Trimalchio served a 100 year-old Falernian: a joke, but might suggest they had vintages. As well as the Italian wines the Romans drank wine from Greece, Asia Minor, Egypt, Spain, Provence, Narbonne and Aquitaine. Petronius said that Rome had laid its hands on the world, and it also stored the world, so to speak in its cellars. In fact, the Romans stored their wine at the top of the house near the smoking chimney; they liked this extra bouquet.

The barrel came from Gaul and was associated with beer, so the most common container for wine was the amphora, coated inside with pitch and sealed with clay. The glass bottle's use spread at the end of the first century BC and with it came the cork stopper.

The Romans proved as thorough in viticulture as in everything. They grafted – perhaps an Etruscan invention – dipping the pruning hook in bear's blood and wiping it off with beaver skin. No one knows where this ritual originated. From the second century BC onwards the Romans regulated the viticulture introduced into Mediterranean Gaul by the Greeks and the Gauls provided the ingenuity and talent. For instance, the Gauls went off into the forests to find wild vines which were then grafted on to 'southern' stock. Before long, the Gauls in the Allobrogica, now the Dauphiné, succeeded in hardening a vine which was frost-resistant. The cunning chieftains cashed in on their discovery to get Roman citizenship. Why not? – it gave them the right to grow their own vines for themselves in the future. Following this example, the Bituriges Vivisci passim of Bordeaux bred a vine which thrived on the gravelly, wind-swept soils of the Graves, Aquitaine and Médoc. As Tacitus put it, '*Grave solum coelumque.*' ('How gloomy is soil and climate.')

Funnily enough, there was during the Roman Empire a parallel situation to the EC wine gripes of today. The citizens of Rome who grew their wines in Italy and the province of Narbonne made it known in high places that the talents of their Gaulish colleagues, especially the Allobroges and Bituriges, were damaging their own export trade and even home consumption. No wonder the less well-off Romans wanted to buy Gaulish wines, which were reasonable, well made and plentiful.

With such a massive amount of documentation on the Romans, we just can't be sure what their food and drink tasted like – very odd – but as the French essayist Suarès says: 'There is no heresy in a dead religion.' Quite, but we do know that their religious fervour for ostentation, gluttony and ridiculous gastronomic acrobatics went so far that some diners had to tickle their throats with a feather once or several times during the dinner so that: ' *Vomunt ut edant, edunt ut voment*', as Seneca disapprovingly put it. ('They vomit to eat and eat to vomit.') But what a lot the Romans organized, discovered and adapted – imagine if they'd known about the Americas . . . tomatoes, chocolate, maize, coffee, potatoes, the turkey . . . Help!

✦ THE TRIVIAL ROUND AND ✦
THE COMMON TASKS

In the *domus* of our friend, let us call him Quintus (as do his intimates), who lives on the Caelian Hill, opposite the Palatine, the bell rings just before dawn. His acquaintance the polymath Pliny, would have been up hours ago, scribbling away – but then he even wrote in his sedan chair . . . Quintus' first caller is his twelve-year-old son, just off to school. He notices the old slave carrying a lantern and the boy's books, probably Virgil or Horace. He kisses him, reminds him he has to recite a poem at the dinner party tonight, and he sighs, for he knows the school is boring, that the lessons are repetitive, literally beaten into the boys, and wonders if he shouldn't assemble a group of friends and fund a school with an intelligent Greek as teacher, as had been done recently over on the Palatine and was constantly advocated by (again) Pliny. Trouble is, Quintus thought, we Romans are so suspicious of the Greeks, giving the boys the wrong ideas . . . *'Timeo Danaos et dona ferentes,'* he muttered to himself – one of the few lines he remembered from the *Aeneid*. ('I fear the Greeks even though they bring gifts.')

At this point, his valet enters with water in a silver bowl for him to wash his hands and face and helps him to dress – his underwear, which he exchanges for what he had been sleeping in; his tunic with a broad purple stripe running down the middle, which indicates his senatorial rank, his black patrician shoes, each with a little silver or ivory crescent on the instep with the same significance. Next he is shaved – in soapless Ancient Rome, a barbarous and agonizing daily event but obligatory for gentlemen (for custom dictated a beardless countenance) and though the iron razor (none, of course, extant) was sharp, facial cuts were common and hair was often removed with tweezers or some other depilatory. Julius Caesar, a strict dandy, suffered particularly. Nero had the world's best barber. Quintus has his own but most Romans went to the neighbourhood shop, sometimes in the open air, and bled when the barber was jostled by the crowd; indeed, there are lawsuits arising from such injury – and, contrariwise, stories of successful practitioners retiring with a fortune. When the Emperor Hadrian grew a beard to conceal a scar and the fashion was allowed, upper-class Romans, who for centuries had been painfully clean-shaven, must have been mightily relieved. His barber also dresses his hair, not as complicated a procedure as that for his wife, whose hair might be piled elaborately on her head, like Marie Antoinette (the times that an angry matron had hit her hairdresser with a mirror or had her flogged for fumbling over a kiss-curl were already part of Roman folklore). Bald men wore wigs and Sulla, once so handsome but suffering from psoriasis, as painful as it was unsightly, had one of ginger curls which, until they realized who he was, made people laugh; alternatively imitation hair was painted on bare parts of the head; but let us give Quintus a reasonable head of hair and allow him to have his simple breakfast – milk, honey and bread – in peace. His valet helps him with his toga, also obligatory for any citizen of standing (only a full Roman citizen could wear one), but often, especially in hot weather, an affliction and needing a certain amount of skill to arrange the impressive folds. Quintus is now ready to meet his *clientes,* which have assembled in his reception hall.

These are citizens, sometimes poor relations, who have difficulty in making ends meet without a private dole from a great man. Quintus is not dangerously rich or powerful, nor does he have the patronage of some great office of state – controlling the water supply or the corn, or being about to govern a province – but he is important enough to have, and in a sense to need, hangers-on for mutual support. His money, which he does not handle himself, comes from rents of property in Rome, estates in Sicily and North Africa and farms dotted all over Italy and is enough to enable him to keep up a *train de vie* as elegant as any eighteenth-century nobleman, including the maintenance of villas in Puteoli and Antium, the occasional heavy flutter on the horses, the purchase of jewels for his wife, the odd visit (in an anonymous sedan chair) to the most expensive brothel in Rome (for although a good man he is not a puritan) and finally, but crucially, the daily gifts to his clients. Originally these came in the shape of parcels of food, which the hungry client might cook in the street outside, but nowadays money was the form. In return for this patronage, which might be brutal and mean or tender and generous, according to the mood and disposition of the patron (clients were not allowed moods), Quintus was applauded whenever and wherever – he would be an unusual Roman if he did not enjoy declaiming his own verse – he spoke, be it at a law court as a character witness or on the floor of the Senate.

Quintus has dealt with his clients – all, like him, in togas but some quite threadbare and in colours which do not show marks – one by one, according to their status. A typical reception of a *patronus* might include a *praetor* (to help in an election campaign), a tribune, a knight (offering an investment in a shipload of silk), a poet, an artist (who had heard that Quintus planned to build a private bath), an architect (ditto), a bum or two, one or two freedmen and even a slave. All would have addressed him as '*dominus*' (Lord); all would have received something, if only an invitation to dinner; a few would have been told to return to the *domus* to receive their present because Quintus needs their presence during the day to help him with his shopping, which today involves the purchase of a new slave. In Rome the men, at all social levels, were responsible for purchases and also the collection of the corn dole. They always left the house, the women rarely did. The wives of the poor had their chores but those of the rich had nothing to do save gossip, intrigue (socially and sexually), look after their money and contemplate divorce, which was often instigated by them.*

Quintus is now ready to go to the Forum, a mile away. He does not take the sedan chair, nor the litter with the six hunky Germans in scarlet livery, but decides, it being a fine day, if cold, to walk. This, in a toga, is no light undertaking** and Quintus, a favourite client on either side, an

---

* The *domina*, at least in Roman literature, was more bossy than bossed. Juvenal, a misogynist, warns against marriage: 'No present will you ever make if your wife forbids; nothing will you ever sell if she objects; nothing will you buy without her consent.' One wife was so mean with the cash that her husband gave a friend his silver shaving bowl while she was asleep and pretended it had been stolen. A wife with a large dowry was in a strong position because she could take it with her to the next husband – and the next and the next . . . (some women had five). Divorce was easy. The husband said to the wife: '*Tuas res tibi agito*' ('Take your belongings with you') and she answered with the same (legal) formula: '*Tuas res tibi habito*' ('And you keep yours for yourself!').

** 'It required unremitting attention if the balance of the toga was to be preserved in walking, in the heat of a discourse, or amid the jostlings of

accountant to hold his purse, servants to clear the way for him, is the centre of an impressive little procession. Should a consul pass, preceded by his *lictors*, he will stop and, if he is wearing a hat, remove it. If he sees a friend and equal, he will embrace him effusively. (In this way, it was often objected, Romans of rank passed their colds on to each other.)

Although this is an ordinary day, with no festival and no Games, the Forum is crowded – with gamblers playing dice, beggars (including a soldier with a wooden leg), a hired claque applauding unconvincingly, a man declaiming some verse plagiarized from Virgil, a group of noisy fellows, linen-clad and with shaven heads, proclaiming the end of the world, a man carrying a tray of loaves, another pushing a tiny cart containing an enormous turbot. On an impulse Quintus buys it. Apart from mullet, turbot is the most expensive fish known in Rome and it will impress his chief dinner guest, a *quaestor* who has just returned* from a tour in Britain and is now at the treasury in Rome.

Rome pullulated with people of every race, voluntary emigrants attracted to the great city from the provinces but also the descendants of prisoners-of-war brought in as slaves, some of whom Quintus might have among his *clientes* and who could only litigate through his sponsorship. Indeed the crowd in the Forum would be a macrocosm of his own household – Gauls, Spaniards, Thracians, Cappadocians (from eastern Turkey), Syrians, Greeks, Galatians,

---

a crowd. The weight of it was an intolerable burden.' (Jerome Carcopino, *Life in Ancient Rome,* Routledge, 1946.) One of the joys of summer was that it could be abandoned the moment one reached the villa.

* Some officials did not return; the earliest (legible) inscription in England is on the tombstone of a *praetor* who died in office, erected by his loving wife and recently discovered by Tower Hill Underground station, where there is a copy.

Numidians, Macedonians; Jews he would not have employed because of their odd habits, strange diet and unavailability to work every seventh day, licensed by their first protector, Julius Caesar.

Quintus sends a servant for a copy of the *Daily News*, posted up by the rostra in the Forum; he is going to attend upon Nero and should know what is (officially) happening. Presently, with his little retinue, he climbs the Palatine Hill to the palace of Nero and makes his way through the curious crowd by the gates – who had nothing to fear from the rapacity and jealousy of their Emperor; indeed they liked him. Quintus hoped Nero would be in a good mood and wondered if he would be searched for a concealed weapon, since the Emperor had taken such a hatred for men of his class. (We are in early AD 64, when the death of his mentors, Seneca and Burrus, and the murder of his mother had removed any restraint from the twenty-seven-year-old ruler of the world.) Quintus is officially a 'friend of the Emperor', who likes to see him at court, and even more, Quintus remembers uneasily, likes to see him applaud his increasingly common performances in his theatre. Our friend is handed to a freedman, who acts as usher, and presented unsearched to the Emperor, who receives him graciously enough with a kiss and even remembers his name. Nero is wearing not a toga but a sort of silk dressing-gown with a kerchief round a fattish neck. His eyes are grey-blue and slightly protuberant, his legs are slender but he is developing a paunch, his hair is yellowish, his fingers are covered with rings, his skin is blotchy and he stinks of perfume, but, one has to admit, as Quintus will to his dinner guests that evening (omitting, because there are spies everywhere, the other details), the man has charm.

Nero apparently has no need of Quintus' counsel this morning, nor (and Quintus thanks his favourite god, Apollo) has he been bidden to dine at the palace, the meal being a marathon which started at noon and often did not end before midnight. Normal Romans had their *cena* (supper) at the end of the working day, which incidentally, for all the 150 types of artisan differentiated by the great Professor Waltzing, lasted no longer than that of the average worker in the European Community today. The *prandium* (lunch) was no more than a snack of bread, cold meat, fruit and vegetables with a glass of wine, served with little ceremony, but for which Quintus returns home, as he could not be seen in any of the thousands of wine shops in the city of Rome. Lunch is not substantial enough nor is the weather hot enough for Quintus to take a siesta, so he returns to the Forum to attend to his business. He tells his banker in the Basilica to send a draft to a nephew studying in Rhodes – the money will be in Athens in four days – and asks him whether, in his view, silk is a good investment these days? (It is; hasn't he noticed the number of weddings announced in today's gazette?) Which reminds him, he must not forget to go to a betrothal at the Temple of Julia for a granddaughter of the great Caesar; he witnesses the signing and sealing of a will, taken for safekeeping to the Temple of the Vestal Virgins, he attends the manumission, before a magistrate, of a friend's slave who had been his secretary for six years, he decides not to appear as a character witness for an official charged with extortion in Syria, because he has heard the jurors have been satisfactorily bribed, and he also funks attending a declamation by an actor of a another friend's poems at a hall he has hired for the occasion, but he goes to the street of booksellers, just behind the Forum, in search of a little light pornography. Books, or more properly, scrolls, on rollers like the Torah in synagogues, were more plentiful in Ancient Rome than printed books in eighteenth-century Europe and cost less. Quintus is not a great scholar but he shares the view that a gentleman should have a well-stocked library.

He has promised his wife that he will buy another cupbearer to replace the current incumbent (called, not too originally, Ganymede), who is growing too hairy and can be sent to the help the gardener, who is growing too old. In the slave market, still accompanied by his little suite of attendants, Quintus notices without interest the adult slaves, chained and naked, shivering in the courtyard with their nationalities, professions and recommendations written on a board round their necks. Having declared his requirement, he is ushered by the dealer into an inner room, where a brazier is alight and the choicest merchandise (equally unclothed, indeed with genitalia scrupulously shaved) is displayed. He is shocked by the price of a fair-haired blue-eyed boy – from Britain perhaps? – and remembers his wife's warning not to bring back anything too pretty, as 'they spell trouble'. The slave dealer comments: 'You can see, my lord, that the boy has been very well looked after.' 'Perhaps a little too well,' Quintus replies. 'I find him on the plump side; a few pounds lighter and he'll fetch a fortune', and with this excuse he chooses a plain but friendly, smiling, fine-boned Numidian, who will match one of his wife's bedroom slaves. The accountant, since blacks are cheaper than whites, nods in approval. (Even so this purchase sets him back the equivalent of £8,000 in modern money.) The new slave will also be called Ganymede.

On the way to the baths he orders nine garlands from a shop which only sells this commodity, a minor industry in Rome; but first he sends the new boy to his *domus* with a slave and a note saying he wants his litter to be at the baths in two hours' time, hoping to be sufficiently fatigued not to face the climb back up the hill. With his valet, Quintus then makes his way to the gymnasium attached to the baths to work out with his wrestler and play with a heavy stuffed ball. This will give him an appetite and keep him in trim. Like all Romans of his class, he has a horror of corpulence, the characteristic of gladiator trainers, slave dealers – and Emperors.

In 33 BC Agrippa made a census of the *thermae* of Rome and counted 170. While a city *aedile* he subsidized the entrance fee to the level of a quarter of an '*as*' – the smallest coin – so that citizens could luxuriate in these palaces of pleasure for little money and for hours of their day. In Quintus' time the grandest of these establishments, the baths of Diocletian and Caracalla, spreading over thirteen and seventeen hectares respectively, were not yet built. The baths behind the Pantheon were favourite with patricians, so it is there he goes, the new baths of Nero being too hot for his taste.

When first introduced, the concept of nudity offended the Romans' sensibilities, smacking, they thought, of Greek decadence and exhibitionism, but the practice soon caught on (though the sexes were separated, not by rooms but by hours of attendance). To wrestle, Quintus strips and is covered with an unguent of wax and oil, then with a layer of dust. He can play a variety of games, a sort of fives or *pelota*, or punch a heavy stuffed ball or exercise with dumb-bells. Quite senior citizens, even sometimes the Emperor, cavorted with their friends, indistinguishably equal in their sports tunics, save that a rich old man might have a slave to hand him a ball he had dropped and would certainly bring his own man to rub him down. Dirty and sweaty, Quintus goes to a dressing room, sumptously decorated, unlike the clinical changing rooms of our era, then to one of the *sudatoria* or dry baths to work up a sweat, and on to the *caldarium* where he lies down and is sprinkled with hot water before his body is scraped with the strigil. Last he runs to the *frigidarium* and dives into the cold pool. The Elder Pliny, Martial and Petronius, who adds that his hero (or villain) Trimalchio picks up his dinner guests somewhere along the routine, all recommend this procedure as conducive to the Roman ideal of *mens sana in corpore sano;* indeed the comfort and grandeur and cleanliness of the Roman baths, egalitarian and almost free, must have offset the horror and stink of much of everyday life in the world outside.

Quintus is carried up the hill in his litter, together with one of his dinner guests he had arranged to collect at the baths and the two clients, both his freedmen, who will receive their reward for attending him throughout the day; this in the form of dinner, which will include an introduction to his 'consular' guest (of honour), the *quaestor* at the treasury, and some titbits to take home in their napkins. On returning to the *domus,* Quintus, just as he is being helped off with his cloak and toga, is hit by the furore which precedes the best organized dinner parties. The cook is put out by the arrival of the turbot (partly aggrieved at missing out on the kickback which would have been a perk to add to his *peculium* if he had ordered this expensive item himself), and Ganymede I has burst into tears on seeing his successor, the newly purchased cup-bearer from Numidia. His wife, Cornelia, called after the saintly and efficient mother of the Gracchi and possessed of all her namesake's tact, has comforted both servants, who have been so long (too long?) with the family. His son has fluffed the lines written for him by Quintus' pet poet and is threatening not to perform. A Roman master would be perfectly entitled to flog the lot of them but Quintus enjoys the Games, eschews the lash in the home and is a fair and just man. (Nor does he, like some of his contemporaries, serve inferior wine and food to less important guests.)

He has put on a loose, light, muslin garment which he might change between courses, because a good dinner can be quite a messy affair, and is checking the seating arrangements in the *triclinium* with his *nomenclator* (usher), who will announce the guests and show them to the couch, one of three, on which they will recline, their left elbows resting on a cushion, at an angle to the table. Slaves will remove the slippers of his guests and wash their feet. *Ministrators* (waiters) will bring in knives, different sorts of spoons, and toothpicks.*

Quintus appoints his guest of honour as president of the occasion, making it his responsibility to organize, monitor and mix the wine, reasoning that a treasury man would discourage too much drunkenness and bad behaviour, and having noticed, with approval but with some apprehension, the glad eyes shot in the direction of the Numidian boy, who seems to have blossomed since his moment of purchase, only a few hours ago . . . The garlands are distributed.

After the hors d'oeuvres, his son, who has been sitting on a stool in front of him, declaims his poem (flawlessly), is applauded, blushes and withdraws. Course follows course and after each the guests are brought bowls of water for their hands and the marble table is wiped. (Tablecloths did not appear in Rome until the time of the Emperor Diocletian.) The conversation is cheerful but guarded since in AD 64 Nero has reintroduced treason trials and in Rome even careful talk could cost lives. But the subject of Quintus' new private bath, with the designs passed round, is a safe enough topic and its inauguration (with, indeed, an *augur*) will be the occasion of a much bigger party, with poetry and music.

The clear Numentian wine, carefully measured out (at first) by the *quaestor* and in its seventh year of ageing, is appreciated

---

* We have to wait till the sixteenth century for forks.

by all except for Quintus' remote cousin from Como – where he has estates near the elegant Pliny, whom he claims to know. Quintus had forgotten what a boor he is and resolves that he should stay remote. The man is continually sick from over-eating the shellfish and gulping the wine and has to be helped by Ganymede I, who has vainly shaved his legs and thighs – and cut himself – in an attempt to postpone his last supper as cup-bearer. The musicians, flute and lyre, please and the gyrations of the Spanish dancing girl draw applause, especially from the *quaestor*, whose measures are growing more reckless with time – apropos of which, Quintus reflects, should not his guests be toying with the idea of departure?

The *cena* has been a success. People will talk about that enormous turbot, so big the cook had to borrow a dish big enough to contain it. The expense, even for nine guests, has been as great as the fish, but so what? Quintus has spent on one evening the annual salary of a master mason, but he can earn that amount ten times over if his shipload of silk comes safely into port. And his wife . . . his wife . . . has charmed the company. She is still beautiful (and so efficient) and maybe he has been neglecting her of late. As his guests pile into the night with their servants and litters and sedan chairs and bodyguards with heavy sticks to deter the villains, Quintus decides he might pay her a visit, later on . . .

❧ INDEX OF PROPER NAMES ❧

Index of Proper Names